The Pursuit of Perfection

The Pursuit of Perfection

The Life, Death and Legacy of

Cormac McAnallen

DÓNAL McANALLEN

PENGUIN BOOKS

PENGUIN BOOKS

UK | USA | Canada | Ireland | Australia
India | New Zealand | South Africa

Penguin Books is part of the Penguin Random House group of companies
whose addresses can be found at global.penguinrandomhouse.com.

First published by Penguin Ireland 2017
Published in Penguin Books 2018

001

Copyright © Dónal McAnallen, 2017

The moral right of the author has been asserted

Set in 10.68/13.12 pt Bembo Book MT Std
Typeset by Jouve (UK), Milton Keynes
Printed in Great Britain by Clays Ltd, St Ives plc

A CIP catalogue record for this book is available from the British Library

ISBN: 978-0-241-97438-4

www.greenpenguin.co.uk

Penguin Random House is committed to a
sustainable future for our business, our readers
and our planet. This book is made from Forest
Stewardship Council® certified paper.

To our parents

Contents

1. Beginnings   1

2. Identities   14

3. Naff and Naffer   26

4. A Name for the Future   45

5. Young Man in Demand   58

6. Coming of Age   75

7. Mind Games   95

8. 'You're going to lift three cups'   113

9. 'Hit him, sir!'   139

10. Role Model   154

11. Cormac's Brother   175

12. Reaching the Pinnacle   189

13. The Mornings After   217

14. Last Rites   246

15. The Wake   265

16. Aftermath   286

17. Remembering Cormac   308

Epilogue: The Future   329

Acknowledgements   333

1. Beginnings

'I was born in the South Tyrone Hospital, Dungannon,
on 11th February 1980 . . . I was the heaviest of my family
at birth, weighing in at 9 pounds 3 ounces.
My Dad came from the house in which I am sitting in now
and my Mum comes from a small house near the Moy. My Mum
is called Bridget Eileen McAnallen (née O'Neill) and My Dad
is called Brendan Joseph McAnallen.
I have two brothers. Dónal, the oldest, was born on 10th July
1978 and Fergus was born on the 16th October 1981. My full name
now is Cormac Joseph Micheál McAnallen . . .'

['My Autobiography', history homework, Autumn 1990]

Cormac was always there.

From as far back as I can remember, he was part of my world. And
he was always competing. Even being the heaviest baby gave him
bragging rights. He beat me by three ounces. From the start, he had
that slight edge on me.

It was only in transit to his baptism, and after a lively debate, that
his name was agreed upon. Names from the old Celtic annals appealed
to our parents. Cormac evoked the high kingship of ancient Tara and
the nobility and scholarship of Cashel. It served also as an Irish ver-
sion of Charles, the name of our maternal grandfather. And the broad
double 'Mac' in his first name and surname suggested a boy who
meant business.

Four more people were killed in the Troubles that week. Daddy
was in Cork, managing a contract, and after a quick trip home on the
night of Cormac's birth, our mother was left to deal with the tornado
of postnatal tasks and emotions by herself. She remembers several

nights of fierce winds, and the incessant creaking and violent banging of barn doors at home.

Cormac grew into a chubby toddler with a tuft of strawberry blond hair.

He was bubbly and bright, but also very sensitive. When Mummy sang slow airs like 'She Moved Through the Fair' and 'My Lagan Love', you could see his face melting. He was also terrified of vacuum cleaners, the upright ones that looked like Dr Who baddies. '*Daca-doon!*' he cried. When parents were cross with him, he burst into tears, but retaliated with a threat: '*I'm gonna thun away!*' Or '*Say your pwayers!*'

If we were all acting up, and Mummy went out the door and feigned to leave us, Cormac would be the first to break. While I waited for her to come back, he'd panic to run after her, or sob as if she really meant it this time.

He grew braver and bolder. Where there was action, he wanted in the thick of it. Strange places and people did not unnerve him, whereas even a bouncy castle seemed intimidating to me. When we met firemen leaving our great-aunt Kathleen's house, I was scared of them and their engine; Cormac got up with them into the front seat.

His relish for a challenge occasionally verged on foolhardiness. Aged five, he ventured into the deep end of the Slieve Donard Hotel swimming pool and nearly drowned. On a return to south Down a year later, he ignored Mummy's repeated warnings to not climb the trees at Tollymore Forest Park, fell, and hurt his arm badly. Again, despite parental instructions, he picked wild mushrooms in the garden and ate them raw. Drinking diluted washing-up liquid was his ultimate act of lunacy, and he relished our disgust.

He could devour a full bag of mandarins or satsumas at one sitting, even if a queasy aftermath lay ahead. Our aunt Maggie recounts the time she didn't know our room number in a hotel, but followed the scent of oranges from the foyer to the correct room.

From the time he was fit to talk, we debated anything and everything. First it was:

'It's a tah.'

'No, Cormac. It's a car!'

'No! It's a tah.'

'It's "Everybody Wants to Run the World",' he said.

'Naw. It's "Everybody Wants to Rule the World",' I countered.

Turns out we were both right on that one.

At the crossroads exactly one mile from our house, Mummy always paused to await our commands. 'Go the low road!' he'd beg. 'Take the high road,' I appealed.

I drew the line at his claim that the 1982 World Cup finals on telly was his earliest memory. 'How could you remember it?' I demanded indignantly. 'Sure you had only turned two!'

If he were alive today, we would still be rehearsing that theatrical quarrel.

*

We grew up in a foul-smelling land. That's how we translate the name of the Brantry (*Bréantar*). It's a rural area of south-east Tyrone; sulphur in the ground may be behind the smell. We were quite remote, over three miles from the nearest village, Eglish. We had fifteen acres in the townland of Tullygiven, but Daddy was in the process of phasing out the family farming tradition around the time Cormac was born.

In a GAA-less universe, we might've claimed dual-county identity. Two miles away lay the Armagh border. Both our parents had lived just over the Blackwater in their earliest days: Daddy, by the river-banks at Clontycarty, outside Caledon, and on the county boundary; and Mummy, in a north Armagh orchard farm at Derrymagone, between Collegeland and Clonmore. When Daddy set up a general construction business in the late 1970s, he chose 'Ardmac' – playing on '*Ard Mhacha*' to portray the 'Mac' family reaching heights, and with a suitably robust sound. In 1982, he opened an office in Lurgan.

Our surname is also most common and can be traced furthest back in nearby parts of Armagh: Tullysaran, Derrynoose and Portadown. McAnallen is a name of obscure origin, usually translated as '*Mac an Ailín*', though '*Mac Conalláin*' has been mooted of late. Likely we are related to the Nallen clans of Mayo, if indeed they were among the many Ulstermen driven 'to hell or to Connacht' by Cromwellian order.

Despite the Armagh connections, we were Tyrone people. Our line of McAnallens had occupied Tullygiven intermittently since the 1790s, if not earlier. By the 1980s, our household were still the flag-bearers for the family name in Tyrone; the few other McAnallens of the county, all relatives, migrated here and there, but we stayed put. Growing up, we'd see our McAnallen aunts and uncles and cousins mostly at family anniversaries and Christmas get-togethers. Kevin, Daddy's eldest brother and Cormac's godfather, used to host us all at the Christmas soirées at Dundalk. He and uncle Seán were partners of Daddy in Ardmac, expanding the company south of the border and over to Manchester. Our aunt Hannah joined them in Dundalk and in the family firm. Aunt Margaret Mannion and family, over in Mayo, we got to see maybe once a year at best. Only aunt Mary remained north of the border, in Dungannon.

We saw much more of the O'Neill side of the family in our early years. We spent a lot of our childhood about our grandparents' house in the Moy. The family had moved to Jockey Lane when Mummy was a teenager. It was a cosy house, radiating warmth, artistry and atmosphere. The door was always open. To us, it was quite a magical place.

Our grandfather, Charlie O'Neill – 'Gandy' to his many grandchildren – was widely renowned as a fiddle-player. By the age of nine, back in 1926, he had taught himself how to play, from listening to tinker fiddlers – itinerant tinsmiths – around his home at Drimarone, near Donegal town. Seven years later, he moved to north Armagh to look after the traditional family homestead, where Constantine 'the Hatter' O'Neill had been burned out amid sectarian feuding in 1806. Later, he had sprayed orchards, worked at the ICI factory in Birmingham, and laboured on the building of the northern M1 motorway. He was still fiddling every day, near and far; he even had a reel named after him, the much-recorded 'Charlie O'Neill's'.

The Gandy we knew was a gregarious and generous man. He kept a fire lit about 350 days a year and boiled his signature soup, densely populated with spuds and oats and chunks of fatty meat, daily in summer as in winter. Oranges and Dairy Milk bars were dispensed as regular treats, the odd pound coin too. He regaled us with fantastic stories of 'the dog-cat and the ghost' and kindred creatures. Then he'd take out the fiddle impromptu and play a highland reel for us in front of the blazing inferno.

Granny taught us how to play cards and recited old yarns and limericks she had learned in the Inver area of south Donegal many moons ago. She mentioned spending her early years in New Zealand's southern isle. Her old-fashioned mannerisms were amusing to us. She encouraged us to submit entries for newspaper crossword prizes, but if we neglected to put 'Master' before our names, they had to be scrapped. Any time a subject for mature viewers came on television, she enquired aloud, 'Is that educational?' Cormac always laughed at that.

Jockey Lane also served as our meeting point with aunts, uncles and cousins. On a given evening, we might see aunt Marie (Burns) swing by with her harp, and jam with Gandy. Uncle Pat was a mean fiddler too, when he wasn't twisting. We heard of many well-known musicians dropping in – like Dougie MacLean giving his first-ever rendition of 'Caledonia', the Scottish folk anthem, in that house in 1977. I treated this story as utter fantasy until MacLean confirmed its veracity in a radio interview, a couple of years ago.

Dull moments were few, whoever was visiting. We lobbied aunt Imelda, a freshwater biologist in Belfast, to play board-games with us. Ditto uncle Charlie, a mathematician turned computer programmer, and once an Ulster junior champion cross-country runner. Aunt Teresa (McCartan) talked of the form of her racehorse, Colleen Glen, and her girls were always good for a laugh with/at their country cousins. When aunt Anna (Kelly) brought a carload of five from Carland, it was all action. Each summer, aunt Maggie (Allchin) returned from Qatar, where she taught and played for the national women's golf team, and Cormac and I got in several rounds with her. Uncle Peter still lived in the house, but we'll save him for later.

One evening, Gandy decided to cut Cormac's childish curls. Mummy was aghast, as though her son had been shorn of his innocence. The curls never returned.

*

> *Friday 20 Nov 1987*
> *My name is Cormac Joseph McAnallen.*
> *I am seven years old.*
> *My birthday is on February the 11th 1980.*
> *I like to play football, basketball, hurling and rounders.*
> *My best friend is John Paul Peter McGeough.*
> *My favourite school subject is English.*
> *My hair is brown and my eyes are blue.*
> *My teacher is Mrs Donaghy . . .*
> *My pets are three cats.*
> *. . . the Master is Kevin McGuckin.*
> *My age is 7 and I am in primary 4.*
> *. . . My favourite TV programme is Grandstand.*
> *. . . We have got a football pitch outside where you can play lots of*
> *   sports.*
> *. . . We have got a tree-hut and a snooker table.*
> *Outside the barn we have a base and a conker tree.*
> *We have got a playroom were [sic] we have got the snooker table we [sic]*
> *   have tennis rackets and five hundred comics.*
> *We have got some books and about thirty toy-cars.*

Cormac and I shared all the same interests and did the same things. His relative maturity ensured that the age gap between us barely mattered. The two of us were stapled together in people's minds even before competitive sport entered the equation.

Fergus followed close behind us in years but seldom in our footsteps. His passions and pastimes were very different.

There was recreation aplenty at home. Daddy took us for walks up the back fields and challenged us to race through the mucky and stony parts: we called this the 'Krypton Factor' assault course. The 'base' – a shelter made of scrap metal, with construction contraptions serving as our weaponry – was where we lived out our 'A-Team' illusions.

Daddy built us the tree-hut in the garden, a sledge also, and converted our barn loft into a spacious games room. Santa Claus produced a small snooker table at Christmas '83. Battle commenced. By 21 March 1985 – even before the Taylor–Davis final at the Crucible – I was leading Cormac by 528 frames to 412.

It would be ever thus: the two of us continuously in contest, constantly keeping score. A table tennis table came down the chimney a couple of years later and, as with everything else, every encounter had to have a winner and the score had to go on record.

We got away with blue murder around home. We 'tobogganed' head-first down the stairs on a duvet, side by side, despite many warnings from Mummy. Our 'hockey' was played in the living room with two upside-down blackthorn sticks and the new-fangled Ariel plastic liquid-dosing balls.

★

I had been at Derrylatinee Primary School a year when Cormac started in 1984. Situated in the Brantry's outback, it was the sort of school that civil servants yearned to close. There were fifty-five pupils, two classrooms, two teachers, and one big stove to heat the place. It was big on idyllic nature walks and calligraphy, and was just beginning to engage with modernity. In Cormac's first year, school uniforms were introduced and a mobile classroom was installed. We had to go on sponsored walks and classroom silences to fund our first computer and a duplicating machine. We were so proud of ourselves.

While corporal punishment was still in force, Cormac received his share. One day in P2, he got into a scrap. 'I tore his jumper and he pulled my hair,' he wrote in an English book. Six slaps each, lesson learned.

The attention to detail in Cormac's school diaries was extraordinary. Recounting an outing to the Ulster Folk and Transport Museum, he listed the sight of a prison, blocks of flats, army watchtowers, 'five tunnels' on the Westlink, the docks, Belfast Lough, 'two big big cranes', Shorts aircraft factory, the harbour airport, and Esso petrol on sale for 6p. A tale of a trip to the supermarket is peppered with references to the countries of origin of various fruits. His observations of the school bird table specified ten species of bird, from greenfinches to dunnocks.

He could also be a dirty fib-dog. One day he wrote that we had gone to see 101 *Dalmatians* in the cinema. We did nothing of the kind, I chastised him. (We saw only two films on the big screen prior to university.)

Our schoolyard games seem so passé today. Tig and other running games themed on the TV shows of the day – 'Iceman', 'He-Man' and 'Knight Rider' – when it was dry. Conkers in the autumn. Marbles in the spring. Rounders and races on summery days.

Marbles held particular currency. After learning the flicks from Master McGuckin, we played 'friendlies', 'keeps' and 'follow the leader' – Cormac's favourite, he wrote at the time. He and I bought them in forty shades from McMullan's shop in the Moy and carried them in emerald-green Tyrone Crystal holders.

Innocent though they were, all of our schoolyard games seemed to be banned at some stage. Tig was outlawed due to some cry-babies. Marbles was prohibited after a window got smashed. Football was taboo except on bright Friday afternoons, and it could be soccer only, for we had but a small patch of grass. Inspired by watching athletics on television, Cormac and I created a 'steeplechase' course, tying ropes between the new mobile classrooms and the nearby hedges. That was banned, too. At one time, hopscotch was the only game allowed outside.

After flying through his first three years, Cormac was moved up (or 'skipped') a year from P4 to P5. This put him one class behind me again; there had been two between us since I had done P1 and P2 in the same year. Cormac coped well with the promotion, remaining around the top of his new class. When teachers called for boy volunteers for Irish dancing, no one stepped up until he did; then others poured forth.

The P7 class of 1989/90 excelled in the eleven-plus examination; the principal, Mrs Eileen Donaghy, referred to them as her 'golden year'. An 'A' grade guaranteed grammar education for Cormac. I had passed the year before. Going from the secluded serenity and decorum of Derrylatinee to a big secondary school in town proved a culture-shock for naive lads like us.

*

From the time he could read, Cormac was often to be found scouring atlases and reference books, like the two dozen grey-and-chocolate volumes of the World Book Encyclopaedia that heaved on our front-room shelves. He was also glued to the geography-themed TV quizzes of the day: *Worldwise* with David 'Kid' Jensen, *Going for Gold*, and *Where in the World* with Theresa Lowe.

He put it all to use. Just look at this story he wrote for a schools competition in 1990:

Hello, I am a piece of wood and I live in Siberia. Will I tell you my story?

Alright then, I will. It all started when I was a seed in Quebec. I fell into the sea and floated into the Atlantic Ocean. Eventually after about a year or so I got washed up on the shores of Ghana. A local tribe picked me up and planted me. After about forty years I was grown to my full height. Then they carved me out and made a hut out of me! I stayed there for 9 years. At that time the country was fighting a civil war and guerrillas wrecked the hut. Soon archaeologists came and looked for remains of the tribe's belongings. The Archaeologist brought me to Vienna where I was put in a museum. Then one night some Russian bandits stole me and brought me to Moscow! From there they brought me on the Trans-Siberian railway to Vladivostok. At the time somebody was going to try to walk to the north pole by foot. I can't exactly remember how but I got into his knapsack. On the way he met a Polar bear. He and his party took off their knapsacks and started to run away. It took the weight off him.

Now I am stuck here and I don't know how on earth I am going to be saved.

THE END.'

Much of what I learned about the geography of the world I got from Cormac. It was he who informed me about the Rocky mountains, the Angel Falls, and the volcano Popocatépetl. When we were about the Moy in those days, people used to introduce us as the boys who knew every capital in the world. We didn't, but Cormac's voracious appetite for learning inspired me to learn more. And it wasn't only me. He taught J. P. McGeough how to spell Czechoslovakia.

Our invented games at home became geography-fests. Cormac's concept of 'toy football' comprised two 'teams' of Matchbox model cars, a marble as a ball and two empty ice-cream tubs as goals. World cup tournaments were staged. Intricate 'draw' ceremonies involved slips of paper bearing the names of most of the sovereign nations of the earth in a democratically unseeded lottery that would put FIFA to shame. Then a straight knockout format was applied. When I was amenable, we took a side each, but otherwise he played out each match by himself, affording a flick to each team in turn, until a winner emerged. Invariably, an obscure far-flung republic triumphed. As we became more nationally conscious, we taped drinking-straws to the tubs and played the whole thing out again under Gaelic rules.

Mummy had taught for a while in Spain and Ireland, and now she devoted a lot of time to our education. She talked to us almost as equals, rarely dumbing subjects down for us. Yet it wasn't all library books and serious stuff by any means. She started us reading comics. At one stage we were buying fourteen per week. From *The Beano* and *The Dandy* to the newer *Whizzer & Chips*; action titles like *Eagle* and *Transformers*; and *Shoot!*, *Match* and *Roy of the Rovers*, which we hid from Daddy, who disapproved of soccer. Later we started buying *Gaelic World*, *Gaelic Sport*, *Gaelic Review* and *Gaelsport*, and the Christian Brothers' *Our Boys* while it lasted.

Our magazine mania peaked with *Winners*, the 72-issue ring-binder collection about sports. On Thursday evenings, Mummy drove us eight miles to the Moy and back to get the latest editions. She played Handel's *Messiah* at full blast on tape till we knew it nearly inside-out and we sang our own oratorio with lyrical references to Tyrone football.

*

Our uncle Peter O'Neill brought so much fun into our lives. He was one of the main reasons we spent so much time at our grandparents' in the Moy. We idolized him.

He played basketball for Dungannon in the National League.

He could spin a ball on his finger for a minute.

He had played in Yugoslavia.

He knew American players, even some black men.

He wrote a column about them all for the local papers.

He printed the *Dungannon Observer* and brought it home on Thursday nights before it went on sale.

He ran the first Belfast Marathon.

He had won enough skyscraper 1970s-style trophies to cover the top of the piano and the sideboard.

He could play 'O'Neill's March' on the tin-whistle.

He could bounce a teacup against his biceps and catch it.

He could fool a fly with his left hand and swipe it with the right.

He taught us the rules of chess.

He wrestled with us on the sofa, two or three at once, like a mini-royal rumble.

He had a stockpile of corny quips for any occasion.

He took us for spins in the car along labyrinthine back-roads just for the sheer hell of finding out where they ended.

He did odd jobs around our house on Saturdays.

He was also a member of Tyrone's senior football squad. He knew the blond superhero, Plunkett Donaghy, and brought him to our house once.

Peter didn't play in any knockout games in the summer of 1986, when Tyrone reached its first ever All-Ireland final. It was the year that we really got into Gaelic games, and we were so proud of our link with that squad.

Six-year-old Cormac caught the championship fever before I did. Tyrone v. Cavan in the Ulster semi-final at Irvinestown was the first big match he attended. Upon his return, he recounted this great game to me and persuaded me not to miss the Ulster final. High up the hill embankment at Clones, when it really was a hill, I stood with Cormac, Daddy and Gandy. Plunkett's dubious goal saw Tyrone through.

We had hopes of a trip to Dublin for the All-Ireland semi-final, but Daddy ruled that Cormac and I were too young to go. We ended up watching it with Mummy and Fergus in a pub at Manorhamilton, Co. Leitrim, of all places. (We had gone on a weekend trip to Sligo.) Against the backdrop of repeated Ulster failures at Croke Park over many years, few people expected Tyrone to beat Galway.

That landmark victory and the build-up to our maiden All-Ireland final was magical – for young boys like us as well as for men who had tilled the Gaelic fields of Tyrone for half a century without a proper harvest.

Our young eyes were impressed by the three blond mullets (two peroxide) sported by members of that team, and the quintet of moustaches, ranging from princely handlebar to Greek waiter to on-the-run. At their helm was the heavily bespectacled *bainisteoir*, Art McRory.

As the hype intensified, a 'Good Luck Plunkett and Peter' banner stretched across the street on the Moy. That was our uncle they were talking about. Over a main road.

We watched the final in the living room. As Tyrone amassed a 7-point lead with twenty minutes to go, the fairytale seemed poised to come true. The subsequent surrender, to lose by 8, would haunt many an older observer for the next two decades.

But Cormac and I were hooked. Going to matches became a ritual, from Ulster Championship to Dr McKenna Cup, and club fixtures too. At our early National League matches, the two of us often stood behind the goals, in the hope that we might catch a ball and throw it back to the goalie.

Cormac's school diary entries capture our enthusiasm in those formative outings. His account of the Tyrone–Derry league game on 8 February 1987 set the tone. 'On the way to Omagh,' Cormac wrote, two days shy of his seventh birthday, 'we passed 31 cars and two cars passed us.' (That wouldn't be the last time Daddy's foot-to-floor driving produced impressive overtaking stats.) That was the day Cormac's name reverberated on the tannoy at Healy Park for the first time. Either before the match or on a half-time mission to purchase crisps, he had got lost.

We both got lost in the dense crowd at Irvinestown in June, when Tyrone's title-defence fell under an avalanche of five Armagh goals. We were shattered. We had thought Tyrone were never going to lose an Ulster match again.

For a school essay on the theme 'The most exciting day of my life', Cormac picked his first visit to Croke Park, for the 1987 All-Ireland semi-final, Meath v. Derry. (I made a protest about Daddy's lowered minimum age – how come Cormac was old enough for Croke Park now at seven, but I couldn't go before when I was eight? – but it served me no good.) Cormac was so excited to stay in Dublin, he wrote that 'when we were going back to the hotel I was head-butting lamp posts'. We shouted for our fellow Ulstermen, especially after the heavily strapped Dermot McNicholl came on, but to no avail.

Our standard expeditionary crew consisted of Daddy, Cormac, myself, our neighbour John Downey and Paddy Gallen. Paddy was a blind man who hailed from west Tyrone but lived close to us in Caledon. Absorbing the atmosphere was as exciting for him as watching the match was for us. He held on to our arms as we mazed through the crowds. On big championship days, he got his commentary from a transistor radio. For lesser National League games and the like, I described the action to him.

2. Identities

Eglish was both our parish and the name of its standalone village. That was where we went to church. But it wasn't taken for granted that we would play for Eglish.

Our family had a long but convoluted connection with the GAA. Our grandfather, John McAnallen, was chairman of the first club in the parish – St Patrick's, Brantry, formed in July 1937. Although a small club, it built one of the first GAA halls in Ulster. Prior to its opening in 1938, it was damaged by a bomb. The RUC raided the houses of local members of the nationalist Ancient Order of Hibernians. There were AOH–GAA tensions over rival dances in the area, but it was preposterous to suggest they'd want to bomb a GAA hall, let alone know how to. Local nationalists suspected 'B' Special constables instead.

In football and otherwise, the Brantrarians and Eglish villagers didn't quite gel. Land around the settlement of Eglish was generally flatter and better than the Brantry's rugged terrain, where hills and woods and lakes provided refuge for dispossessed men in the 1640s and 1790s, and that rebellious streak persisted still.

In an effort to bring all of the parish together, the club was renamed St Patrick's, Brantry/Eglish, until it dropped out of junior football in 1941; it came back in 1947 with the same dual name but folded again in 1950 due to emigration. When a new club emerged in 1955, it was known simply as St Patrick's, Eglish. By then Granda John was long adrift from club affairs, but he followed Tyrone to Clones for their Ulster breakthroughs in 1956–7, and on to Croke Park.

The concept of 'one club for life' is promoted today as if it were the historical norm. It's a romantic fabrication. In truth, players back then transferred to the team of their friends or the strongest club within range – parish rules be damned. Daddy played one or two youth games for Eglish, and no more. One evening he left a field of hay for a minor match, but didn't get on. The hay was lost, he got a scolding from his father, and didn't go back to Eglish. He tried out with a scratch Brantry revival team, but it came to nought. In 1966 he rowed in with the Benburb club, which was cobbled together from student priests in the local priory and lay misfits of four parishes. The 1968 East Tyrone Junior Football Championship final with Benburb was the apex of Daddy's career. He was centre-back that day, and club secretary; uncle Sean was corner-back. They lost to Killyman by a point. The Benburb club dissolved the next year, once the seminary shut. Uncle Sean joined Eglish, but Daddy turned westward to help set up the Aghaloo club in 1970. He became its first captain.

All the while, Daddy was missing out on the Eglish revolution. The quiet hamlet where road bowls (or 'bullets') had been the main game was becoming a village and a small sporting powerhouse. An old gravel-pit was turned into a decent playing field, and opened as Fr Connolly Park in 1964. A youth club, set up in 1965, spawned new teams. Eglish basketballers won the Tyrone youth championship for three years running. Eglish camogie club went on to win forty-five of the next fifty Tyrone senior titles. Meanwhile, the GAA club ascended from junior ranks in 1964 to a fabled triumph in the Tyrone Senior Football Championship of 1970. Modern Eglish was now a place with people and facilities and tradition.

Daddy ploughed away in the junior ranks with Aghaloo, a club that had no home as yet. Weeks after Aghaloo men bought some ground in 1973, club-member Francie McCaughey was killed by a bomb on his farm near the Brantry. Many locals believed that he was singled out because of his part in the land purchase.

As small boys who had no family ties to the Eglish club, we didn't really notice when it reached consecutive Tyrone championship semi-finals in 1984–5. Worse again, we first supported the Moy, Eglish's deadly rivals, because uncle Peter played for them. Moy–Eglish relations were then at an all-time low. Their league game in 1986 ended in a brawl and both clubs were suspended till the end of season – causing Eglish's first-ever relegation. At one derby match, we shouted for the Moy in front of Eglish neighbours, to Daddy's embarrassment. Thankfully, no one else remembers.

But now that I think about it, it was on the Moy field that Cormac first practised with an O'Neills ball. Sometimes with me, but other times on his own, he took one of Peter's footballs in hand and dandered down the Benburb Road to kick into the near-end goals. That was Páirc Thír na nÓg. The Field of the Land of the Youth.

*

From as soon as Cormac started school, if not earlier, Daddy took us to Irish classes in that draughty old Brantry Area Rural Development (BARD) building. When they had run their course, he moved on to more draughty *ranganna* in An Port Mór, Tullysaran and Armagh, and we had to tag along. We didn't look forward to the classes much; often we were the only children there. But they did give us an early advantage in the subject at school and enhanced our sense of Irish identity for life.

We were in the graveyard every Sunday after Mass, praying over three family plots. Easter Sunday was different: that was when the republican commemorations took place. Our uncle Dan, Daddy's brother, figured in the 'Tyrone roll of honour' as 'Volunteer Dan McAnallen'. Daddy was there out of duty, and he took us along. For years, he had said the prayers in Irish. When we were old enough, he asked us to say them instead. I declined. But even as a boy, Cormac wasn't afraid to stand out and say them in front of everybody.

We knew why we were standing there. We were there as relatives, who would have been in the cemetery anyway, saying prayers. We saw different republican representatives there. But did we, as young lads, *really* understand the significance, or all the trappings? Honestly, no. Dan's death, and the aftermath, weren't much talked about in front of our young ears.

We knew uncle Dan as a red-sideburned young man, smiling in a framed picture in our front room. We saw the silhouette of that face etched into his black gravestone. We read the gold inscription that he was 'killed in action' at Pomeroy police barracks in August 1973, aged twenty-seven. We heard also that a young lad of sixteen, Patrick Quinn, died with him in the blast. That they received the last rites in a house. That no hospital could've saved them. That their dead bodies were left on the side of the A4, a few miles away at Killeeshil.

Beyond that, Cormac, Fergus and I learned only snippets about Dan as we grew up. Only in recent years have I got a more detailed picture, for his full story's seldom told. Small wonder. People tend to prejudge a dead IRA man as either a heroic freedom fighter or a bad article altogether. There's little in between. And the sudden dead get no chance to frame their own stories.

In other circumstances, Dan's days would have ended very differently. He plumbed for an English company, and counted several Protestant workmates as good friends. He married before he tasted alcohol. He organized bingo sessions and '25' card drives as parochial fundraisers. He was a fanatical football follower. When Tyrone won the All-Ireland Junior Football Championship of 1968, he and Sean led a pitch invasion of Croke Park. That first national title at adult level meant a lot to success-starved Red Hand supporters, and Dan was delirious. He never played for a club, though. Football wasn't played at the schools he attended, and the minor grade passed him by.

He buccaneered through all facets of life. If he saw a scrap between two strangers he'd wade in for the underdog. He had no involvement in politics until the civil rights campaign reached his doorstep in 1968. The Caledon squat protests chimed with his own experience of having to go to Keady, County Armagh, for a council house. He stewarded at the first civil rights march, from Coalisland to Dungannon, in August. Subsequent marches were blocked by security cordons and batons, Stormont refused reforms, loyalist vigilantes bundled in, and tension mounted. News of the Bombay Street burnings in Belfast in summer '69 convinced some young men, Dan included, that physical force would have more effect than peaceful parades; internment and Bloody Sunday hardened their views. So Dan metamorphosed from marcher to martyr within five years. His was the 920th or so lost life of the Troubles; three thousand more would die yet.

On his funeral day, Tyrone and Cork contested the All-Ireland semi-final at Croke Park. This was to be a defining day for football in the county: only its third senior semi, and the minors were playing too. Dan had planned to be there to cheer on his heroes, including centre-back Mickey Jordan of Eglish. Instead, he got a minute's silence before the big match, observed by the 30,000-strong crowd. Under constant drizzle, Tyrone collapsed to a 15-point hammering. Cork went on to wear a set of Tyrone-style jerseys in the final, due to a clash of colours with Galway, and captain Billy Morgan said in his winning speech that the GAA was 'not doing enough for the North'.

Dan left a young widow, Bertha, a modest and quiet lady. His ailing mother – our grandmother – died of cancer two years later. The bitter residue of his death lingered, amid a generally baleful atmosphere north of the border. Like other similarly bereaved families, the McAnallens could expect more suspicion and surveillance from the Crown forces thereafter. Once-routine journeys were now more tortuous. Faced with driving to Aughnacloy and crossing the border checkpoint to get to the Aghaloo field, Daddy gave up football shortly after Dan died. In other aspects of everyday life too, bearing our distinctive surname did not make life easier for family members.

Cormac and I did not know all that then. We saw Dan's picture on a poster in our aunt Mary's flat on our visits after matches at O'Neill Park. We read the title of 'Captaen Foirne Briogáid Thír Eoghain' on the gravestone in Eglish cemetery, without comprehending it. Our parents made a conscious decision not to fill in the gaps in the narrative for us. Martyrs have begotten martyrs in Irish history and they did not want to mourn another one.

Immersion in local historical, cultural and sporting affairs would surely keep us safe. We should live for Ireland, not die for her. Perhaps then we might enter a better roll of honour. Or even win as a 'Captaen Foirne'.

★

Daddy and Mummy were big believers in community and tradition. If they weren't on the phone organizing something, they were writing or out attending a meeting.

I remember our coming with them to some early meetings of the BARD association, of which they were founder members. They helped to organize an annual BARD festival and establish a community centre.

They also hosted several big barn dances at our homeplace, which we awaited with great excitement.

Daddy moved on to researching the history of the McAnallen clan. He was on the phone many evenings, connecting with all our American and Australian cousins. He published his research in booklet form in 1985, and organized the first worldwide family gathering in the same year.

Next, they helped to form the O'Neill Country Historical Society, which covered border areas of Tyrone and Armagh. This region was connected to the last Gaelic chieftains of the O'Neill dynasty, such as Hugh and Eoghan Rua; and also the birth of the Orange Order, whose Dyan No. 1 lodge lay just down the road from us. Recording and recognizing this rich historical tapestry became a mission for our parents and other like-minded people. They set up a heritage centre in Benburb, and their annual historical journal, *Dúiche Néill*, is still going strong thirty-two years later.

Daddy took us along with him to various historic sites, museums and heritage centres. These trips could be rather dull for impatient young boys like us. I watched him painstakingly use Daz washing-powder to trace the faded letters on gravestones in the old cemetery in Eglish, then write down the inscriptions.

There was the odd eureka moment, however. On a visit to Tully-hogue, the ancient inauguration site of the O'Neill kings, Daddy directed Cormac to look for remnants of the O'Neills' ancestral chair. Cormac reported back with the news that he had found a stone slab under the long grass in the specified area. Upon checking the indentations on the rock and cross-referencing its location with Richard Bartlett's map of 1602, Daddy was satisfied that this was the real thing. While Cormac was probably not the first person to see these remnants since Lord Mountjoy's forces destroyed them 386 years before, they had not been identified in the late modern era. His discovery would act as a spur to efforts to preserve the site in more recent times.

*

Living in the north sharpened your sense of identity from a young age. The Tyrone nationalist mindset encompassed a collective grievance over partition, Stormont misrule and neglect. It taught us that Tír Eoghain was the last Gaelic kingdom of Ireland to yield to conquest, the torch-bearers, standing in the *bearna baoil*. Daddy named our home 'Ballaghkillgevill', in homage to a phase of the Battle of Benburb in 1646, a few kilometres away from us.

In long-suffering Dungannon, security barriers closed off streets, and the town centre was a 'control zone', where unattended vehicles could be regarded as car-bomb suspects. This could cause a real rigmarole: once or twice, when old enough, I had to act as the fraternal enforcer while Mummy went into Wellworths, but keeping the cyclonic Cormac inside proved a chore.

British army and RUC patrols formed the most striking impression of the Troubles. Being stopped and questioned on country roads on dark nights wasn't remarkable. Nor were inordinate delays and car-searches in places like Aughnacloy. We didn't witness much direct hostility as boys, but there was always fear, especially after events like the shooting dead of Aidan McAnespie. When armed soldiers walked down our remote lane or through our fields and into our yard, we'd be very alarmed.

The Troubles had an indirect impact on school, too. Entering P6, I looked forward to having Cormac as my teammate for the cross-community schools quiz. Our partner school was Mullycar, the local Protestant primary. I had taken part and lost narrowly in 1987. With Cormac, we'd be hard to beat in '88. Expectantly, I asked one day about the quiz. To my dismay, the teacher said we weren't going, as it was run under RUC auspices and this caused contention. Fielding questions from police constables had surprised me the time before, but only in passing. The change in policy followed the fallout from the SAS's Loughgall ambush on an eight-man IRA unit. At the time, I was just deflated not to compete.

*

After Tyrone's 1986 odyssey, Daddy erected two sets of wooden goalposts, cut from local trees, in our back lawn. Suddenly we had a 25-yard pitch: ideal dimensions for boys of our age. A vegetable garden to the left and a row of apple trees to the right formed natural sidelines, and hedges at either end were our terraces.

It was just Cormac and me usually. Daddy kicked with us for a short time before retiring on the grounds of age. Our nearest neighbours lived half a mile away, and none had an interest in football. Some of our two dozen cousins were willing but were all too far flung to give us a regular game. On the rare day that Fergus gave in to our pleas, he stood in goals to kick the ball out for us to contest, and no more; and he swung at the ball with such indifference that persisting with that experiment seemed futile.

Practice got more serious with the arrival of two pairs of Mitre football boots, red-and-white shorts and socks, courtesy of Santa, in 1987. Mostly we took turns shooting for goal. Sometimes we played straight one-on-one matches, and it was then that the first glimpses of Cormac's playing style became evident. In soloing the ball, he burrowed his burly body past my taller and stiffer frame.

This marauding style probably explains why he excelled with the oval ball on the lawn. 'Cormac normally beats me at rugby,' I recorded in my school diary in April 1988, so it was a 'big shock' for me to win by 66–21 that time. During Wimbledon fortnight, that same green patch served as a tennis court. We recorded every result of the All-England Championships in the newspaper pull-outs, year after year. Likewise, for Italia '90, I filled in the same results of every match in at least eight different souvenir brochures.

Therein lay one of my problems. My instincts were slightly more bookish. I'd happily spend as much time with my head buried in wordsearches and compiling anagrams of 'Crunchy Nut Corn Flakes'. Cormac had the more insatiable passion to play, and he got exercised about the fact that I didn't *always* join him on the lawn, and showed more interest in football when we had visitors. Cormac could never be sated. We have a picture of him in his grey First Communion suit, kicking a ball on that lawn as if he were in a county final.

As our sporting landscapes widened, his enthusiasm tended to spur my interest, rather than the older brother leading the younger, as might be expected. Whatever about 1982, it was he who spread World Cup '86 fever to me. He wondered at John Fenton's goals and Cork hurlers before I did. His fascination with international athletics and world records stirred mine. Most grand prix track-and-field events in those days were televised, and we watched them all. Cormac rhapsodized about pole-vaulter Sergei Bubka, middle-distancer Said Aouita and sprinter Ben Johnson. *16 Days of Glory*, an American documentary series about the 1984 Los Angeles Olympics, enthralled us for weeks before the 1988 Games. The revelation of Johnson's doping did not douse our zeal.

Then there was basketball. The sport had begun to catch on in Ireland, and it was an exciting time for us to get hooked. The Dungannon club, then operating as 'Cookstown Glenavon Hotel', entered the National League in 1986/7. The club shot up from the third division to the top flight in successive seasons. Peter, as club PRO and still a fringe player, took us to matches in the intermediate school in Dungannon, against teams like Annadale and St Gall's of Belfast, Marian of Dublin, and Marathon of Limerick. He played the game with us in the Moy too. We ambled over to the ring outside Cartmills' house, beside our grandparents in Jockey Lane, to shoot a few hoops and, if Peter was about, some older lads would join in.

Peter also introduced us to the Moy Youth Club, in the parochial hall just a few yards further down Jockey Lane. He was in demand to teach the skills to local teenagers there, and he took us along one night. Although Cormac was only seven, and ten was supposed to be the minimum age, he had no fear about mixing it with the older boys. On his very first night there, he played basketball with Patrick Hughes and Colm Miller, two lads who were at least five or six years his senior. He was really pleased to be accepted by them. Sadly, both Patrick and Colm would die in car accidents in their late teens. At least six members of the youth club from our time would die at a young age, all but one of the others before Cormac.

It was just outside the Moy, at Collegeland in Armagh, that we started doing summer work in 1989. The McGeary fruit farm had been an institution in the area since the 1960s, and half of the sixteen-strong family still worked there, pulling strawberries. Leo, the main man, spoke constantly of football and the past Tyrone and Armagh players who had graduated from his fields. 'To play in an All-Ireland final,' he advised us, 'you have to be able to solo through a hedge.' We didn't try it, but the message would stick with Cormac.

★

There was one more important legacy of '86. The Tyrone County Board appointed a coach, 'Doonan' Gallagher, to tour the schools, and local primary school leagues were organized for the first time. Until then, Gaelic games didn't really feature at Derrylatinee.

With so few pupils at our disposal, we had to merge with Roan in Eglish to form a team. When we Derrylatinee greenhorns visited the village school before games, it felt like a clash of civilizations; we thought them slightly lawless with their bad attitudes, bad words and even an American football helmet in the playground, yet they looked at us like we were the yahoos. Kitted out in black and white stripes, our combined team looked quite striking. Sometimes we were called 'Jossy's Giants', after the Geordie boys' team on BBC back then.

I started playing in 1988, and nine-year-old Cormac came on board a year later. He lined out at right corner-back and I as goalkeeper. We slew Kingsisland, Brockagh, Moortown and Castlecaulfield/Carland in turn. Cormac even sallied forward to strike a point in the last of these. In our young minds, we were invincible.

Our first shot at a title rested on an away match against the Moy, lads whom Cormac and I knew just as well as our teammates. We lost by a landslide. Worse still, I bungled spectacularly, hitting kick-outs straight to Moy boys and letting in a flood of goals.

Enlisting with Eglish was the natural progression. The two of us turned up for duty at an under-12 tournament in the Moy in June 1989 and both debuted in defence. It was another massacre: we scored a meagre 1-1 against our neighbours' 4-10. Moving on to the grade 3 under-12 league, Cormac made the left-half back berth his own, while I floated around. For the game away to Derrylaughan, the rotating captaincy was bestowed on Cormac. He was truly chuffed to be picked to lead the Eglish team, aged just nine, having hardly pulled on the club *geansaí*.

The manager who appointed him to that role was Paddy

McIntosh. Neither of us knew him before that campaign, nor how central he would be to our future development. Paddy wasn't a native of Eglish, but a townie who grew up in Dungannon. He first came to the village to play basketball with former schoolfriends in the late 1960s, then joined the Eglish football team in time to become the championship-winning goalkeeper in 1970, and he ended up getting married and living in our parish.

Coaching youngsters became Paddy's vocation. Unlike most under-12 managers of a quarter-century ago, he didn't see the season ending with the last league game. After Mass every Sunday through the autumn and winter, he took our indoor Gaelic football sessions in Eglish hall. He coached the skills and refereed our games, of course, but he mentored us individually too. He sat us all down on the floor of the hall and gave us each a personal appraisal of our attributes and areas for improvement, always accentuating the positives.

Few people earmarked Cormac for sporting greatness. He wasn't selected for mini-sevens games at half-time on big matchdays, and didn't win any skills contests. But his puppy fat concealed an innate athletic engine. When Daddy took us to Kilbroney Park in south Down in the thick of winter for the Ulster NACA cross-country championships, the difference between us emerged. In the under-12 event, I went out in front, but suddenly panicked when the going got tough and dropped out. Cormac, as a newcomer, held on and came third in the under-10 race. On a warmer day, at the Mary Peters Track in Belfast, he excelled again, collecting silver medals in the 60 metres and long jump.

A dentist, visiting our school to discuss oral hygiene, gave out plaque-disclosing tablets which stained teeth blue. Hours later, Derry-latinee/Roan journeyed to Moortown to play a football game. Teams from the shores of Lough Neagh were reputedly hard nuts and Cormac hadn't won either of his under-12 games there the previous summer. When he and J. P. had got changed to play, Mrs McNeice noticed their teeth were blue and asked what was going on. 'We want to show our teeth and scare them, Miss,' came Cormac's reply. Despite this effort, they lost. Days later, Cormac's arm was fractured at school – while playing football, of course. He underwent an operation and three months in plastercast. '[B]ut somehow I was glad it happened,' he wrote months later, with a seemingly spartan insanity. Whatever doesn't kill you . . .

He was back to fitness in time to join Eglish under-12s in summer 1990. Thanks to the parish baby boom of 1978–9, we had essentially the same team as the previous year, but for a couple of players. With Cormac holding the left half-back spot, we steamrolled our way through the league. Having lost to Derrylaughan by 17 points the previous year, we turned the tables to win by 48. It was the third and bottom division, but we knew we had the nucleus of something special. The talent was there. So too was the discipline. And the camaraderie. The minibus back from our away games resounded to our reboot of the hit of the season:

> We're all part of Paddy's army /
> We're all off to . . . Galbally [or wherever we were playing] /
> And we'll really shake them up when we win the . . . football cup /
> 'Cos Eglish are the greatest football team.

3.   Naff and Naffer

'My personal interests are football, Athletics, Basketball, Hurling
and most sports. My ambition is to become a professional
footballer or to be a pilot. In 1990 I went to Donegal and played
golf every day for a week and came to the Sea, climbed the big
mountain up around Downings. I would love to go back there.
I sincerely hope with the start of the [Gulf] war that I will be
able to fill in any further details about myself.'
[from 'My Autobiography', school project, Autumn 1990]

When Cormac walked into St Patrick's Grammar School, Armagh,
on 28 August 1990, he was – at ten years and six months – the youngest of over 750 boys there, owing to that skipped class at primary
level.

Cormac and I were probably the first day-boys from Eglish parish
at school in Armagh. People often asked why we crossed the county
frontier, when most kids in the area went to Dungannon, Donaghmore or Ballygawley. Well, we lived as close to the Armagh schools
as the Tyrone ones. Also, our parents knew several teachers in
Armagh, and two of their siblings went there; they took part in
choirs and other cultural pursuits in the 'city of saints and scholars';
and they brought us to the cathedral on special occasions, such as the
funeral of Cardinal Ó Fiaich a few months before Cormac started
secondary school. The school was sited right behind the cathedral, at
the back of 'Sandy Hill'.

I had longed for Cormac's arrival throughout my first year in
Armagh. When I started there, I didn't really know anyone, and
while I made friends and learned my lessons, I still felt like a real outsider. Townie taunts about my (supposedly) backwoods Tyrone
origins and (allegedly) culchie accent and (definitely) unconventional

haircut left their mark in my gauche, gullible soul. Some mornings, the fear of going to school was mixed with anticipation of how things would be different when Cormac came under my wing.

I felt much more confident with him about. Each day we sat side by side on the No. 74 Tullymore Crossroads bus to and from Armagh: 'fratres in unum', like the school motto. I liked the idea of having to 'look out' for my little brother in a big school. Not that he really needed my help; he could take care of himself. A sudden infusion of Tyrone blood in Cormac's year also eased the transition. The Moy and Benburb lads, most of whom played sport as well, became our natural centre of gravity.

We were playing darts on the morning of Saturday, 19 January 1991, when the postman landed. We unfolded the results of our Christmas tests. For some reason I wrote them side by side in my diary as follows:

	DÓNAL	CORMAC
RE	77	93
French	75	90
Science	77	74
Music	78	97
Maths	60	93
English	63	A
IT	C	B
Irish	77	74
Art	73	82
Geography	73	82
History	74	84
Classical Civ.	73	98

Maybe it was simply worth recording as the big news of a dull day. But revisiting it now, it appears I was looking over my shoulder. We weren't taking the same exams, but I saw the new kid in town out-scoring me in most subjects. He would be my yardstick, and I his.

Cormac didn't stand out all that much, or excel in one particular thing. Even so, in most years Cormac received awards as one of the top three in his class.

His second year art-pad contains a drawing of Croke Park, with circles for spectators' heads, but this time with more structure. The Nally Stand is packed to the rafters; the Hogan, half full; the rest, empty. From the numbers noted at the top, it's clear he was counting heads in the crowd, and at 11,600 he was one-sixth of the way to capacity when he got sidetracked. An unfinished masterpiece.

Despite his high marks, he was no teacher's pet, and he didn't quite present himself like a model pupil. He had a peculiar way of holding a pen between his fingers, and teachers were constantly urging him to improve his handwriting. I invented my own word to tease him about his scrawl: 'Stedgly'.

His tie was often crooked, with sweat visible under his grey jumper and dripping off his head after break or lunchtime soccer games on the old tennis courts. He fought tooth and nail for every ball and argued the toss with anyone who cheated or messed about (as many did). Hearing the lads recollect him in this way now, I realize that I was the same – but at the time I couldn't understand why people thought us so similar.

As we got used to the place, we felt lucky to be at St Patrick's, as it catered for many more extracurricular activities than most schools: every kind of sport, except notably soccer and rugby, and plenty of music, drama and quizzes. We were also blessed with generous and understanding educators.

One of Cormac's talents – his remarkable recall – emerged in English class. One day in third year, Miss Fox cast the class's minds back to the time they studied 'The Lake Isle of Innisfree' two years before.

'Does anyone remember the words, to say it now?'

Heads down, muffled silence. Then a hand rose at the back of the room. 'Miss, eh, I think . . . I could have a go at it.'

'Go ahead, Cormac.'

'I will arise and go now, and go to Innisfree . . .'

It's said he recited it through, exactly.

That class did their fair share of poetry. Miss Fox was their form-teacher in 1B, English teacher for three years, and editor of the school magazine. As a first year, Cormac's poem 'Who wants a War?' was printed in the school mag. There was conscientious idealism in spades, though the lyrics – 'Chemical and nuclear, blowing up the world' – are more Cranberries or Black Eyed Peas than Owen or Sassoon. He improved. Three years in a row, his poems were published in Ulster schools' anthologies. They were decent compositions for his age. The best of them was called 'The Future' – of which more anon.

★

Playing what we played and living where we lived, near neither bus-stop nor club, required constant ferrying. Our parents went those extra miles, even the odd outrageous journey, so that we could play always. We demanded nothing less.

The family was on holiday in Donegal in the 'Twelfth' week, July 1992. Cormac agreed to go on condition that he get a lift back for our under-14 friendly away to Glenn, Co. Down. I wouldn't take the chance that they'd change their minds about making such a massive trip for a friendly, so I skipped the holiday and stayed with our grandparents. The team bus waited for Cormac until we had to leave without him. It looked like wise heads had decided to stay in Donegal. But as we warmed up, this pinball figure hurtled up the pitch, yanking a liquorice jersey over his head.

Paddy McIntosh often retold that tale to illustrate our extraordinary dedication as players. But the real dedication was Mummy's: she drove those 115 miles on a Wednesday evening, stopping in Letterkenny to buy new boots for Cormac, and then back. Mummy, being the most genuine and considerate of people, made countless sacrifices for us.

Our father's style was different. He tried to use gentle taunts to spur you on. Halfway through a plate of dinner, he'd interject, 'You're not fit for it!' Sporting praise was hard won. Cormac could notch three points in a league game, only to be pressed in the car home as to why he didn't handle another ball better. Even as I write this, he doesn't ask, *How are you getting on with the book?* No, it's only ever, *Have you not this book writ yet?* But in accompanying us everywhere, he was our biggest and proudest fan, who brooked no criticism of us from anyone else.

Hard work was taught by example in our house. There was always something happening, and it was usually quite loud. As Cormac crammed for A-Level Maths, our house was hosting historians for the 350th anniversary of the Battle of Benburb, while re-enactors jousted in nearby fields.

Our parents inculcated honesty, integrity, respect for others and empathy for the underdog. Most of all, they taught us to be and think for ourselves, to debate a point out fully, not follow the herd or be shallow sycophants.

We didn't wish to be the cool kids. We were naff and naffer. We wore white socks with black shoes. Truly, we had a sheltered existence. We never troubled teenage discos, nor did we care.

Our lives were as intertwined as twins', aside from the gap of nineteen months and a few inches. Outside classroom hours, we were stuck together. Walking the 2.6 miles home from the bus stop when a lift from family or friends was wanting. Stopping for a few moments on the Battleford Bridge, the Armagh–Tyrone boundary, to soak up the splendour of the Blackwater gushing eastward. Taking shortcuts home through fields and over streams. Later, bussing home in the dark from training sessions, Monday to Thursday. Heading to the Moy on Friday evenings, and later to basketball club youth coaching in Dungannon.

Our summers revolved around work and sport. We didn't go to Gaeltacht courses, contrary to what some people imagine. Instead, each year we toiled hard with McGeary's of Collegeland, on their strawberry fields mostly, picking mushrooms the odd afternoon, even footing turf on a rare day. Cormac also worked a few days at the spuds with our neighbours, the Downeys. But the strawberries were our main fix, for seven seasons.

On those balmy afternoons in the drills, I was struck by a sense of our brotherly bond and the inevitable passing of youth. I didn't want it to end. One day, as the two of us sat alone, facing each other in the back of Leo's van on a journey, I expressed sadness that our childhood was nearly behind us. Cormac wondered what I was on about.

Perhaps my recent fourteenth birthday had turned me all sentimental. I found it hard to articulate why the spectre of adulthood caused me anxiety, but something told me that what we had between us would be lost along the way.

Sport defined the rest of our holidays. Week-long pitch and putt in Donegal in '92. Petanque throughout our family break in Brittany in '91. Watching every minute of the Barcelona Olympics. Pool-table marathons played out against the soundtrack of the O. J. trial on TV. Powerful debates over whether Chester Williams' place in the Springbok squad truly signified a watershed for apartheid; he said yes, I was a nay-sayer. On his craze for cricket, I demurred further.

Cormac and I had never been to an eleven-a-side soccer match of any description, but we managed to persuade Daddy that the 1994 World Cup coincided with an urgent need to catch up with American relations. They kindly made Philadelphia, Poughkeepsie and Washington D.C. our bases. Our tickets entitled us to see the Group E winners, which, for a few Houghton-inspired halcyon days, seemed sure to be the Republic. Luis García Postigo scuppered that and put Mexico top of the table. Bulgaria became our adopted team. We saw them shock the Mexicans and we leaped at Letchkov's winning goal against Germany in the quarters at Giants' Stadium.

Hurling was the one sport we missed out on. We craved to play it, and pucked about at home, but without a local club outlet we didn't acquire the skills needed to make Armagh school teams. Aged sixteen, Cormac finally got to line out for Clann na nGael, a new hurling club based around nearby Killeeshil. His debut, against Carrickmore in a minor league tie at Eglish, typified the sorry state of the game in Tyrone: the referee failed to show.

One-on-one, we kept playing and competing through our teens about home. I still held the upper hand in most things, clinging on to a vestige of alpha-male status. Only in table tennis did he put the hex on me with his quick reflexes. For a wrestling opponent, he looked elsewhere. His class had their own king-of-the-ring bouts at lunchtime, and even on the minibus to and from Seagahan Dam with 'Liamy', the science teacher who couldn't give a damn. Even when triple-teamed, Cormac never gave in. He stayed over with his close friend Paul Toner from Tassagh for Wrestlemanias and battles royale. He loved the theatrics, and the faux analysis of 'scientific wrestling' by Doink the Clown and the Repo Man. The Undertaker was his favourite, then Million Dollar Man Ted DiBiase. He pranced about the house in Hulk Hogan poses, tearing off his top, flexing biceps, affecting a grimace of superiority while nodding in self-adulation and urging us to work hard, say our prayers, and eat our vitamins. He put on a preposterous pair of dungarees as his 'wrestling suit' and made Fergus his practice partner – or victim. At least one bed was wrecked in the process.

In those days, he loved winding up our younger brother for sport. He'd challenge Fergus to an A-Team quiz, ask a ridiculously unfair question, and then taunt him. 'That's it! I know more about the A-Team than Fergus does!' Fergus fumed, like B.A. after a plane ride. Nightly, between his renditions of 'Bohemian Rhapsody' and The KLF's 'Justified and Ancient' on a plastic pink echo-mic, to Atlantic 252 in the background, he would saunter over to Fergus's room, call out, 'You owe me rent!' and threaten flustered Ferg with eviction.

He was mischievous with me too, and liked to push his luck to provoke a reaction, by spitting water at me or saying something rude. On occasions I got too aggressive and forceful with him. Mummy continually reiterated that one blow could be fatal, and asked how we would feel then. Daddy laid down that brothers shouldn't quarrel, for we'd be long enough apart. He meant it: in 1992 he barred me from going to the Monaghan–Derry championship game as punishment for hitting Cormac.

But I wasn't a scrapper by nature. The only times I ever waded into football scuffles, it was to defend Cormac. Otherwise, even if 27 other players mucked into a melee, I'd detach myself from the idiocy and futility of it all. He didn't get involved much either.

I was protective of Cormac, ludicrously so. In that summer of '92, just turned fourteen, I took a Tipp-Ex bottle to my new copy of Liam Hayes's autobiography, *Out of our Skins*, and blanked out all 36½ expletives in the vain hope of keeping twelve-year-old Cormac pure of mind.

Nearly any interest or pastime I had, however nerdy, he followed my lead. Collecting coins and GAA programmes were listed as hobbies on his maroon PVC National Record of Achievement file, which all Northern Irish pupils had to compile. His profile matched mine almost word for word.

For some reason, I entered his name – more so than my own – in a plethora of competitions. Hence Cormac McAnallen first appears in sports magazines of the early '90s as the winner of videos about Gaelic games, George Best, Gary Lineker and Gordon Strachan.

I watched out for him in other ways, too. The day after the 1995 All-Ireland final, the school prefects were announced – eight for sixth form and eight for seventh. Although pupils cast votes, we all believed the prefects were somehow anointed from above, as teachers' pets tended to be picked rather than the popular class jesters. I was named but Cormac wasn't, to my vexation. Still sour over the football, I vowed no more injustice. Hastily, I vented to Mr Savage, a senior teacher, about the unfair exclusion of a model pupil who had given his all for the school without currying favour, and I dared to question the selection method. I had some gall, and still I can barely believe I said it, for Savage had cultivated a stern image – 'Savage by name, savage by nature', as Cormac said. Savage assured me that the result was genuine. In his final year, Cormac was ordained a prefect.

Faith mattered to Cormac. Like most rural Irish teens of that era, we were reared to observance: Sundays, holy days, sacraments, Brigid's crosses, religious education and clerical mentoring. But his belief came from within and largely resided there. Of his own accord as a teenager, he said grace privately to himself before and after evening meals. This ritual helped him to remain grounded and to keep sight of true priorities. I recall him espousing the Catholic emphasis on charitable good works as a way to salvation. Obeying precepts and examining one's conscience mirrored and complemented the discipline preached by sports coaches. He was praying and playing, 'ambitious for the higher gifts'.

Between provincial and all-Ireland tournaments in Gaelic fooball and basketball, Scór, and Pioneer and schools' quizzes, he was seldom off the road in pursuit of medals, plaques and crystal paperweights.

By the age of eighteen, he had covered every Irish county on competitive outings and contested head-to-heads with sixty-plus schools and teams of all sorts from all but six counties.

*

For all that Cormac played, he did not have the look of an athlete. At ten, he was a stocky broth of a boy with tufty hair and a moon-faced smile. He was also freckled and susceptible to sunburn – indeed, the softest-skinned of the family. In my memory, this Cormac is always wearing that classic green Meath jersey with gold pinstripe squares that he bought for £10 from Begley's shop in Dungannon in 1990.

By twelve, he had a barrel chest and a medieval mop-top. In that year's Eglish under-12 team picture, he was tall, not the tallest, but more notable for his puppy fat. He was never slow, though. He ran cross-country for the school team and people began to talk of his great engine.

Coaching obviously pushed him on a lot (more on the men responsible anon). But he also took great inspiration from the 'Kerry's Golden Years' video. We had bought it at the old Croke Park shop when he was about ten. Cormac watched it almost daily till he could recite Michael O'Hehir's lines and re-enact the scenes in our practice games at home.

Before a free-kick: 'Here cometh the equaliser.'

After a chip-up: 'reminiscent of the late Paudie'.

Around the goalmouth: 'Oh danger for Dublin there!'

Following a sloppy goal: 'the greatest frace [sic] of all time!'

For a screamer: 'Jackie . . . wang!'

Post-action (in a Jimmy Keaveney chirp): 'I don't care if we never win another bloody match!'

Running about with up to seven teams at once firmed him up. Within three years, he changed a lot, thinning out and pushing six feet. Still, when on *Blackboard Jungle* in 1995, the bio line that he played basketball concluded with the caveat: 'He says he makes up for his lack of height by sheer determination.' A few months later, sixteen-year-old Cormac was a taut 6' 1" and 13 stone.

He had become fitness-minded as an early teen, before that was the norm. He ran circuits of the lawn and apple trees, just to see how far he could go. 'I just ran forty-five laps,' he'd tell me with glee, then beat it next time. I never joined him. He loved to get dirty, too: when the ground was waterlogged, he went out 'muck-sliding' by himself, ever striving for a longer, filthier slide. Meanwhile, he began practising intensely with his left foot and kicking at the barn door for accuracy.

Cormac also owed a nod to his grandfather and his hearthside homilies. 'If you want to play football, get out the skipping rope!' he barked at us lustily. He had been fighting fit in young manhood, a phenomenal swimmer, and he played for the Moy and a clutch of north Armagh clubs – though his accounts of punching a ball over the bar from the corner flag stretched credulity.

Perhaps no one else ever followed Gandy's drill, but Cormac did. He was fourteen when he rounded up a rope and started skipping. Before long, he mastered the running skip as well as the basic jump. His footwork wouldn't have won any awards, but hard practice pumped up his physique and pepped his step at a pivotal point in his development.

*

Scanning through the pictures of past teams on the school walls, Cormac saw famous faces. As well as Armagh stars, there were big names from Derry, Antrim and Tyrone. He was proud to read how much former Tyrone heroes like Eddie Devlin and the solo-running sorcerer Iggy Jones had done to forge the school's football tradition.

In 2004, he would write a piece for the MacRory Cup final programme:

> I was very aware from first year of just how important MacRory [Cup] success was to the school. As the seat of Cardinal MacRory himself, and with the school's excellent record in the competition's early years [. . .] you were reminded every day by photographs and trophy cabinets of a proud tradition that was to be upheld.

That tradition had flatlined by the time we started at St Patrick's

Grammar. One Monday in September 1990, he got a clue as to why. Wanting to dissect the previous day's Cork–Meath All-Ireland football final, he found others dwelling on Liverpool 4–0 versus Man Utd. He had supported Liverpool since their 1986 double, but the idea that an English soccer league match could stir pupils more so than the national GAA final perplexed him. Where was the passion for Gaelic games he was used to in Tyrone? Was he at the wrong school?

St Patrick's Grammar was the product of a merger, two years earlier, of St Patrick's College and Armagh Christian Brothers' school, and the infusion of new pupils bolstered the school's dreams of football glory. The senior team reached the MacRory semi in Cormac's first year; he went along to lend support, while I stayed at home. St Patrick's lost to St Colman's of Newry at Lurgan on that murky day, 2 March 1991, but he was hooked.

Junior football in the school was in a miserable state overall. Second- and third-year teams were sent out to their slaughter. Forty-point defeats weren't uncommon. There was no whole-school coaching masterplan, no gatekeepers of the game such as Adrian McGuckin in Maghera or Ray Morgan in St Colman's. While Armagh school sides invariably improved as they matured, they were playing catch-up.

Cormac made his debut for a first-year team that beat Keady high school in a pre-Christmas challenge, then he played a game for the 'B' team, but kept in the mix for the 'A' side and figured in blitz tournaments in the spring.

In his second year, Cormac secured the full-back berth on the D'Alton Cup (under-13½) side. Fr McAleer managed this Tyrone-dominated team. There was a quintet from the Moy: Ryan Kelly in goals; Karol McQuade wore No. 4; Paul 'Mini' Holmes, No. 6; Paul Mellon, 7; and Karol's older brother, Francis, No. 11. Rory O'Donnell of Edendork donned the 15 jersey.

And me too. As I had a July birthday, I could play for the school year below me. I came in at right corner-back, as Cormac's wingman. Following a sharp growth spurt, I was the beanpole of the team – I towered fully three red bricks above Cormac in the official squad picture – and I felt a bit daft to be in the corner; but I was just glad to play alongside him.

In that spring of '92 we qualified for the quarter-finals with ease. Then we met St Patrick's, Maghera, the modern masters of Ulster colleges' football. They diced us up by 15 points at Coalisland.

Cormac's progress in schools football was far from linear. He got his worst roasting ever in a friendly at St David's, Artane, in October '92. 'Rayo', a titanic target-man, pinched three goals off Cormac in half an hour; I moved back from midfield and was chuffed to snuff out his scoring. As my lanky physique filled out, I had leaped ahead of Cormac again on school teams; inside six months, I had gone from second-year sub to fifth-year corner-back.

A few weeks later Cormac received a call-up to the fourth-year panel. This was a sizeable step up for a twelve-year-old into an under-15½ competition, but he was disappointed not to be a starter, while I played at full-forward. We qualified for the quarter-finals to meet mighty Maghera again in January 1993. After a torrid twenty minutes, Cormac came on at corner-back and shored up the defence, but the damage was already done and we endured a 14-point punishment.

Cormac, like myself, could play for the school-year below him; in fact, for his second tilt at the D'Alton Cup in spring '93, he was still one of the younger players. He moved to midfield and was appointed captain. Promising players were peppered around this new team, including Philip Jordan, Kevin McElvanna, Paddy McKeever and Paul McCormack . . . five future All-Ireland medallists, all told. As a unit, somehow, they malfunctioned. A chequered league campaign prefaced a lame quarter-final defeat to St Michael's, Enniskillen. A year later, that group didn't even reach the last eight of Corn na nÓg.

A further blip in Cormac's progress chart occurred in autumn '93. In the Rannafast Cup fifth-year (Ulster under-16½) competition, he sat on the sideline for all six games, while twenty-three others featured, and I switched between full-back and full-forward. Once again, we perished in the quarter-finals. This time, St Patrick's Academy, Dungannon, thrashed us by 17 points. Not getting on hurt him all the more that day in Eglish, our own ground.

At last, nearing the end of the 1993/4 academic year, our fortunes turned. The school was still under a cloud since the senior team's MacRory Cup final meltdown at Armagh on St Patrick's Day. We were there, among the thousands, wondering whether our school would ever win anything on a field.

The new Ulster under-15½ championship allowed us to dispel such doubts. We had essentially the same promising squad from the D'Alton Cup two years earlier. For once, a quarter-final brought joy: we blitzed the Academy by 10 points in Dungannon. Cormac missed our semi-final win over St Macartan's of Monaghan, being on Ulster basketball duty. That decision made him fodder for locker-room ribbing by our captain, Barry Gordon. But our managers, Brother Ennis and Damian Woods, reinstated him at corner-back for the final, while I was up at full-forward. On a scorching Saturday, 28 May 1994, we beat St Colman's by a point on rock-hard Páirc an Iúir. For the first time in years, Armagh had won a schools' provincial football prize.

Except that no cup had been forged for the new competition. Brother Ennis was also the Ulster Colleges Council president, with some plenary power, and he sensed a publicity coup for our school. He sent Ronan Hart, an older pupil, to his car boot. Hart burst into our dressing room with this tall old wooden contraption, a long-forgotten, but now recycled prize. We roared. We had won the Nannery Trophy.

When you win at that age, you look only upward. We could almost put money on our winning the Rannafast Cup in the autumn. A 13-point tanking of St Macartan's in the quarter-final set up another tilt at the Academy in Middletown. Fifty minutes in, the scores were level. Surely we had the edge. But Dungannon goaled again. Cormac was corner-back on paper but his man was roaming out-field. To Cormac fell two of our best chances to equalize, but he fluffed them. We were gutted to lose by two. Cormac would reach another Rannafast semi-final a year later, and again a team of future Armagh and Tyrone stars fell short.

The MacRory Cup was the one that really counted. Cormac got his first lash at the premier competition in 1995/6. The school's forty-two-year itch had now become interwoven with Brother Ennis's personal crusade. We knew him simply as The Brother. A Westmeath native, he had taught in the North for almost four decades, shouldered thankless tasks like coaching Antrim footballers and Tyrone hurlers, and had several frustrating near-misses in his bid for MacRory glory. He gave his all and had his teams spoiled rotten, without getting them over the line. He taught Maths and persuaded Cormac, like many players before him, to choose it as an A-Level subject, on the basis that 'all good footballers are good at Maths'.

'Expectations were not terribly high,' Cormac wrote later, 'but we topped the group and put in a hard winter's training.' A tender fifteen, he didn't get on at the outset. The third game, against St Michael's, Enniskillen, saw him blossom. I injured my thumb and he replaced me at centre half-forward after ten minutes. He did well and fisted a point in Armagh's best MacRory performance in years, a 2-10 to 0-6 triumph. His reward was the No. 10 spot the next day out against Abbey CBS, Newry.

That winter catalysed Cormac's rapid maturation. Membership of the flagship school team makes you feel like a man. It's not just the rigorous regime of slogging up slopes and treading quagmires. It's being treated as important – like Des Mackin, the behemoth who bestrode the school with impunity for five years. It's attracting a fan club, old and young, male and female. It was car stereos and house parties looping mix-tapes of hyper trance, then going out at night as a team, drenched in Lynx and Cool Water. It was also open access to alcohol. In this milieu, I could see greenhorn Cormac growing up in a hurry, looking and sounding different. I had resolved to abstain from alcohol for good, so I surprised myself when I told him that if he wanted to drink, I wouldn't make a fuss. He didn't take long to start.

Our 17-point obliteration of Omagh CBS in the quarter-final sent our spirits too high. We ran out the tunnel at Coalisland to meet St Mary's, Magherafelt, semi-final rookies, puffed up with complacency. In hail and sleet we were dire from the get-go, not passing second gear, while Kevin Madden and Paul McFlynn flung over their points. Cormac and I were marooned side by side in the full-forward line for half an hour, little going our way. Late on, I was hauled off, then he was too. That was my last year, and I'd be gone before most of the team would make one last bid for the MacRory Cup.

That campaign had a gratifying postscript. The Brother organized a ten-day summer trip to America for the MacRory Cup squad, calling on his network of east coast contacts to put us up. The Artane Boys Band played a fund-raising concert for us. We also collected sponsorship for a 5k run that only five of the Tyrone lads and two Armagh boys did at all. One boy blew his sponsorship money on drink. That set the tone.

We stayed first at Manhattan College, went up the World Trade Center, and played an adult New York 'county' XV at Van Cortlandt Park. This was more an Average Joe team, but they observed the homicidal rites of Big Apple football – even on minors. The orb was barely airborne before the lump-extraction began. One head wound later, a clump of Cormac's hair was shaved off. In Boston our host, a fifty-year-old ex-teacher from Monaghan named Brendan Crawley, had converted his basement with disco decor. The squad had to kip on the floor, so, sadly, our teachers had to relocate for two nights. Brendan ordered in three kegs and invited a posse of au pairs. The cops called twice. Soberly I spun the discs. Next day, I filled in for Brendan at work, dusting a few Boston mansions for a cool $90.

That trip was Cormac's introduction to team bonding, I guess. A big season lay ahead.

★

For a few years of his teens, Cormac gave as much energy to basketball as to football, and reaped greater rewards from it.

Basketball was nominally the school's second sport, but in the 1970s and 1980s it was St Patrick's College's most successful code. Pictures of Ulster champion basketball sides and international players sat beside the old-framed footballers on the 'good' wall of the school's lengthy main corridor. Past pupils like Eugene Young, Paul McErlean and Joe Brolly had excelled in both sports. Each year they returned to play in the annual past-pupils' blitz on our wooden court, and we marvelled at their skills.

In Cormac's second year, that quintet of future All-Ireland foot-ballers coalesced again on court: Philip Jordan, Kevin McElvanna, Paul McCormack, Paddy McKeever and Cormac. Maths teacher John 'Sammy' Collins recruited Chris Faloon, the curly-maned Donaghmore entrepreneur, to train them. After they lost the Ulster semi-final, the coaches advised them to sign up for Dungannon basketball summer camp to hone their play.

Cormac and six other St Patrick's boys did as instructed. This annual camp was a big deal: over a hundred adolescents from around Ulster came to learn from leading Irish and American coaches, all organized by Frankie O'Loane, the pillar of the Dungannon club. At the end of the week, Cormac lost the junior boys' one-on-one final to his school colleague, Declan McAuley. Time for more practice at the hoop Daddy had just put up in our back yard.

St Patrick's cruised through the 1992/3 Ulster under-13½ cham-pionship, culminating in a 26-point drubbing of Our Lady's of Castleblayney.

I played in the Ulster under-14½ decider that year. We lost to Castleblayney at Maysfield, but my 23-point haul represented a per-sonal redemption. Twelve months earlier, in the under-13½ final, against 'blayney too, I had been making my first start; after a few errors, some smart-alecs in the crowd from St Malachy's of Belfast had a go:

'Dó-nal is an inter-nation-al'.

Clap, clap, clap-clap-clap, clap-clap-clap-clap, 'Dónal!'

(And, while on the bench) – 'What do we want?' / 'Dónal' / 'When do want him?' / 'Now!'

I put a brave face on it as the tale reverberated around school, but felt rather mortified. Cormac wasn't present, but he heard about it. So inasmuch as I made up for it the following year, it mattered to me that he witnessed it, and that he would be in some way proud of me. When we discussed the game afterwards, I fished for compliments from him. Then I understood that an essential dynamic of our rela-tionship was my innate desire for him to look up to me.

On return to summer camp in '93, Cormac won the junior 'hot-shot' and MVP awards. In 1994 he was selected for Ulster in an under-15 interprovincial tournament in Waterford. It's remembered for his two-handed overhead shot from top of the D, tossed backward like a bridal bouquet. Swish! A year later, he was named Ulster under-15 captain, and first reserve for Ireland under-15s – but no call-up, much to his dejection.

At that level, most of the players were all hip-hop skills, designer trainers and fancy moves. Cormac was the no-fuss, budget-price opposite. His ascent owed to hard work and sheer aggression. His teammates were constantly impressed by his ability to outjump and outmuscle much taller opponents under the boards.

Cormac's school team won the under-14½ title in 1994 and the under-15½ crown in 1995. The following year, they gave St Malachy's the stuffing they deserved in the under-16½ ('Cadet') final at Maysfield, to achieve a four-in-a-row sequence. By then, Cormac was top scorer, averaging 19 points.

Winning Ulster titles in basketball and travelling around the island for All-Ireland tournament matches complemented the making of Cormac as a Gaelic footballer. His man-marking and spatial defensive nous were enhanced. He honed his passing and movement in attack. Racing up and down the court did no harm to his stamina. Above all, he learned to outmanoeuvre bigger opponents under the basket – vital preparation to mix it with the big boys in the midfield cauldron of Clones.

★

Following Tyrone through the early '90s involved many thrills but mounting frustrations. The under-21 teams of that era engendered real excitement about the county and attracted a loyal band of travelling supporters. Cormac and I were in Mullingar when Kerry trounced Tyrone in the 1990 final. At Newbridge in '91 we were entranced by their cosmic display to get revenge on the Kingdom. After they ground down Galway to retain the cup in '92, we loitered in the Longford Arms till late to talk to our new heroes. These were Tyrone's first national titles in our lifetimes, and we sensed that greater glory lay around the corner.

We were already subscribers to the cult of Peter Canavan. On those road trips we saw him perform inimitable magic tricks that no one else could even attempt. We argued he was Tyrone's greatest already; older folk quibbled. And he was among us, tangible at every other turn: watching us on stage in Scór in Ballygawley hall in December '91; refereeing our D'Alton Cup game against Omagh CBS in March '92; cutting the cord at the 'Tour of Eglish' bicycle run in July '92, and drawing Cormac's name as winner of an O'Neill's ball; and selling a ticket to Cormac at Dunmoyle two years later, on a day when we attended four club games. Yet, when asked to name his favourite player, Cormac didn't want to give the standard answer. Instead, he would volunteer Tyrone corner-back Paul Devlin, for he saw in the unsung Moortown man a dour doggedness to aspire to when playing the same role.

All the while, fans became ever more frustrated with a series of senior team setbacks. We had hard-luck stories aplenty: Raymond Munroe's disallowed goal in Armagh in '90; Damien Cassidy's few extra steps to net for Derry in '91; Anthony Tohill's freak goal in the devastating NFL final collapse of '92; and a string of injuries a year later. Plunkett Donaghy's stroll to goal put paid to Armagh at Omagh in 1994 and liberated us Tyrone lads at St Patrick's after four years of taunting about our championship duck. Defeat by Down in the Ulster final brought us back down to earth.

Daddy drove us to every Ulster final, regardless of who was playing. And as other Ulster counties advanced on a remarkable run of four All-Ireland titles for the province, we followed them. We urged on Down from the upper Cusack Stand at the '91 semi-final. We boarded a school bus to cheer on Armagh – yes, Armagh! – in the '92 minor final, and celebrate Donegal's senior title; Cormac clambered over the Croke Park fence to celebrate, and collect some coloured centrefield sod as a souvenir. (It's still in a jar.) In 1993, we waited in the Moy square for three hours with Fergus and Mark Jordan, before anyone else, for the homecoming Derry team. And in '94, we flocked to Newry to meet the Down side at the GOAL charity game.

We wanted to do something distinctive as Tyrone supporters, not rely on generic merchandise. Cormac had long been intrigued by the

Cork fans' inventiveness in brandishing Japanese and US Confederate standards – for aesthetic reasons, full stop. We scoured a book on world flags until we found the right one. Tonga: a red field with a white canton charged with a red cross. We got Mummy to stitch together our Tyrone flag with a difference. That Tongan flag travelled the country in Cormac's hands for three or four years.

Tyrone's golden year arrived in 1995, sort of. On the day we 'beat Derry with thirteen men' at Clones, Cormac and I jumped around in ecstasy on the Hill terrace, hugging each other – and strangers too – once Jody Gormley's insurance point looped over. Surely Tyrone would complete a cycle of five All-Irelands for Ulster and claim its own first.

For the final against Dublin, the pair of us stood behind the Canal End goal, with Fergus and the Moy lads from school. We danced with delight as Sean McLaughlin's late equalizer sailed over. Seconds passed before we realized the score had been voided – the referee awarded a free out, mistakenly thinking the ball had been handled on the ground. The final whistle sounded. We stood on for ages in a daze of shock and anger. How could such a colossal injustice be visited upon our poor county, to hand a twenty-second title to Dublin?! Daddy was staying the night, but Cormac and I went to hitch for home in dismay, and were spared the thumbing only when our neighbour Seamus Donnelly gave us a lift.

Cormac had a small consolation. We had both entered the first-ever Gaelic 'fantasy football' competition, run by the *Irish Independent*, and followed it closely. In the closing weeks, Cormac's selection sneaked into the national top ten. He had picked several Tyrone men and Cavan free-taker Ronan Carolan, and won himself a blue sweater.

As Tyrone fans we suffered yet more trials in 1996. The first team to retain the Ulster title in two decades, and the most experienced of the last four, Tyrone were favourites to beat an old-meets-new Meath mash-up. What horrors we had in store. The blood, bandages, crunched bones, and collapsed spine of that team left a scar on the collective psyche of a county. Compounding the agony, Tyrone people were advised to man up and stop whingeing. But we could see that another generation might pass from the county jersey without the holy grail.

4.   A Name for the Future

We started at the bottom with Eglish. The club had won consecutive minor county championships in 1986–7 – a stunning coup – but barren numbers left the club barely able to field at youth level thereafter.

This is how low it had fallen. In the 1990 Féile na nÓg under-14 championship, Eglish were drawn against lowly Fintona. Cormac was ten, and I was eleven, and we read about it that day. We begged Mummy to take us in case we might get a game, but we couldn't find the Dunmoyle pitch and arrived well into the first half. Yes, we both got on. In a 47–0 drubbing. I recall the ball crossing the halfway line twice.

Our young crop were the next great black-and-white hopes. Paddy McIntosh stepped up with us to manage us as under-14s in 1991. We marched to the county grade-two league final, but Loughmacrory downed us by a dozen points. Cormac and I were both on the left wing of a defence that shipped 5-10.

We were effectively demoted to the new grade three in 1992, due to a careless county board decision. We won every game by double figures. In the Féile knockout, we skinned a couple of higher-ranked teams before choking against Errigal Ciaran on a sweltering May day. Still, we spoke of our unshakeable belief then that we'd be in grade one for our minor days and might even win it.

We had the right mentors to improve us. We were a well-mannered bunch to begin with, but Paddy's zero-tolerance policy ensured that we stayed that way:

No swearing.

No backchat to anyone.

No surnames or nicknames, however innocuous, when addressing colleagues; first names only.

Train or get no game.

Get stuck in, but never strike an opponent.

Paddy built up such a rapport with each of us on a personal level that we didn't want to betray his trust. When addressing us individually with a Coke can glued to one hand and a fag in the other, he'd dispense wisdom and preface it with, 'I'm telling you this as a friend,' which made you feel important.

Under Paddy's scrupulously fair regime, the strong players were asked to give special coaching to the weak ones. Like a biblical shepherd worrying about his one lost sheep, Paddy pressed us to encourage our brother Fergus to join the Eglish football fold, long after we had abandoned that cause.

In these campaigns, Paddy had a good foil in Kieran Daly, his fellow mentor. Kieran spoke little but his words impacted and enforced. One evening, as we stood outside the hall before a Féile match, Kieran saw a player spitting and sent him home on the spot. In 60-plus competitive games in eight seasons under these men, we only had two sendings-off. We were warned that other clubs didn't always uphold such standards. 'When you boys go to the lough-shore, yiz are gonna get sput at,' Paddy advised us.

This thesis was tested at an under-16 league match at Ardboe in September '93. We had a surprise lead in the second half when the referee sent off two natives for verbals; when he got another earful, he whistled game over. Chaos ensued. Our lads became fair game for retribution. Marty McCann was head-butted, a gang of four set on Eugene Daly, and we were locked out of the dressing rooms for a quarter of an hour. Paddy had already gone, abruptly, having received the news that his brother had died. The whole episode was surreal and scary for us fourteen- and fifteen-year-olds, and to this day we have no idea why it all happened.

Cormac had started that campaign on the bench. Everyone else saw him as an automatic pick, but Paddy didn't want him hurt in the crossfire of a local derby. It took just fifteen minutes of Ryan Mellon scything us open for Paddy to reverse that policy.

Promotion slipped our grip that year. With almost all the same hands, we returned to grade-two under-16 fare in 1994. From August into autumn we made silage of opponents; then we spluttered to a horrific halt in the championship semi-final, losing to our bogey side,

Brackaville, by an agonizing point. We made no mistake in the league, beating Donagheady in the final.

Cormac was eligible for each age-level for two years after me, and on these teams he was becoming a more central figure. He was corner-back on the 1993 under-14 team that won grade three and reached the county Féile semi. He was a rock-solid full-back for them as under-16s in 1995, winning the grade-two double. Their manager was the rather laidback Brian 'Reddy' Murtagh. (Cormac yearned to ring up Murtaghs', ask for Brian, scream down the line: 'ARE . . . YOU . . . REDDYYY?!' – and hang up.)

Back with my age group, Cormac ascended to minor competition in 1995, in grade two. We came under the wing of Patsy Jordan, who had managed all the minor teams from the champions of 1986–7 and through the long wilderness years when pickings were slim to non-existent. The bitter pill of a narrow league final defeat to an Edendork/Killyman combination was sweetened by the realization that all bar one of our team would be eligible again next time around.

A smouldering subplot on the touchline left a cliffhanger at the end of '95: who would manage us in '96, our year of destiny?

★

Saturday, 21 September 1996, was the day that Cormac became talked of as a future Tyrone player. That day, Eglish contested the county minor final at O'Neill Park, Dungannon.

Such a prospect had appeared to be very distant eight months earlier. A row over who would manage the team caused a big division within the club and threatened to ruin our season.

Paddy McIntosh, having coached us all the way up the ladder of youth football since Cormac was in single digits, let it be known that he wanted to take us now as minors. He had been involved in the 1995 minor set-up for a while, but left as he felt his input was diluted.

Managing us to success as minors had been Paddy's ambition for a long time. We all knew that. Our group had become one of the most important things in his life. So much time and emotion had he invested in us, and so carefully had he crafted our team, that he had become part of us too. If he missed out on this chance, he'd be devastated; and if we failed to win without him, the 'what ifs' would multiply. So it distressed the squad to think he would not be involved when we reached our peak.

As in most clubs, there were layers of factional friction at play. Paddy played up his persona as the classic players' man, club outsider, outlaw. Habitually, during his private chats with players, he looked over his shoulder, sidled a few feet outward and advised, 'Never talk beneath an open window.' His suspicions worked on our fertile teenage minds like an *X-Files* plotline.

A hastily written letter was handed to the club secretary, bearing twenty-odd names, and requesting Paddy Mac as our manager. It had come from within the squad; most players, when canvassed, assented to support it, but did not see it, or sign it; neither did I, before you ask.

What we, as impressionable young lads, thought logical, wasn't necessarily seen as such by others. Paddy was not due to 'lose' his job, as he had never been the minor boss; the existing minor coach would be pushed aside if we got our way. We weren't considering things like that in depth. Moreover, the club didn't have a specific policy of assigning coaches to ascend up through the age levels with a team.

Worse still, the letter also presumed to name Paddy's backroom set-up.

We hadn't made any threats, but damage was done and people were hurt. The entire minor panel was summoned to face the committee. In train we trudged up the narrow, creaky stairs to the meeting room. We sat in a long line along the right-hand wall, the club officers staring back at us. Outrage poured forth at our sheer audacity. No one had ever heard the like of it. Who did we think we were? Minors were to be seen, not heard. We weren't even old enough to vote, let alone make decisions for the committee!

If emotions weren't heightened enough that evening, we also received a letter of resignation from Paddy. 'I sincerely do not want to subject you to any more inconvenience that would unsettle your team,' he explained in capitalized blue biro. Whatever the club would do, it 'cannot erase the great memories we have shared over the years together'.

Nevertheless, seeing that the job had become almost a poisoned chalice, the committee appointed Paddy as our manager, with Kieran Daly alongside him – the partnership we had grown up with. Club grandees told us bluntly that after all our words we'd better deliver.

By our mutiny we had cranked up the pressure on ourselves. In our maiden league game, unfancied Galbally sprang a shock 1-point defeat on us. Right fools we'd appear if this form persisted. The defence required surgery. Cormac sidestepped from the right corner to full-back and Greg O'Neill moved to No. 6. That would realign our spine for the rest of the season. But when our old foes from Ardboe ambushed as at home with two second-half goals, Paddy flipped his lid. His special team had never lost at home before. This time, we were detained *inside* our dressing room; in half an hour of the hair-drier, fresh laws were laid down.

The improvement was immense. Once we got going, we were some team. We slammed eight goals past Naomh Muire, beat Clonoe by 9 points, Brackaville by 10, and Dungannon by a dozen. In the league semi-final, we eclipsed Errigal Ciaran. The minor championship draw panned out ideally. We coasted through the aperitif rounds and avenged Galbally with aplomb in the semi. We were in two grade-one finals. How bizarre, how bizarre, as OMC played out on the radio.

Coalisland Fianna would be formidable final opponents. As reigning champions with thirteen of the winning panel still involved, they were the hot favourites. We had beaten them twice in the league, but this time, unlike the previous two, they had a full deck to play with.

Two promising teams produced possibly the most constipated football final ever seen in O'Neill Park. The jitters infected both teams. Wide after wide stacked up. Time after time, Cormac came barging out of defence, bouncing the ball once, banging off a shoulder, bounding into a counter-attack. He stepped with an extra spring, unseen to us before.

On 50 minutes, Dermot 'the Great' Donaghy – all 6' 5" of him – cherrypicked from altitude above the square and sank the pigskin in the 'island net. They pilfered a late penalty but it grazed the post and wide. Then it was all over. By 1-5 to 0-3, the lowest final score since footballs had a natural tan, we had won the county title. By common accord, Cormac was Man of the Match.

His transformation into that man had not taken place overnight. Since the spring he had become a regular on the Eglish senior team and had proven himself fit for any company. The Tyrone GAA public hadn't really noticed, though, as that Eglish side was wallowing in mediocrity.

In mediocrity, and in obesity. Never had Cormac and I seen so many fat men as on the May day when we made our adult championship debuts for Eglish. As we stood in the dressing rooms at Galbally, gearing up for gladiatorial combat, mounds of flesh belched out of at least eight men who were due to play.

The sight symbolized what had become of the minor champions of 1986–7. As a group, they never fulfilled their promise. Injuries and emigration had taken a toll, lads skipped to the States for summer jaunts, and lack of pressure for places bred a degree of inertia among the remainder. Some had a part in Eglish winning the 1992 intermediate championship; but their season in division one yielded one draw and fourteen defeats. By 1996, when those 1980s golden boys should have been in their playing prime, Eglish was plummeting down the second division. The team manager, exasperated by this lethargy, resigned on the eve of the championship.

Small wonder then that our group of minors got fast-tracked on to the first team. Cormac came into the side as a corner-forward, and I flanked him at full-forward that deluged day in Galbally. The leather barely came as far as our line, but Eglish escaped with a draw. In the replay, we both moved back down the field, but Eglish was edged out.

As the younger breed found their feet, and Cormac became a fixture at right half-back, the team clawed up the league table. At Fintona in October, he learned the vagaries of the GAA disciplinary system the hard way. The opening of the host club's new dressing rooms occasioned much pomp and parading, and a championship-type atmosphere pervaded: they had to win to stay up, we were hunting promotion. While GAA President Jack Boothman, the Bishop of Clogher and a local horde looked on, the referee applied the rules with unwonted rigidity against us. One of our fairest players was sent off for protesting a dodgy call by the linesman. And for two iffy fouls, Cormac received two bookings. Even with thirteen men, we won that game.

Thirteen days later, with Cormac suspended and badly missed, we conquered Carrickmore by a point to clinch the minor league title. As double champions, we stood supreme within the county. We progressed to the Ulster Minor Football Championship at St Paul's club in Belfast, losing out to brilliant Ballinderry – the eventual winners – in our second game.

Cormac also had his first-ever success as a skipper that year. For a much smaller, weaker Eglish under-16 team, he was the man: midfield general, free-taker, top scorer and multi-tasker. In their grade-two league final victory over Killeeshil, he had a notable duel with a lad called 'Hub' Hughes; but another young buck, Stephen O'Neill of Donagheady, put them to the sword in the championship semi.

No matter. As the dust settled on an eventful year, Cormac was becoming known around Tyrone and Ulster as a name for the future.

*

For early evidence of Cormac's pursuit of perfection bearing fruit, look no further than his teenage talent for quizzes. They were what truly made him tick.

He approached every quiz as seriously as any match. If there was a clash, he missed football and basketball games to take part in quizzes. The pull to participate lay in the test of wits, the raw competition, and representing his home patch. As on the field of play, I was usually by his side.

'I'm just a good guesser,' Cormac would say with modesty when complimented on his quiz prowess. But his were well-educated guesses.

He made a vital instinctive interception to steal our second victory in the 1995/6 season of *Blackboard Jungle*, displaying several attributes that would later mark him out as an athlete: anticipation, speed off the mark and precise execution.

And leadership. In the concluding one-minute buzzer round, Coláiste Éinde from Galway had wiped out our 8-point lead; incredibly, the opposing captain, Cormac Ó Comhraí, had nipped in with the last six answers.

Ray D'Arcy: Well, an amazing tie-breaker situation . . . Those scores are correct; both teams on 44 . . . I will ask the next question on my card here, and whoever buzzes, if they get it right, they automatically win, if they get it wrong they lose . . . Right, so the next question will decide who goes forward . . . Fingers on the buzzers, here's the question: 'Who captained Scotland in the 1995 . . .

Buzz

Ray D'Arcy: . . . Armagh –'

Cormac: Gavin Hastings

Ray D'Arcy: – is correct! That wins you the game! . . . And congratulations to St Patrick's Grammar School from Armagh. Well done, Cormac – well interrupted there! We'll see you back here for the final of Group 10.

Cormac knew that we couldn't afford to wait to hear the full tie-breaker question. He was willing to take the huge risk required. Once 'captained Scotland' was uttered, it was 50/50 soccer or rugby; and mention of 1995 hardened his hunch for rugby's World Cup, which preceded filming by just a few weeks, in a quiet year for major tournaments.

His quiz career had started four years earlier in parochial halls and community centres. Back in the early 1990s, when most rural juveniles took the temperance pledge, the quizzes of the Pioneer Total Abstinence Association attracted brainboxes from every parish. You needed encyclopaedic general knowledge to succeed against this competition.

We thought of ourselves as the hardy bucks of Pioneer quiz-dom. At provincial and national finals, we sat with just pen and paper, surrounded by tables of timid teenage Free Staters chomping crisps, sucking bags of sweets, and slugging Lucozade and Tip-Tops. This carb-loading for geeks irked us no end: was this a quiz or a bloody teddy bear's picnic?

Our first mega quiz quest was to Listowel, Co. Kerry, in May 1992. The under-13 Eglish Pioneer team had qualified for the All-Ireland final. Terry Daly drove a minibus with a crew of nine: the team of Cormac, Mairead Daly, James McIntosh and Gary Daly; his wife Mary, Paddy McIntosh and Patsy Jones, the Eglish PTAA organizer; and Gerard Jones and I as stowaways. The team came thirteenth out of sixteen teams. They didn't know Frank Whittle invented the jet engine, or Christopher Cockerell invented the hovercraft. Me neither.

In 1994, a team comprising Cormac, Gerard, James McIntosh and myself came third in the All-Ireland under-16 pioneer quiz final at Roscommon. We were well pleased. The more questions about Ireland and sport, the higher our prospects of success. If it were simply on Gaelic sport, we felt almost invincible. In the Ulster juvenile GAA quiz at Threemilehouse, we scored 79/80 to bag a new set of jerseys for the Eglish under-16 team.

The GAA's Scór na nÓg fitted our bill. Scór quizzes tested your mettle and character as well as your knowledge. Each team-member had to stand alone at the microphone, under the lights, before a hushed audience, and answer within ten seconds. Cormac thrived under this sort of pressure.

In his debut season, we erred in forming two teams, and Cormac – nominally representing Eglish Camogie Club, with no sense of irony – bowed out meekly in the county semi-final. Next time out, we merged into an 'A' team of Cormac, Gerard and myself, to greater effect, winning the county final after Cormac brought us into a three-way tie-breaker by naming the president of the European Commission: Jacques Delors.

From then on, we took it seriously. More so than any other quiz, Scór questions could be predicted. In other clubs, youngsters were coached by quiz veterans. We taught ourselves. Many winter nights were spent at each other's homes, reciting lists of winners, battles, famous authors, and rivers and ridges of each county. Cormac's super-absorbent mind sponged everything in. Tell him some trivia once and he knew it for good.

We retained the county title and returned to the Ulster final in '94. Woe betide, we lost by two points to Killeshandra of Cavan, though we got as many questions right. Cormac had another clean sheet, but the name of Robert Emmet's housekeeper beat us.

We had one more stab at Scór na nÓg before Gerard and I would be too old. In the Patrician Hall, Carrickmore, we scored 58/58 to seal the provincial crown at last. Onward to Athlone RTC for the All-Ireland in February 1995. We felt proud to represent Tyrone and Ulster on a national stage, against St Joseph's of Westmeath, Straide of Mayo, and Abbeyside of Waterford. Fortune favoured us this day. We got no stinkers until Cormac's last question.

'In what county is the fishing village of Clogherhead?'

Louth. It was the only answer we missed all year. Still, the final scores read Eglish 52, St Joseph's 48, the others well adrift. We celebrated our All-Ireland title with a discreet underarm fist-pumping motion befitting Scór. Our prizes were Celtic Cross medals, just like All-Ireland players received.

Wherever age-limits allowed at school, Cormac and I joined forces. The two of us, alongside Diarmaid Sheridan, made a strong team for the BBC Radio Ulster Irish-language schools quiz, '*Fios*'. Cormac was becoming razor-sharp on the buzzers. Even if the right Irish terms eluded him, he didn't hold back.

'*Cén bhliain ina raibh an* "Wall Street" *Crash*' *i Meiriceá?*'

Buzz.

'Nineteen twenty-nine.'

'*Tá an ceart agat. Naoi Déag Fiche 's a Naoi.*'

We won the Ulster title − but our appearance on primetime television was a bigger deal. Of the many schools quizzes back then, *Blackboard Jungle* was the biggest. The programme's broad appeal lay in the cascading, jangly indie-guitar-riff theme tune, the gettable questions, and a format that made for close contests. We had watched it three evenings a week, nine months a year, since it first aired in 1991.

Our time came in the 1995/6 season. Internal trials produced a new team: Cormac, myself and Darran McCann from Armagh City. We had a tough act to follow. The previous year, our elders had performed admirably to reach the semi-finals. Against that backdrop, we aimed to win a few games and, sure, let's see. Like countless other young culchies who descended on Donnybrook studios and tingled as they went for make-up and saw stars walk by, our first objective was to not embarrass ourselves on the small screen.

'The first time I went on *Blackboard Jungle*,' Cormac said in an interview in 2000, 'I was incredibly nervous – more nervous than I have ever been or will be for a football match. Whenever you go to ask a question on camera, you start doubting everything you have ever known.'

His doubts evaporated quickly. After our debut victory over St Joseph's of Newtownforbes, Cormac was on my case, lobbying to take over from me in the individual specialist round. We had won by 19 points, I had scored 4/6 and expected to improve; I was also the captain. But so heavily did he breathe over my shoulder that I let him at it in that next match – the battle of Gavin Hastings – to answer questions on Geography. And fair play to him, he scored 5/6. In the group final, against Edmund Rice College of Ennis, Cormac unleashed a blizzard on the buzzer: he nabbed seven correct answers in one minute, and I was the only person who broke his run. 54–28 it finished.

Next up: Loreto Secondary, Kilkenny. I don't recall the details of our victory, but Google says that same school entered one of the next Young Scientist exhibitions with a project on why boys respond faster than girls on quiz buzzers. I trust we provided some solid evidence for their findings.

We were now in a de facto quarter-final against mighty Terenure College. This was the first time Cormac donned a Tyrone jersey in competition. We trailed by 5 points after the first round, and Terenure were just as tenacious on the buzzers. In an epic minute of high scoring, we got 12 points and they added 13. We pocketed a Discman each, but I was devastated that my one shot at the title was spent.

When Cormac and Darran re-entered the *Jungle* a year later,

Michael Collins from Armagh filled my place. They hoped to emulate the previous year's progress; anything beyond would be a bonus. But when they crossed paths one summer night in Cookstown, Cormac vowed to Darran, 'We're gonna win the minibus!' He was three-quarters serious. The quiz-coach, Mr McGonigle, got his history classroom rigged up for buzzer practice at breaktime and after school.

The second game tested them to the limit. With ten seconds left on the clock, they trailed St Colman's by a point. Captain Cormac to the rescue: Scott's voyage, *buzz*, South Pole; Southfork soap, *buzz*, Dallas; Chicago's state, *buzz*, Illinois. Correct, correct, correct, then the final whistle.

In the pool decider against St Nathy's, Ballaghadereen, he was flawless; asked how many 'New' states in the USA, he could be seen on screen coolly counting them to four in a New York minute. Semifinal showtime didn't faze him in the slightest. While his teammates stacked up their share of points in the ordinary rounds, he scored ten on the buzzers to beat St Michael's, Ballsbridge, by 56–49.

Who should await in the decider? Terenure, once more. In the green room, the D6 bluebloods maintained a cool distance, unlike other teams; they weren't here for small talk, just to win. The Dubliners built up a 5-point lead, but this time St Patrick's turned it around to take the front, 43–42, with only the buzzer round remaining.

Cormac and Michael got the first three to go 49–42 ahead. *Flying now.*

Then Terenure blazed their way to the next six correct answers. *Mayday.*

With ten seconds to go, Armagh trail, 48–52. It's an identical scenario to this moment in our defeat to Terenure a year ago. St Patrick's need the last three questions to win.

Ray D'Arcy: Tuborg, Tennents . . .
Buzz
Cormac: Beers.
Ray D'Arcy: Correct. Lager, Lager, L –

Buzz
Cormac: Born Slippy.
Ray D'Arcy: Correct. Which candidate slipped and fell in . . .
Buzz
Terenure: . . . Eh . . .
Final whistle
Terenure: SHOIT!!

That shout by Ross O'Carroll-Kelly was cut from the broadcast. But on the box you could see that for the next six seconds, amid the audience roar, Cormac thought it was a draw and remained completely in the zone, turning to his colleagues to coax them to be ready for the tie-breaker.

Then he raised his arms in elation, shouting 'Yes!' upon realizing that Terenure's docked point handed victory to Armagh, 52–51.

'Born Slippy' turned out to be the guess of the series. Inside a few milliseconds, I suspect, he reasoned that asking the name of that summer anthem – and not the group – was the snappier, better question for a buzzer-round.

For victory, the team won a television each, while the school received a £2,000 Waterford Crystal trophy and, of course, that white Renault minibus.

Later Cormac remarked: 'I never got the joy of travelling in it, as it was my last year. I have only seen it parked outside the school. I might not have won any major football medals at the school, but the minibus was my legacy!'

5. Young Man in Demand

Within the 1996/7 MacRory Cup campaign lay the roots of the Armagh/Tyrone duopoly of Ulster football for the next decade. The SPGA side included seven future All-Ireland medallists, three from Armagh, four from Tyrone. The Dungannon Academy team they met in the final had two, both for Tyrone.

In a 'truly wild' semi-final swept by gales, Cormac wrote, SPGA 'used all our strength of mind and body to hold out' and beat St Macartan's. Roll on the first-ever Armagh–Tyrone decider!

> The fortnight leading up to the final was the essence of MacRory football. Being the centre of attention within the school, the art department making banners, the buses that I had travelled on in previous years being booked to carry first years to support us. Back in Eglish, loyalties were divided, although most probably went for Dungannon due to the Tyrone-Armagh aspect of the game. For all of us, it was the biggest game of our lives to date. We were very aware of how the events of March 17 1997 would define our memories of school, and our football careers, and prepared very well. The day arrived, and after a warm-up on the Glen Road we approached Casement Park. The crowds streamed into the ground – they were here to watch us! – and we got ready. The Casement changing rooms that day, with the wood panelling and the nerves of thirty young footballers, seemed as hot and cramped as a sauna room. Captain John Toal slapped faces and eyeballed us until we were bouncing, before Brother Ennis calmed us with a prayer . . .

In this St Patrick's Day battle of St Patrick's schools, Armagh probably held the favourite's tag, having won the league match between the schools, and with more Ulster Colleges All-Stars in their line-up. (Cormac wasn't considered for an All-Star; he was automatically disqualified by dint of a tame sending-off in a club game the previous autumn.) In Eglish, interest was particularly intense, as Cormac would be opposed by club-mates J. P. McGeough and Conall Ó Máirtín for the Academy.

The derby attracted a bumper crowd of 6,000. They would be kept on their edge of their seats – or, like me, on their feet – from the first minute, when the aptly named Martin Early slipped in to goal for the Academy.

> Two points down at the half, I was confident we could bridge the gap. Five minutes in, we got our chance – a penalty! Up stepped Shane Kelly, but he dragged it wide. Minutes later, another speculative ball into our defence was grabbed by Richard Thornton and finished. That put six in it . . . A great solo run by Paddy McKeever and goal finish by Paul McCormack was the lifeline we needed. Still ten to go. But McCormack and Kelly were both sent off as frustration grew. We fought hard to the end, but Dungannon kept a two point cushion to win by 2-9 to 1-10.
>
> I don't think I've ever been as disappointed by a loss as I was that day. Club and county matches come and go, but you usually get another try next year. This time, however, there were no more chances. As we watched Paul McGurk lift the trophy, it dawned on us what it would have meant to have seen the Armagh crowd down saluting us as winners.

Cormac's account didn't mention his own part. At centre-back, he kept tabs on the Academy playmaker, Brian McGuigan, and was later moved to full-back to firefight the Thornton threat. And, diplomatically, he glossed over the raw ire in the Armagh camp: with themselves, for sloppy play and kamikaze discipline; and with the referee, for some decisions, and a few words.

Armagh smarted with the belief that they had thrown it away. But the Academy proved worthy champions, cruising to the Hogan Cup through runaway victories in the national semi-final and final. At any rate, those were the best two college sides in Ireland that year.

Cormac didn't bow out of school life empty-handed. St Patrick's had an easy passage to the Ulster under-19 Schools Basketball Championship final. Cormac lorded the boards as Armagh amassed a solid lead in the opening half of the decider. Before the second-half tip-off, a Castleblayney player elbowed ball-handler Ryan Kelly in the face. RK was such a clean player, his teeth sparkled. This blatant, brutal attempt to take him out sparked a melee, and Cormac was among the players sent off (more than a little harshly). St Patrick's won comfortably and became Ulster champions anyway, though not as Cormac would have wanted.

Such small regrets had subsided by the time he received the school's 'sportsman of the year' trophy, presented by Packie Bonner.

Cormac's last act at St Patrick's was to finish out his A-Levels. He scored As in French and Politics, and a B in Maths. What to do next? On Daddy's promptings, he enquired about architecture, and put together a dossier of drawings and photographs of our house. For whatever reason, it didn't work out.

He turned back towards the idea of arts at Queen's. Just as I was already doing.

*

In 1997 he was chosen as a county minor. This was a big deal. That feeling of affirmation, of being someone of worth, a local hero joining the cream of the county. That sudden groundswell of goodwill coming at you. That sense of immense possibility. That glimpse of the future.

It started on a Saturday in early December 1996, when four pupils of St Patrick's, Armagh, bundled into Frankie McQuade's Avensis in the Moy. Frankie and his family were diehard Red Hand fans, especially his youngest daughter, Colette.

Only one of Frankie's brood was on board this day: his third son, Karol. In the back seat sat Philip Jordan, Ryan Mellon and Cormac McAnallen. It was destination Derrylaughan for the opening Tyrone minor trial. Cormac had stayed overnight at Granny's in the Moy. The five other Eglish triallists travelled separately.

Frankie's fledglings ventured more in hope than expectation. The three backseat boys were in their penultimate year of eligibility and might be deemed unready. There was also a hunch that pupils in Armagh might start on the back foot: only one of the eight players from Tyrone on their SPGA squad had been given a run for the county minors in '96.

Plus, a trial is a bit of a lottery. Given one shot to impress, you might have to operate from an unfamiliar position, while others show off. Ryan started this trial at wing-back, and Philip at corner-forward – opposite ends from where they would ply their trade in time to come. Cormac lined out at centre half-back, familiar turf, but with 150-odd lads on show he couldn't be overconfident.

In those days, there was no phone call from a selector: players learned of their progress from a sidebar notice on the back page of the *Irish News*. The 27 December edition revealed that Cormac was among the eighty-one lads through to the next stage. Only he and Ryan of the original carload had made the cut. They were named with the other Eglish lads on a 'Leinster' team, from south-east Tyrone, to meet a north-western 'Connacht' squad two days later.

Over three Sundays, 'Leinster' proved the strongest of the four trial teams, and Cormac acquitted himself well. Step by step, he gained in confidence. When they beat 'Ulster' at Beragh on 12 January, he scored a point; in defeating 'Munster' a week later, he notched a brace.

He had done himself justice and felt positive. The affirmative news came through. He had made the grade; so too had four Eglish colleagues. Once his MacRory Cup campaign concluded, he could join up with the Tyrone minor panel and wear that Red Hand crest.

*

By that point, I knew that I would not become a Tyrone player. Writing about this subject is about as pleasant as chewing glass; but if I were to dodge the matter, I'd neglect an important juncture in Cormac's development.

In January 1996, the Armagh school team beat St Patrick's, Tuam, in a challenge match at Enniskillen. I played and scored well. Cormac came on as a sub in the forwards and got thumped by his marker. I intervened to put a stop to that. Some of our mentors, who thought me prone to pussyfoot about, were pleased to see me in fiery form.

Errigal Ciaran quiz team were appearing in the Ulster Scór na nÓg final that evening, and I went to Killeeshil to provide a late grind. That same team, including Mark Harte, had beaten an Eglish team captained by Cormac and thus ended our club's reign as All-Ireland champions. No hard feelings, though. We willed Errigal towards the Ulster title and they won it that evening.

Mickey Harte, who was the Tyrone minor manager at the time, gave me a lift home, with some of his family in the back. Sloshing through the puddles of a day of incessant rain, that normally fifteen-minute journey edged closer to twenty. Talk turned to our MacRory Cup campaign, and how we'd meet Mark's team, Omagh CBS, in the quarter-final. Then our morning victory arose. *Please ask me how I did*, I willed. I was thinking up 'modest' answers in my head. *Oh, well, Mickey, quiet day at the office, y'know. Just two in the onion bag, and two more over the bar.* Instead, he asked about the progress of Mark Jordan and 'Mini' Holmes, two of the five Tyrone players on our first fifteen. Nothing about Ryan Kelly, our goalie, and nowt about Cormac or me.

As I got into the house and the Harte car headed for Glencull, I had an epiphany. What Brother Ennis had heard was proving true. Two months earlier, he had asked Fr McAleer, the assistant manager, about the Tyrone contingent's prospects. Jordan and Holmes were the two names that got the thumbs-up. So the message seemed consistent. The rest of us were up against it. We had noticed that minor trials had begun without us, but still we hoped.

There was a chink of light. We pasted Omagh in that quarter-final, three weeks later. Operating between midfield and full-forward, I poached two opportunistic goals. Cormac also played solidly at wing-forward. Perhaps we would prove our worth yet. But a fortnight on we flopped hideously against Magherafelt in the semi-final, with both of us being substituted.

After that, nothing. There was a convention that college players might get a county call-up or trial, once their teams bowed out. But no call sounded.

Many years later, Mickey Harte seemed to suggest that Cormac had a minor trial in '96, when he was playing corner-back for the school, and carrying some excess weight. In fact, county managers issued the invitations to trials and Cormac wasn't listed. He was playing forwards for the school. And, as mentioned previously, by the end of 1995, the skipping fanatic was flying fit.

In truth, Cormac's omission was owing to other factors. Playing on slightly out-of-the-way teams – Eglish in lower-grade youth leagues, and Armagh in schools competitions – he hadn't been seen much by the county managers. And, having just turned sixteen, he was still young and raw. During that MacRory Cup campaign, he criticized me for not passing to him enough. He feared he might lose his place. Mummy intervened in that row and told me to rectify it. I was supposed to help him.

The '96 minors were really the last team Cormac didn't get picked for. He wasn't distraught, as he had two years left at that level. He was sorrier for me. My last chance had gone, and it hurt.

Tyrone lost to Fermanagh at Omagh in the first round of the Ulster Minor Football Championship. It was a GUBU result. There were guys out of position, out of sorts, and two had been on the sunbed the previous week. Fermanagh weren't even strong: they capitulated to Derry, who lost to Donegal, who lost to Laois. Tyrone had fallen to the bottom of the pile.

Lads who missed the cut, from Dromore to Donaghmore, thought they could have made the difference. Several Eglish players would have had a decent shout; only one, full-forward James Muldoon, got in. Brother Ennis, who managed Armagh minors as well as our school side, told Ryan Kelly, Cormac and me that he would have chosen us at that level. We believed him. Eleven lads from our school squad made his Armagh minor panel.

Armagh wasn't Tyrone, of course. But when you're a player, you have to have faith in your ability. Such was Cormac's rate of improvement that year that he could have done a job well in summertime. Maybe I could have mullocked around midfield, won some ball, and marked tightly. I was disciplined, willing to learn, and even wore my socks tied up – just as Fr McAleer ordered. We didn't get a trial to prove it.

In hindsight, my limitations are clearer to me today. My gait looked languid, my chassis carried excess baggage. I didn't have the *va-va-voom* pace or party-piece tricks. My catch-and-kick method didn't fit either: I thought it purer, more exciting, more *Gaelic*, to lace a 60/40 ball to the square than to hand-pass laterally about midfield.

I wouldn't be dredging up these memories today if Cormac were still with us. But 1996 was the year our trajectories changed.

As Cormac developed into a county minor and much more over the next couple of years, I shrank into the role of his junior. The change happened so fast that I barely even noticed. Through years of sport with club and school, I had ploughed up the left in fourth gear while this newer model rushed up behind me in the fast lane. Although he was consistently higher octane in his class, I had kept my nose ahead on the road before us. When he pushed to overtake, he sped on to a superhighway, I got shunted down a by-road.

My experience was far from unique. It was the classic case of the GAA star's brother. In the claustrophobic GAA world, one's identity is marked out by club and county status, and all else is subservient to that. One is automatically linked and compared to the ascendant sibling, however much one tries to be oneself.

Wind-up merchants could smell my vulnerability. Cormac had barely dirtied his county jersey when the first jibe landed. It was on a sunshiny day in June '97. The *Blackboard Jungle* minibus was being presented at the school in Armagh. I arrived fresh from passing my driving test. Everyone was in good chirp. A past form-teacher crept by.

'Are you not tired of being upstaged by Cormac by now, Dónal?'

Ouch! No need, nor answer, for that.

Others' more innocent questions could also leave a scratch.

'Are you Cormac's brother?' ever more strangers asked upon meeting me, hearing the surname. 'No, Cormac is *my* brother,' I'd retort sometimes, not entirely in jest.

'Are you the footballer's brother?' Now, that was really cutting. With those few words, I was reduced to a non-footballer.

Hundreds of GAA club players nationwide could tell a similar tale. I experienced it earlier than most because Cormac rose so meteorically.

*

For two months after Cormac joined up with the Tyrone minor squad in March 1997, there seemed little to set this group of players apart.

He debuted at centre half-back in a narrow victory over Antrim at Casement Park, five days after the MacRory Cup final. Subsequent results in the Ulster Minor Football League – including a draw with Armagh and a home defeat by Louth – set no pulses racing. Nine days before the championship, Tyrone took a 13-point thrashing by Cork in a challenge match. It was sobering stuff.

So too was the story with six minutes remaining of Tyrone's pre-liminary-round match against Down at Omagh. Cormac was solid at No. 6, catching, intercepting and distributing. But that wasn't enough. And Mickey Harte's seven-year stint was set for the bacon-slicer. Until a Stephen Donnelly howitzer from outside the 20-metre line saved them. In an amazing late show, Tyrone beat Down by five points. At the final whistle, Cormac was pulled aside by Gary Walsh, the former Donegal goalkeeper, to give an interview for BBC Radio Ulster. Some of the local press named him as their Man of the Match. So the journey began.

The next match, against Armagh at Omagh, was, in Cormac's words, 'a day that will never be forgotten'. He had soldiered with half of the Armagh side for years of school, and knew them better than most of his county colleagues. It was a proud occasion for Eglish too, to have five players in a Tyrone squad: Cormac, Brendan Donnelly at No. 4, Conall Ó Máirtín at midfield, and J. P. McGeough and Marty McCann on the bench. Add to that Mattie McGleenan's iron fists at full-forward for the senior team, and the club had never had it so good.

Omagh was gridlock that day, so the minor team walked up the Gortin Road to get to Healy Park. The ground was filling up to its 22,000 capacity for the derby ties. A sizzling sun and the aroma of burgers and onions made the atmosphere closer still. Useful vantage-points were not to be had. I stood in the corner of the poor man's side of the park, with an impaired view of the far end, but almost in line with the critical incident in the 14th minute.

Paul McGirr was a Tyrone colleague whom Cormac was just get-ting to know. They were kindred spirits: country lads, clean-living but with a sharp wit. Paul, not unlike Cormac, came in with something of a dual county identity, having played for the Fermanagh vocational schools team. They had no idea how much their lives and legacies would be enmeshed.

Paul's tragedy is well remembered. How he stretched to flick the ball past the Armagh goalkeeper, collided with him, lay there as the ball trundled into the net, and never got up. As medics set to work, it became clear he was badly injured. Eventually, he left on a stretcher, but few believed he was in urgent danger. Fatalities didn't occur on football fields.

The game restarted and Tyrone won by 1-10 to 0-9. Paul's 1-1 proved decisive. Cormac was relieved to get through, to have kept things tight at the back, and to hear that Paul was already in the county hospital; there he would surely mend. Victory steaks eaten, the Eglish lads rode home in Tommy Rafferty's taxi, and thoughts turned to evening festivities in Cookstown.

Cormac was at home by himself, nearing 8 p.m., when the landline rang. *Paul's dead.* Sheer disbelief and horror engulfed him and the other minors, then the county and the GAA world. The rest of the family was eating out, hearing conflicting rumours. We rang Cormac. He told us about the ruptured liver and the fatal truth.

He sensed the anguish from both sides. He had played alongside the Armagh goalkeeper for five years. 'Mixer' was a quiet but funny guy, the one-liner king of our school-team trip to America the previous summer. After two years on the sub-bench for school and county, he had arrived. Sunbeam on a gorgeous green carpet pitch, all applepie for his first major game. What unfolded was an awful affliction for a seventeen-year-old.

Yet, bravely, both he and Cormac were back at school over the next couple of days. Cormac had to focus on his last week of A-Levels, between evening bouts of grieving in public and in private. The corridors were usually serious during exams. They were even more sombre now. Senior boys sympathized with both Cormac and Mixer. They found words harder for Mixer. What could they say? Teenagers aren't equipped for this. Cormac made sure to tell Mixer of Tyrone compassion for him, to reiterate what Mixer had heard at the wake the previous day.

Cormac attended the wake at Dromore, almost an hour away, on the Monday and Tuesday nights. He had never seen a boy's dead body before and, like his fellow players, he found the whole experience harrowing. Shaking hands with distraught and exhausted McGirrs, not knowing what to say. Inching through the home, passing by a pantheon of GAA figures. Ascending the stairs with trepidation. Catching sight of a young but ghostly corpse, drained of life and blood. Struggling to recognize him as the sprightly teammate of a day or two earlier. Trying to recite prayers with meaning. Touching his hands, cold and limp as rubber gloves. Joining Tyrone colleagues on chairs on the landing, tears welling in eyes, amid silent tension.

I was there too for a while. I queued for an hour to get in on the Monday and felt deep sorrow for the family. It was the first monumental wake I'd visited. I hoped never to see another.

Cormac stayed overnight in Dromore on the Tuesday night. At the funeral the next morning, he and his fellow players formed a guard of honour, wearing their Tyrone jerseys. Opposite them, admirably, stood their Armagh opponents of a Sunday past, Mixer and all. Cormac and colleagues were honoured to bear Paul's coffin in procession.

Cormac was glad to get that week over. He sat his last A-Level exam, French literature, on the Friday afternoon. A few hours on, he joined up with the team for a meeting at Cookstown, to take stock of what had happened, to consider how and where to go from here. They would press on, but would not forget. Speaking years later, Cormac was convinced this episode provided a springboard to success for Paul's teammates.

> It was a horrible, sad time for everybody. But the bond that developed between us in those few days became really tight. Whenever we did eventually get around to thinking about the next match, players knew each other an awful lot better, for better or for worse. We came to trust each other and depend on each other . . . the events surrounding Paul's death were one of the things that kick-started everything. There's a bond there that we'd feel would give us an advantage over other teams.

From then on, they developed a fanbase unknown to minor teams anywhere. Fifteen thousand people packed into Clones ground in time for the minor semi-final, Tyrone v. Monaghan. Out from the old hillside dressing rooms, down the metallic steps and on to the pitch, the Tyrone players walked slowly and dramatically in line, black armbands on sleeves, the No. 25 jersey substituted for No. 12. The crowd stood to applaud. Tyrone made a blistering start, and won 4-14 to 3-7. Before the headline game, the minor and senior teams lined up for a minute's silence.

An injury scare briefly marred Cormac's countdown to the Ulster final. He was punching metal clips at the Ardmac factory in Dundalk, alongside his cousin Niall McAnallen, when he clipped his own hand. Luckily, he got the all-clear for the big day.

Ninety seconds into that decider, Tyrone prospects appeared very dicey. A fearless Antrim side, with some well-worked set-pieces, had made the net bulge twice. Yet, Tyrone led at half-time. With six minutes to go, Antrim punted high in search of an equalizer. Cormac caught and, several fluid movements later, the leather wended its way into the hands of Darren O'Hanlon, who buried it. Game over.

Cue euphoria. The crowd cheered with relish. Paul McGirr was name-checked in the captain's speech. The players toddled around the park on a lap of honour, punctuated by a couple of Klinsmann dives. Tyrone had a new set of heroes, who had earned the right to celebrate.

My perspective on the summer revelry wasn't quite as romantic as others'. They had their nights out, overnight stays in each other's houses, and Monday clubs with liberal pouring of libations. Either side of that Ulster final, Cormac went AWOL for a couple of long weekends, no call home. Daddy in particular was agitated; there was talk of a pub lock-in in Dromore. When Daddy and I challenged Cormac as to where he'd been and what he was at, he cracked back that I resented his success. Looking back now, I realize I was somewhat envious – not of his achievements, but the fact that newfound hangers-on were edging me out of his social circle.

My pride in Cormac's successes was incalculable. Listening to supporters' comments at the All-Ireland minor semi-final pricked it sorely. Injuries forced a reshuffle of the pack, and Cormac moved to midfield for his Croke Park debut. In his absence, the half-back line leaked; Kerry half-forwards Noel and Tadhg Kennelly were kicking points from obscene distances. From early on, some Tyrone sages around me were axe-grinding. 'McAnallen's no midfielder,' they enunciated. 'They should never have moved him out of centre half-back'. One or two made it more personal by trying to fault his fitness. 'McAnallen can't keep up with it at all.' I wanted to bite back but kept shtum, since I knew some of them. In truth, he won plenty of ball and linked up well.

Tyrone trailed by 3 points with 5 minutes to go, but showed tremendous calm to claw back the deficit and draw. Cormac was satisfied. 'It has been drummed into us never to give up,' he stated before boarding the team bus. 'We have not given up all year and there is no reason why we should start doing so now.'

The following Saturday, Eglish played Killeeshil in a league game at Edendork. Paul Hughes, an older brother of Tyrone minor Kevin, didn't turn up. At just twenty-three he was the heart of two clubs: secretary for Killeeshil and co-founder of Clann na nGael Hurling Club, for which we played flittingly. On the way to our league game, he died in a car crash. Another family plunged into grief, another club with a huge void, another tragedy for Tyrone.

Just seven days later, incredibly, Kevin 'Hub' Hughes played like a hero in the Tyrone–Kerry replay. He was Cormac's midfield partner for the first time, in a match played at an astonishing pace. Ten minutes in, Cormac soloed through and shot from forty yards to open his account for the year. Tyrone opened a 4-point lead; Kerry hit back furiously to lead by 3; Tyrone riposted with 4 in a row. At full-time, it was 0-15 each.

Extra-time, 15 minutes each way, more frenetic still. Cramp crippled Cormac, and he came off in the 68th minute. But he returned in the 76th, after the turnaround, with the scores tied again at 0-18 apiece. The game had reached that point where systems and strategies went out of the window, and unfeasible things became possible. So when Cormac was fouled, 60 metres out in the 80th minute, he opted to take the free-kick himself. Over the bar it flew, implausibly: Tyrone by 3. Kerry plugged away, but Mark Harte's eleventh accurate free-kick of the day sealed it: 0-23 to 0-21 – the most scores ever in the All-Ireland stages. Tyrone folk invaded the pitch and chaired 'Hub' about. We didn't want to leave our sacred site. To beat Kerry at any level in

Dublin made Tyrone people dizzy with joy. We were emancipated from the stigma of alleged mental frailty on the big stage.

In a post-match interview, Cormac called it 'the hardest game I've ever played in'.

The final was against Laois. They were reigning All-Ireland champions, and warranted serious respect; but only two of the previous season's fifteen were back, and we had begun to think our minor team was nigh unbeatable. As the five Eglish panellists assembled with their parents at 'chapel corner', prior to departure on the Saturday, they couldn't see their team losing.

But in the pressure-cooker of Croke Park, the nerves hit them. There were rearguard blunders by the dozen. Only 30 seconds had passed when Laois goaled. Cormac appeared more sure-footed than most, though not exactly rampant.

Promptly on the restart, Thornton's goal put Tyrone 3 points ahead. Surely they were on course for their glorious destiny. Then, for fully twenty minutes, Tyrone failed to score. Laois prevailed by 3-11 to 1-14, and deservedly so, for they were more resourceful.

Tyrone players sat down, sobbing. Cormac was hurting too, but crying on the grass wasn't his style. Underneath the immediate angst, knowing that he had another year left at that grade may have softened the blow. But around Christmas the pangs hit him. As he wrote in his diary:

> It is only now hitting me just how much of a loss the All-Ireland minor final was. I did not really have a comprehension at the time, but as time goes on, and our achievements become more out of focus, the disappointment rankles even more.

He was glad to have another opportunity to put the record straight.

★

Exploits with Eglish kept Cormac's winning habit alive. 1997 became the club's *annus mirabilis*, the best of our lifetimes.

The adult team set the pace. The fat club of yore was no more. Our managers, Anthony Daly and Jim Fay, veteran servants of Eglish and cameo players for Tyrone in the 1980s, whipped us into fine fettle. Our ground was closed for redevelopment, so we had to travel away for training and matches all year, but this challenge seemed to galvanize our collective spirit.

Young blood was refreshing us, too. Our average age dropped to twenty-one and a half years. We were brimful of ambition and were favourites for the intermediate championship. As we progressed that summer, Cormac showed extreme versatility, stretching from one end to the other as our needs evolved. He lined out next to me at centre half-forward in our opener against Stewartstown and clipped over 2 points in a runaway victory. In our quarter-final against Trillick, he wore the No. 15 *geansaí* but roved about midfield to good effect. Then for the semi-final against Clonoe, he moved to No. 4. His man-marking tightened the screw, and we secured an 8-point victory.

We faced Killeeshil, our neighbours, in the intermediate championship final at Carrickmore in early August. Cormac stayed put in the corner to sandbag our back unit and mark Kevin Hughes. After Big Mattie busted the net to put us 6 up, many of us presumed Killeeshil, as underdogs, would crumple. But they were a gritty lot who flexed their muscles. They earned a penalty – conceded by Cormac – and put it past Mickey McCann. Midway through the second half, they drew level. We nosed ahead again. In a tense finish, sub Felix Daly ferreted in behind the Killeeshil defence and filched our second goal to clinch the Paddy Cullen Cup.

Our bonus prize was gaining automatic promotion to division one. Not only did we think we belonged there, we expected to be top guns for years to come. Winning that title was simply a means to an end, as far as Cormac was concerned. For one night only, we celebrated with the squad in the Moy, Cookstown and Dungannon. There was a thunderstorm late in the night. We were convinced that the clouds were parting for our senior careers.

*

Between club, college and county, Cormac was a young man in demand, playing a twelve-month season.

With the club, he was driving teams to levels that we thought weren't possible. For Eglish to win the county minor championship once in '96 was an accomplishment. To retain it in '97 and reach the club's first-ever Ulster final would defy logic.

Paddy McIntosh had bowed out, having achieved his dream. Conor Daly, the new gaffer, seemed much wiser than his twenty-three years, and not simply due to his hairline. He was all business, heir apparent to Eglish Builders' Merchants, electrical-shop owner, organ-player in church and organ-grinder of the GAA club – our secretary, senior goalie and much else besides. Assisting him were Barry Fay, our nippy senior forward, whose 'heart to heart talks about life' Cormac enjoyed; and Patsy Jordan, the club's long-standing and softly spoken minor coach, who always addressed his charges as 'chaps'.

The new regime was more relaxed than Paddy's. Cormac and the other county minors could be talked to almost as responsible adults, given their experience. The biggest challenge was reassembling them all from myriad commitments, uninjured, as a club minor team.

The draw fell kindly once again, and Cormac stood sentinel at centre half-back as Eglish consummately ousted Omagh, Owen Roe's and Brackaville in turn. The stage was set for a repeat of the '96 decider. Coalisland coveted revenge for the last time.

All the early signs indicated they would get it. The final at Edendork was only 10 minutes old when an Eglish player was sent off for striking. The Fianna piled forward. With 21 minutes to go, Eglish were 6 points behind and appeared sunk.

Then Cormac took a blow to the face. Blood gushed from his nose. Conor Daly dressed the wound, stared him in the eyes, told him to move position and stick it to them. Cormac gritted his teeth and stared back with what Conor remembers as 'a look of venom'.

So began 'the comeback of the decade', to quote the understated *Tyrone Courier*. 'McAnallen switched into midfield and took the match by the scruff of the neck. Coalisland had no answer to his power and physical presence.'

Everywhere he roamed, he had a magnetic effect on the ball. He plucked it from the air, picked it out of rucks, pinched it from tackles.

He rolled with the punches that came his way too. Soon enough, James McIntosh goaled to narrow the deficit. In the 50th minute, Cormac sent over a monster free-kick from outside the '50' to give his team a 1-point advantage, but psychologically it was worth far more. A few moments later, he had a hand in a five-man move that ended with a Kieran Jordan corker. Eglish went on to win by 5 points.

The *Dungannon Observer* declared Cormac Man of the Match for a second county final in a row. 'In Cormac McAnallen,' the paper stated, 'Eglish had an inspirational figure with the heart of a lion who never lost his focus and surmounted all obstacles to produce an amazing second-half effort which was the decisive factor.' The *Courier* extended again to say, generously (or not?), that 'the Tyrone minor star produced the best twenty minutes of football he is ever likely to play'.

The instant bliss of back-to-back success soured temporarily. A skirmish broke out, some Fianna players flailing for post-match retribution, and Eglish lads replying. Like other Eglish fans, I climbed the fence, to mind Cormac as much as to congratulate. I needn't have worried. He linked arms with a Fianna opponent, wished him well, and ushered him away from the ongoing fracas. On the match video, it stands out as a peace gesture in a war zone. Tempers calmed, and celebrations commenced.

Eglish squeaked through the Ulster quarter-final against Seán Stinson's of Antrim to set up a semi-final against Clontibret. Cormac had a tough tussle, and an opponent was sent off for hitting him late. The match lay in the balance when he kicked into a brisk, icy breeze to score his second point and the winner. Press reports hinting that Eglish were lucky to prevail riled some club members; but Cormac privately admitted there was 'more than a grain of truth in it'.

A team talk from former Derry player Tony Scullion, who had joined the Eglish backroom, stirred their blood. Cormac wrote down in his diary that evening: how Scullion was backing Eglish unreservedly against Ballinderry tomorrow, even as a Derry man. How their victory would mean as much to him as his own All-Ireland victory. How his kindly advocacy 'inspires so much confidence before games. He seems to particularly admire me, and always singles me out for special praise.'

New Year's Day 1998 was cold, wet and windy, as it ought to be. Nowhere else was it a day for Gaelic football. Undeterred, a large crowd flocked to west Belfast to see two small rural parishes strive for provincial supremacy, with a trace of Tyrone–Derry spice thrown in. All of Eglish hoped, but knew their odds were long. Ballinderry, the reigning champions, was a youth football foundry. They would be All-Ireland senior club champions four years hence.

A Ballinderry goal in the first minute dictated the momentum. In the bleak midwinter clabber, Eglish now had about as much chance as a fox chasing hounds. There was a small fightback, and Cormac's customary free-kick point from long range, but never enough. Eglish's dream season ended in defeat, 1-4 to 2-7.

> Despite the obvious empty feeling, I still find it hard to feel as 'gutted' as some of the lads, as I have already evaluated the year as being a successful one, not having expected to get anywhere near as far as we did. It is a similar feeling as that I experienced after the All-Ireland final, but as I see now, the regret gets deeper as time goes by.

6.   Coming of Age

Thursday, 8 January 1998

The test, like the Psychology exam, was not as tough as I expected. I answered the two questions on Early Modern Europe, and had more than enough material to fill out two answers, despite my lack of revision. Afterwards, as I had promised myself, I lazed around all day, winning one and losing another game of Monopoly. I lost my last January money on Maverick. This pattern continued right throughout the day, punctuated only by occasional bouts of sit-ups. The lazing around in Belfast is so wasteful, and if there was something better to do I would certainly be doing it, but it is appealing all the same, and oh-so-easy to indulge in.

Cormac matriculated at Queen's University in September 1997. Nowhere else bleeped on his radar. Two-thirds of his school year in Armagh gravitated towards the Belfast colleges almost without a thought. Queen's was within an hour of home, and I was already there. For Cormac and others with Gaelic football designs, Belfast also represented the obvious option: one could play on for local club and county, as well as for a powerhouse student team.

He signed up for arts, and for his first-year subjects he chose history, philosophy and politics. Two major impediments stood in the way of his academic progress: sporting commitments, of course, and the social scene.

Student Belfast was, and is, a unique place: a nine-month self-contained republic. This red-brick tenement jungle bulged with thousands of supposed scholars, their antics notoriously spewing on to the thoroughfares. Two recent TV series have striven to simulate student Belfast. But the cast of ten who crammed into 65 Malone Avenue's three storeys in 1997–8 were more akin to 'The Young Ones'.

They were mostly SPGA alumni, and mostly from Tyrone: Cormac; Ryan Kelly (now 'Archie'), Francie McQuade and Barry Currie ('Beansy') of the Moy; and Rory O'Donnell ('OD') and JP McGeary from Edendork. Stephen 'Jacko' Hughes, Mark 'Leo' Mulgrave, Nicky Daly and Johnny McGivern formed the Armagh quartet. On paper, that crew comprised a potent mix of high achievers: three of St Patrick's straight-A A-Level pupils, the 'student of the year', the 'sportsman of the year', and a World Transplant Games badminton bronze-medallist, inter alia. Six of them were in the same politics tutorial group. Their parents were so pleased.

And yet, squashed together under one roof, they became submerged in sloth and the banter of boys who knew each other too well. After landing on Sunday nights, everyone baled into Cormac and Francie's room, lights off, and played 'murder in the dark' – i.e., a complete beating session.

They ripped one another apart in that house, no exceptions. Cormac got his share of stick from the start. 'Paddy' they called him initially, after the new *Emmerdale* character, back when he had hair; after that, he was simply 'Macca'. A range of bright shirts and luminous tops, purchased on his first downtown clothes-shopping sprees, left him wide open. His freestyle kitchen recipes got roundly slated: he'd throw peas/beans/sweetcorn into a big pot of mash or rice, eat it with a heap of seafood sauce, and leave the rest for the next day's dinner, while housemates held their noses. They were no domestic goddesses themselves. They kept a binbag in the middle of the floor, and fired plates and cutlery and all into it.

In the bedsit bedlam, Cormac let his studies drift. With only a few hours of lectures and tutorials per week, arts undergrads hadn't a taxing timetable, but they needed discipline to adhere to reading lists, assignments and revision. Putting a structure on his own daily schedule proved difficult. There were simply too many distractions.

Getting out of the house was the first hurdle. Daylight hours whittled away on cards, board games, mind-crushing telly and slagging. When he geed himself to walk to Queen's new Seamus Heaney Library, chinwags with countless passing associates broke his groove.

There were early-evening darts matches in Archie's room, with stage-names and walk-on music; Cormac was 'The Shark'. There was lots of nightlife: Renshaws on Mondays and Tuesdays; and the M Club as the midweek Mecca, if you queued before nine and avoided the bouncers – Cormac and Willie Lyons of Coalisland were chucked out for sham-fighting along to 'Sunchyme' ('Hey-a-ma-ma-ma') – while latecomers resorted to Lavery's, opposite. There were also long nights in. Once, Cormac kept a Monopoly marathon going till 5 a.m., long after everyone else lost the will, so he could overtake Francie and win. Very late bedtimes wiped out next mornings and good intentions to attend class. And so the cycle continued.

Anxiety about progress in studies and sport, money, relationships and general direction in life simmered under the student mirth. A rare diary sequence offers a snapshot of his outlook and outgoings at the onset of this milestone year in his life:

Friday, 2 January 1998

Was unable to move for most of the day after a mixture of footballing fatigue and rigours of the night before. Read the rather uncomplimentary report of the match in Irish News, which credits Ballinderry with almost all of the game's finer points . . . I got a call from JP about 6.00 with the intention of going out again. Needless to say, I jumped at the chance, and went down for a few games of snooker before heading off to Clubland. Had a fairly good night, plenty of messing about and 'henching' with JP, including an ingenious scam to get our coats, involving JP pretending to have dislocated his shoulder, while I called an ambulance.

Saturday, 3 January

Up early and into Dungannon . . . Got the stuff out of the house in Belfast (eventually), but will probably have to head up there again tomorrow. Haven't even started to study for the exams, which start on 6th . . . Went home and slept for hours before taking exercise. I learnt that I have been scrubbed off the reckoning for the Tyrone u-21s. Can't say I'm particularly worried.

Sunday, 4 January

Later than usual start for a Sunday, with Fr B switching Mass from 10 to 11 o'clock ... I received the news that myself, Ciaran Gourley, Mark Harte and Noel Clerkin have been called into the Queen's senior panel, and most likely staying there for the Sigerson ...

Monday, 5 January

Meant to get up a day early and do a solid day's work for the Psychology test tomorrow. However, a combination of laziness, frequent breaks, conversations and an extended lunch break led to me getting about 2 hours work done in the designated time from 10.30 to 6.00. Lucky the exam lasts only one hour ...

Pasta shells & Miracle Whip – Pizza Hut buffet meal

Tuesday, 6 January

Did a little revision before leaving for Psy exam. As it turned out, the three questions were all on topics I had revised for, with my preferred choice being the question on abnormal behaviour. The hour flew, and I was home pretty sharpish. As is to be expected, I did little for the rest of the day, my only other excursion being to visit the Errigal boys. I got an awful shock when learning that I had only £10 left in the bank of my January allowance. Lucky enough, then, that the opportunity arose to do their dishes for £5, and I jumped at it. . . .

Sweet and sour rice, peas & chicken burger

Wednesday, 7 January

. . . after wasting the morning lying in bed and in front of the TV, I decided to go to Sigerson training instead of studying . . . I scored 2 points in a game of backs and forwards, before scoring a point from an acute angle in the match. Afterwards, I stayed back for a spot of penalty practice with Davy Wilson and Chris Rafferty. I scored 9/10, I think, my only miss being the hitting of a post. . . .

Sweet & sour rice, peas & chicken burger – tuna & salad sandwich

Thursday, 8 January

. . . I just realised how little I do for my work today when I saw Ryan, Jacko and Johnny heading off to the library for 3 hours in the evening . . . I suppose that that is the sort of attitude that will have to be adopted if I want to eventually get a good degree.

Fried fish & chips, beans – tuna & salad sandwich, banana sandwich

Friday, 9 January

Another unfulfilling day. Only got up at 12.45, and got stuck into a game of Monopoly (which I lost!). Sat around some more, slagging and playing cards . . .

Went out, with the aim of going to the Factory, but we were turned away there . . . [and] . . . ended up in (yes, you've guessed it!) Lavski's. Needless to say, it was totally crap, and we didn't know any-one (at all) there . . . We must be the biggest house full of losers ever to set foot in Belfast.

Roland Scholten (my tip) and Richie Burnett made it through to the semi-finals of the darts. I'm still in with a chance of claiming the money. God, how I need it.

Fried fish, boiled spuds & beans

Saturday, 10 January

I sat the politics exam, and most probably passed, after having sat just 30 minutes of revision. It says more about the difficulty of the exam than any great wealth of knowledge in Politics going into the test. My money for January ran out, so now I must work two weeks in Ardmac to boost the funds. This will require missing the craic in Belfast for a fortnight . . . I turned down the option of going to the Carrickdale with the Eglish ones, both for the practical financial per-spective and from a desire to keep myself in good shape – I have a real mission not to be doing any excess drinking to the detriment of football.

Fried fish & beans – fish, baked potato, beans

Listing what he ate for dinner marked a new departure for Cormac. He wasn't on a strict diet, but taking notes on his intake was quite a radical protocol for a seventeen-year-old, back in 1998, before team nutritionists were part of county youth set-ups.

'It is definitely a very scary time to be living in Northern Ireland, and no one, it seems, is safe.' So Cormac pondered privately on the latest of the Troubles. He was thinking primarily of the loyalist murder of Fergal McCusker in Maghera, on 18 January. Following the assassination of its leader Billy Wright in December, the LVF had embarked on a campaign of sectarian killings. McCusker, aged twenty-eight, was the fourth victim.

Cormac was wary. 'It will be becoming more dangerous in Belfast, and one will have to be especially careful when walking home after going out.' Rumours of a threat being made to Queen's Gaelic players travelling on Citybus – and disembarking opposite a loyalist estate – heightened his state of vigilance. Going home one dark evening, he thought he saw a suspicious car parked at a junction. He had never witnessed a violent encounter during the Troubles, but a strange half-encounter could leave a chilling effect, which one wouldn't want to talk about, for various reasons. Ironically, it was in that brief period after the supposed dawn of peacetime that many of our generation felt most at risk.

*

Cormac's reputation as a Queen's fresher footballer grew after a derby match away to fresher champions Jordanstown in November. He stole the show, weighing in with three scores in a surprise 7-point victory.

At Queen's senior squad's next Wednesday-afternoon session at 'The Dub' playing fields, team-manager Dessie Ryan halted a training game. The canny Ryan was visibly unhappy about the stodge he had just watched. He announced that he was going to get some freshers from an adjacent pitch. Some older players were baffled by this seemingly random act. I was in the game, and guessed whom he might recruit. Back he came with Cormac and two other newbies. New teams were picked. Anthony McGrath, a fourth-year wingback from Donegal, saw this baby-faced boy trot towards him, and thought his luck was in. A few minutes in, Cormac got the ball about the '50' and blasted it over.

Three days later, he got word to turn up for Queen's senior Ryan Cup league match at home to UCD. Being at least two years younger than the other players, and having never played in a premium-grade adult match, he didn't expect to feature. But Queen's played beautifully and amassed a huge lead – 14 points, maybe more. Time to run the bench. The shout came down the line. Cormac was on, in the forwards. He did the basics right, and had a hand in a symphonic movement that produced a point.

It was the right company to quicken his learning curve. At least ten of this panel were then inter-county senior players. Five of Armagh's future All-Ireland medallists were there: Diarmaid Marsden, Barry O'Hagan, Aidan O'Rourke, and Justin and Enda McNulty. Training sessions only began when the south Armagh brigade arrived, invariably late. Kieran McGeeney, himself a Queen's graduate, sometimes dropped by to take part too.

Dessie Ryan exerted more influence on Cormac than most. From Lough Neagh's shore, he had coached Queen's to win the Sigerson Cup in 1990 and co-mentored Tyrone and Ballinderry teams, but declined numerous offers to take charge of club and county sides. He was motivated by neither ego nor money. Around the fields of Ulster that Dessie has tilled, he was, and is, revered.

At first glance, he wasn't your typical football boss. Then nearing sixty, with a short, wiry frame and quiet demeanour; attired in woolly hat and wellies, he'd pass for a small farmer. But he was hardier and fitter than men half his age.

Once he spoke, you knew that he was a deep thinker. His team talks were replete with tales of Sigerson past, of hotshots like James McCartan, but also the unknown Liam Conneally of Clare once crashing in a winning goal – it was his way of hypnotizing us to believe any of us could be a Sigerson hero. His personal touch invigorated young players, making them feel special. He'd pull you aside for a few minutes of individual tuition to improve an aspect of play, like a tackling skill or a tactical element of your position. He had a pocketful of tricks to get out of tight spots on the pitch. From the outset, he clicked with Cormac. 'Dessie Ryan is obviously the sort of trainer who is tactically and motivationally astute, and who knows what the right approach to take is,' Cormac wrote after his first full session. 'He kept complimenting me, and I must say that I did seem to impress him.' A week later, he could see he was already in the manager's plans:

Took the day off, essentially, to attend Sigerson training in Belfast . . .
At the training, things again went very well. Dessie lined me out at centre-half forward, and I scored three points in the game we played. I may even be in the running for a starting place if things continue in this vein. This, no doubt, would unnerve me considerably, as it was something beyond my wildest dreams when first coming to Queen's. However, it is certainly a chance I would jump at.

Everything moved so fast. Three days later, Cormac led the line at centre-three-quarters away to the Down senior team at Newcastle. Micheál Magill, a no-nonsense All-Ireland medallist, was his opposite number. Initiation ceremonies couldn't come much tougher. Out the other end, Queen's lost by 5 points, but Cormac had scooped 0-3 and plaudits aplenty. A week on, a double test: away to Meath on Saturday, being marked by Nigel Nestor; and against Cavan before a big crowd at Kingscourt the next day. Cormac's shot compass faltered in both games, but overall Dessie was happy with his contribution to sound victories for the team.

Dessie tells me now that he didn't know that Cormac had rarely played at No. 11 before. He just wanted him in the engine room and, with sturdy men already in other central positions, the offensive pivot seemed the best place for him to stoke the fires. Cormac was still slightly apprehensive about being the golden child and incurring the ire of much older panellists, whom he had leapt over in the pecking order.

He held this spot and made his Sigerson Cup entrance against Trinity on the Dundalk pitch next to the railway line. Aged seventeen, he was one of the youngest Sigerson debutants in the last half-century, if not the youngest. Daddy was watching, in some disbelief that his son was out there among the big guys. Cormac was relatively anonymous for chunks of the game, but a tap-in goal and late point maintained his credit rating and left Queen's firmly in the black.

On 11 February 1998 – his eighteenth birthday – a last-sixteen game at home to DCU carried a danger warning. Rising stars like Tomás Meehan, Paddy Christie, Shane Ryan and Seán Óg Ó hAilpín populated the opposition defence. But Queen's careered through them regardless, to register a 10-point triumph. A report on *UTV Live at Six* featured Cormac's point and a shout-out for his big birthday.

His best was yet to come. In the quarter-final win over Waterford IT at Kilmacud a fortnight later, Cormac glistened and got 2 points. 'It was one of those games where I took my time on the ball and did things properly instead of just giving it away first time,' he ruminated to himself. Even in the glow of success, though, he was slightly over-awed at the prospect of a semi-final versus UUJ, being marked by Seán Lockhart.

Queen's filled up for an epic voyage to the finals weekend in Tralee. The day before the game, the team commandeered the sodden Castleisland rugby field for practice, and churned it into a mudbath – cue angry letters from Kerry to Queen's. The hours counted down. 'The sense of anticipation inside myself is unbelievable,' he wrote. As the bus drew close to the semi-final venue, with rays of sunshine piercing the windows, the squad sang its anthem, 'Angels', *a cappella*.

Ugly feeling between the finalists had been brewing for a couple of weeks. A Jordanstown official boasted widely that he would object if a particular Queen's player was fielded. It turned out that the player had quietly left his course. Fair cop, you might say, until you'd peruse the other team lists and ask for student-cards. The pot had called the kettle black. Such petty gamesmanship stirred as foul a mood and game as any Cormac ever contested. The marshiest pitch in town sucked the affair even closer to the gutter.

So it degenerated. Angry words were exchanged, blows too. The eligibility spat 'spilled over to the match with too many men in both sides quite frankly losing the run of themselves', stated one reporter, aghast that the 'appalling off the ball incidents' led to just one dismissal. Playing with the wind, 'the Poly' stretched 8 points ahead. Six minutes from the end, a goal from Peter 'Posh Spice' Campbell opened a lifeline for Queen's. Ninety seconds later, Cormac clipped another, soccer-style, to net. But Jordanstown held on to reach the next day's final.

That two-month campaign had brought Cormac on a lot. He had trained, learned, played, sparred and caroused with a host of inter-county senior players. From a new position, he was top scorer in the semi-final and Queen's second highest scorer overall. With a minor campaign in front of him, he had a massive head start in experience over his peers.

★

In the summer of 1998, Cormac wrote the following in his diary:

> The secret was a conversation I had with Harte, in which I told him that I thought we had not been psyched up enough the first day. In an effort not to be over-hyped and lose poise, we were kept too calm, and were consequently blitzed by a Down team firing on all cylinders. In the replay we went out psyched to the eyeballs and did not give an inch all through . . . I scored a '50' near the end, which was the final nail in the coffin, and immensely satisfying to be seen to be doing the business . . .

Wherever Cormac is now, he might be livid with me for reading his diary, let alone putting it out there for a wider audience. In any case, I wouldn't have included the quotation, had Mickey Harte not gener-ously revisited the incident in print himself.

In that conversation with his manager, Cormac argued as well that the routine of holding team warm-ups at a pitch en route to matches was a waste of energy. Few players of eighteen would even try to identify such a defect in team preparation; fewer still would tell it straight to the boss.

Mickey Harte was a formidable figure. Even today, some senior panellists shrink before 'The Beard'. But in the year and a bit since he and Cormac had become acquainted, a mutual respect had developed. To the manager's credit, he heeded the suggestion and changed tack. The pre-warm-up warm-up was duly dispensed with.

Even back then, Mickey acknowledged Cormac's fruition and their special, symbiotic relationship. Look at this interview at the tail end of the 1998 season, for example:

He really took the role [as stand-in captain] in his stride. The interesting thing was to watch him emerge as a leader. He proved a great liaison man between us and the rest of the squad and he was always the one who would come to us and talk about things that were and were not working about training. He really belied his years in the way he approached everything.

*

First impressions didn't set Cormac purring about Tyrone minors' prospects in 1998. Only four of the '97 final team remained. Sitting out a trial at Ardboe in January, he counted up players gone and wondered how they'd be replaced. He saw lots of wannabes on show, but scarcely a wunderkind. When he returned to play in a trial in February, he noted his fierce competition for the midfield spots in Hub Hughes and Owen Mulligan.

Mickey Harte harboured no doubts about where to put Cormac. Why fix what wasn't broken? Throughout the spring's Ulster Minor League, Cormac moored midfield, with Mulligan, Hughes and even Stephen O'Neill as pro tem partners. He noticed during this campaign that whenever he played well, so did the team, and his lapses could affect the whole. He trafficked a lot of ball and averaged 2 points, but fretted about not catching kick-outs – possibly caused by wintertime glove-wearing.

Tyrone won the competition pulling up, and approached the championship with confidence – then barely scraped a draw with Down. After almost flopping out, Tyrone spent a week in introspection. Relief rapidly turned to irritation. Cormac had his own issues to settle. He was sensitive even to implicit criticism, and felt that press and fans undervalued his off-ball legwork, while colleagues played for applause.

It was the classic syndrome of 1997: I had probably done more running than anyone else, but had not done the sparkling showy things which earn ratings, partly due to a lack of confidence.

Deeply hurt by the criticisms I had received in the local papers, I vowed that I would go out and be undeterred by self-belief, to have the confidence to go for scores, and to impress upon the others the need to get truly stuck in instead of poncing about and trying to look good.

Seven days rested, Tyrone, and Cormac, turned up at Newry with a snarling intensity. The midfield duo of Cormac and Hub picked up where they left off last year, with interest. Cormac showcased his catalogue of skills in 3 long-range points: one from play, after a '50' played one–two with Brian McGuigan; then a free-kick from the hands around the 45-metre line; and finally, a '50' straight over the bar. 'Another McAnallen special', the *Tyrone Times* called the last.

The next-round match against Armagh at Clones was a non-event, thankfully, after '97. Cormac thought he didn't have a great game, and somehow he cramped up with 15 minutes left, 'but we won at such a canter that I did not even have to expose myself to a sprint during that time'.

Hub took the steering wheel that day. Such was the intuition and cooperation between them: when one attacked, the other tracked back. John Morrison, the Armagh guru, effused in the *Ulster Gazette* about how 'Tyrone's almost total control was orchestrated by a dominating and unstoppable midfield pairing . . . giving immaculate ball to a mobile front line or supporting play themselves to pick up exquisite long range points.'

Cormac begged to differ. His diary adverted to 'plenty of soul-searching as to why exactly I wasn't performing in front of the big crowds' – that is, at Clones and Croke Park. Within a month of that cogitation, he had tweaked his mindset accordingly:

Playing at Clones and hearing the roar of the crowd . . . is a completely different experience from playing in an ordinary club game. You need to be able to handle the occasion. It is important to cope with the pressure, be single-minded and always remain in the right frame of mind.

If the other team scores, you must learn to put it to the back of your mind and stay focused on your own game. Last year's experience has certainly helped me to remain calm during a match and to keep a clear head.

He exorcized his demon in the Ulster semi-final. Talent seeped out of

Derry's team: Kevin McGuckin, Fergal Doherty, Niall McOscar and Paddy Bradley, to name a few. Cormac drove his county into an early lead which scaffolded a 5-point triumph. The *Tyrone Courier*: 'McAnallen was a colossus at midfield, defending willingly, winning possession, feeding the front men and hitting four wonderful points to underline his massive potential as a star of the future.' His third and fourth points, both from outside the '50', bolted on his image as a giant in minor-land. This time, he spared himself the rod afterwards. As they waved bye-bye to Clones, he led them singing 'American Pie', and the bus drove to the Ardboe levee, the day his pseudo hoodoo died.

In its place, something – or someone – else was born: Captain Cormac. Most supporters forget that Brian McGuigan was the original skipper. When he got suspended in the spring, and couldn't collect the league trophy, vice-captain Cormac did the honours. McGuigan returned for the championship opener, played at centre half-back, then broke his collarbone. Cormac stepped up for the coin-toss with the Derry captain.

In the final against Antrim, Cormac kindled another furious start. In the fifth minute, he kicked a 40-metre point from play. In the seventh, he converted a free-kick from similar distance. In the fifteenth, he shovelled over a '50' from near the right sideline – his 'wrong' side. His *pièce de résistance* came in the thirtieth minute. Mugsy's pass met him tearing through the middle, for an obvious tap-over. But no. From 18 metres, he torpedoed it straight between John Finucane and the left post. The half-time air was sweet perfume. Tyrone led by 2-6 to 0-1, Cormac scoring 1-3. Tyrone glided home, 13 points to the good.

It was time to ascend the steps of Gerry Arthurs Stand again. Cormac lifted Corn Uí Mhuirí with one hand, in unison with Brian McGuigan, whose return from injury as a sub four minutes from the end provoked the game's biggest cheer. But Cormac, who had rehearsed this moment, was the one who made the winning speech:

Tyrone football has had some bad press this year but hopefully we helped set the record straight here. The team today and throughout the campaign has tried to play honest, positive football and we are delighted to have won the Ulster title. I would like to pay tribute to our managers . . . and a special word for Brian McGuigan whom I am filling in for today.

The bad press that Cormac referred to stemmed from violence at club games. It mattered to him that his county played the game, and was seen to play, with honour. Alas, that record didn't stay straight, especially after he left the scene.

Perhaps the most startling of Cormac's feats was to end up as the Ulster championship's second top scorer, with 1-12. This was a converted defender who allegedly couldn't play midfield a year before, hadn't played up front and took none of the close-in free-kicks.

Before that summer was out, there were much bigger things to worry about in Tyrone. The Omagh bomb on 15 August visited multiple deaths on the county. Several of the deceased were GAA members, and the tragedy rippled out directly to families, friends and clubs throughout the county, particularly in the west. Most folk, it seemed, knew somebody who knew somebody who died. By chance, the county minor team had a rendezvous in Benburb that day. Around that time on any other Saturday that summer, they would be finishing training at Omagh CBS and heading home. Cormac and Hub would be sitting on the floor of Philip Jordan's white Peugeot 205 van, surrounded by four kitbags, as they chugged through those traffic lights at the bottom of Market Street.

In the aftershock of the calamity, the Tyrone minors' All-Ireland semi-final date with Leitrim became imbued with extra symbolism. They were, right then, the principal sporting envoys of their county, and they had already wrestled with the pall of grief. As people rummaged about for 'the right thing to do' in the wake of the bloodiest atrocity of the Troubles, some looked on the game differently. From somewhere the idea was mooted that Tyrone should withdraw. While it didn't gain traction, it had to be treated respectfully. This was Cormac's later perspective on the quandary:

> We talked about whether we should continue to play after the Omagh bomb. I know at the time, and maybe still today, there are people who feel we shouldn't have played on. I suppose you're damned if you do and damned if you don't.

We had to make a decision. Would it really have pleased anyone had we pulled out? . . . I was fortunate because I never knew anyone who died or was injured. But I respect that people had different feelings.

Eight days after the bombing, black armbands draped the upper arms of both teams at Croke Park. Leitrim, too, was dealing with tragedy: senior footballer Shane McGettigan had died after a construction accident near Boston. Having paid their respects, the Tyrone players did the needful for the next hour, albeit less efficiently than on other days. Cormac contributed three to the team's hatful of wides, but his high catches, general spanner-work and two more hallmark long-shot points more than redeemed him. At the last, the electronic scoreboard read Tír Eoghain 1-14, Liatroim 1-3.

Cormac was becoming a darling of the media. For the fourth match out of six, local papers adjudged him Man of the Match; and he received the Ulster GAA Writers' Award for August – an accolade rarely given to a minor. Each pundit sought to exceed the last in hyperbole. In the *Irish News* pen-pics before the final, he was rated 10/10 – 'Outstanding footballer who appears to have all the attributes necessary for greatness.'

The tributes owed something to Cormac's constant amenability to interview, and his measured words. After becoming captain, he found himself thrust into the spotlight as the public face of a young team that had enchanted the GAA public and was feted like a senior side. 'At first I was nervous and found the attention strange,' he con-fessed at the end of the season. 'I was finding myself listening to every question because I was afraid of lifting the papers the next day and finding myself in a controversial situation.'

It happened once, when he observed that the Laois side they'd be meeting in the final probably wasn't just as strong as that of '97. Apart from that slip-up, he stayed strictly on-message in the home straight.

The midweek announcement of the team for the final nailed down an issue that lingered still in the air. Sunday week before, the recuper-ating Brian McGuigan had woven magic in Ardboe's Tyrone senior championship final victory. Assuredly, he and his kin hoped for a minor final recall; but it didn't come. Mind you, jerseys 1 to 15 were hard won: Ryan Mellon, who did well in the semi, was back on the bench, joining Philip Jordan, who kept it warm all summer.

'I was just thinking I'd love to be starting and I wasn't starting,' Brian said later. 'I'd love to be captain and I wasn't captain. As the years went on I realized that Cormac was a better captain than me. He was a bigger leader.'

By default or design, Cormac retained the captaincy. Mickey Harte hardly wanted to change the formula:

> Cormac has been a real revelation. If someone told me back in May that in the absence of Brian McGuigan we would still reach the All-Ireland final I wouldn't have believed them. But Cormac has taken the bull by the horns and inspired others around him. He has come on a bagful since being made captain.

As the good-luck cards found their way to the skipper, the scale of public anticipation registered. Self-doubt appeared in a flicker: 'What if I don't do it now?' Then he reasoned to himself, apropos the well-wishers, 'Would you prefer them for you or against you?'

Such thoughts pinged about as Cormac prepared to address his troops. On the weekend itinerary printout, he made a few notes:

DON'T BE AFRAID OF LOSING – LIFE GOES ON
GO OUT AND GIVE IT EVERYTHING – 100% TO
THE FINAL WHISTLE

Cormac led his team out at 1.15 p.m. Laois were on for a rare three-in-a-row. True to form, Tyrone darted out of the traps. Mugsy and McGinley clattered the roof of the net in the first half, and that 6-point margin held to the close, 2-11 to 0-11. Tyrone had won a fourth All-Ireland minor title, twenty-five years after the previous, fifty after the one before.

As the final whistle peeped, corner-forward Aidan Lynch had just released the ball around midfield. 'Cormac McAnallen found the ball in his hands,' commented Keith Duggan in the *Irish Times*, and 'clasped it as though it contained the very preciousness of the moment and ran to the sideline'. No embracing or piling up on the grass for him. Keeping that ball as a memento was the first mission. The referee, Mick Curley, went after him.

'Hold on, the ball has to be given to the captain,' advised Curley.

'I am the captain,' Cormac replied with a smile.

Up to the cup, he led the way. The Archbishop of Cashel and GAA patron, Dr Dermot Clifford, told the congregation that he was never so pleased to present the cup, given the hardships Tyrone had overcome. Wincing with joy, and straightening his arms to their limit, Cormac raised the Tom Markham Cup.

Next, the biggest speech he would ever have to make. On the Friday afternoon, he had sat down with me to write it out. He wanted to use more than the token *cúpla focal*, while also including a fair share of English for the wider audience. We took a while, and a couple of disagreements, to hammer it out. I ran the Irish text past my friend from Armagh, Peadar Ó Baoill, and we threw in one or two Ulster idioms. A slight concern bugged me. He hadn't used much Irish in three years, apart from the odd quiz. He didn't 'think' in Irish. And his oratorical experience was slim; when asked to speak at the *Blackboard Jungle* presentation at school in '97, he was thrown. He might stumble, *anseo nó ansin*. He might even lose the notes he kept in his sock.

On the day, though, his intonation was perfect; his pronunciation not far off. He boomed out those words so confidently and fluidly that people took the match-programme at its word that he was indeed 'a fluent Irish speaker'.

A Uachtaráin Chumann Lúthchleas Gael, a chairde Gael, agus muintir Thír Eoghain,

Bliain ó shin, bhí díoma an domhain ar mhionúirí agus tacaithe Thír Eoghain i ndiaidh cluiche ceannais na hÉireann a chailliúint. Anois, thig liom a ráit gurb iontach an mothúchán Corn Thomáis Uí Mhorcacháin a thógáil in airde! [He raised his arm in triumph.]

. . . I know I speak on behalf of the team when I say that this is a culmination of a dream for us. It's been a rollercoaster two years – we and all the people of Tyrone have gone through the low points, and I think we deserved at least one high point.

He closed off by thanking 'a wonderful Laois team' who had set the standards for the previous two years. After the Tyrone team lapped the pitch, pausing to climb on to the old Hill 16 fence to salute the fans, Laois reciprocated by giving them a guard of honour off the pitch.

That speech struck a chord with much of the 60,000-plus crowd, especially the Tyrone battalions. A northern youngster speaking in flowing Irish at Croke Park was a real rarity. To some old hands, who knew decades of being made to feel less Irish than their southern confreres, the oration amounted to a re-statement of their identity. So they told Cormac. He didn't really expect it to attract much attention. But this minor team was feted like no other, receiving front- and back-cover treatment in daily papers over successive days. At the Burlington Hotel's Monday lunchtime reception for the final teams – where the Tyrone lads had gawked in awe at Maurice Fitz and the Kerry men a year before – Cormac was now a star turn, as old codgers lined up to laud him for his speech as much as for the win.

The homecoming underscored the special place of this squad in Tyrone hearts. Over 5,000 fans swelled Aughnacloy's wide main street on the Monday evening. No one under thirty had welcomed back cup-laden heroes before. The bus eventually inched into town at 9.30. Cormac linked arms with Brian McGuigan for the walk up to the stage, conscious of his own accidental captaincy, and lifted the cup high to each side, beaming.

Cormac was last on the microphone and was well warmed to it by now. 'You don't know how much we appreciate this: seeing all our own people coming out and welcoming us home like this.' In wrapping up, he projected, 'Hopefully we can stick together and have some more happy homecomings in the years ahead.' A final, most poignant moment came when Francie McGirr, the late Paul's father, walked up and shook hands with the players before lifting the cup.

The trophy tour began in earnest. The following Saturday, Cormac led the Tyrone minors out to play a rest-of-Ulster minor team in a charity match for the Omagh bomb appeal. Then he and a couple of lads were thrown on as subs for the Ulster/Galway senior select against the Rest of Ireland in a compromise-rules challenge. People could already foresee a time when he would join up with the major-league acts for real.

Cormac took the cup back to Eglish that evening, as the first club member to captain a winning county side. A big banner draped the back of the stage:

WELL DONE CORMAC
YOU DONE YOUR CLUB
AND COUNTY PROUD

It was nothing if not true to the local dialect.

The club ran it as a 'This is Your Life' type of event. Niall Donnelly of UTV Live, our local man on the telly, introduced different people who had moulded Cormac. First out from behind the screen, Daddy emerged and gave a wave to the crowd. Brother Ennis, Paddy McIntosh and Mrs Donaghy followed after, each paying their tributes.

On his tours with the cup, he visited family, including Granny in a Dungannon nursing home. There was one last place to go. A few months later, after attending the Dromore club dinner-dance as a guest of honour, he went with colleague Kevin 'Herbie' O'Brien and his mother to the grave of their fallen comrade, Paul.

Cards jammed our letterbox. Former mentors conveyed their delight in Cormac's deeds and general disposition. Youth coach Patsy Jordan rejoiced to see a young lad from the townland of Tullygiven, his patch, captain a team to all-Ireland success. Several teachers in Armagh wrote most magnanimously, each having turned, against the grain, into Tyrone supporters for a day. A letter from the Conradh na Gaeilge national executive congratulated Cormac on his good example in speaking Irish so lucidly that he was widely understood.

Weeks passed and the fable of Cormac's fluency grew. Soon, it became said that the acceptance speech was entirely in Irish. Then, legend had it that he conversed in nothing but Irish at home, with his family of native speakers. He was invited to appear at Gaelscoil events and introduced as a *Gaeilgeoir* guest at other functions. He didn't like to disappoint, but several times he had to correct the *fear a' tí* politely before taking the mike to talk mainly in English. The myth persisted. Whatever he said, people lapped it up.

Minor celebrity and his newfound role as a sporting ambassador brought Cormac to a lot of new places. He hit the catwalk, with some Tyrone minors and Derry seniors, for a charity fashion show. He flew to Manchester with the cup for an evening at the Irish centre. Then he breezed over to Chicago for Wolfe Tone's GAA Club dinner-dance, in the company of our parents, Enda McGinley and a pack of All-Ireland senior medallists from Galway.

There was also a vague scent of Oz. John Tobin of Galway called eight under-19s from around Ireland for an Aussie Rules trial. Cormac was flattered, went to see how he would get on, and thought he played well. None of the triallists made the grade in the end. He wasn't really downhearted. But if the offer of a year's contract had come, I think he'd have gone down under.

Back in the black north, at a stuffed McEniff hotel banquet in Bundoran, the Ulster GAA Writers Association named him as their 'Personality of the Year' for the entire province. That was a shock. 'I see awards like that as a reflection on the team, not me,' he said in acceptance. Already, he knew he should share the love.

The more he gave away, the more the media returned to him. The year held one last nice surprise. A couple of days before New Year, the *Irish News* carried a full broadsheet colour-piece on Cormac, based on an interview he did with Alex McGreevy in the Elms Bar. The article was awash with praise for his intellect, eloquence and maturity.

> I'd like to think I have my plans in place. My studies are most important and then playing for my club and Tyrone. I don't think I'll be part of the Tyrone senior team, maybe I'm too young. But I do want to play alongside Peter Canavan, a player I admire very much.

The subheading of the feature? 'Captain Cormac Comes of Age . . .'

The banner headline? 'Man of the Year'.

7.   Mind Games

When it came to recording details of matches we played in, Cormac took after me.

In under-12 days, I wrote down the result, my position and my score after every match I played – one line per game. Aged thirteen, I bought an A5-sized folder, 'Keep Your Own Football Records', for 50p at a school jumble sale. It was designed for soccer, but I knew of no GAA equivalent. For each game it had a separate card with spaces for the team list and even the referee and attendance details. I filled them out dutifully and slipped them into the plastic sleeves.

When the folder was full, I started using A4 pages to document all as before, and added extra lines for the team-colours, weather and ground conditions. I stuck loyal to that format, match after match, filing each sheet away in a red binder.

Cormac catalogued only in spurts at first. 'Appearances up to 4/11/91' was his first record, a single foolscap résumé of sixty-one competitive Gaelic matches to date: 'eleven caps' for primary school, ten for secondary, and forty for Eglish teams.

That was it until about four years later, when he drew on his ele-phantine memory and borrowed my archives to list all his match-results and personal scores of the previous six years in a spiral-bound A4 notepad. After each game from then on, he logged the opponent, venue, result, his position and his personal score.

After Eglish played in the Ulster minor final on New Year's Day 1998, Cormac added a 'Perf.' column, to rate his personal perform-ance on a five-star scale. He gave himself three stars for the first game, and that became his average over the year. Four stars was the most he ever awarded himself that year. When the five-star scale came to seem too crude, he started marking himself out of ten – and then he introduced half marks.

After the team disappointments of '99, he wanted to move onwards

2000 MATCH INDEX – EVALUATION

TEAM	OPPONENTS	VENUE	STATUS	DATE	SCORE	PERS.	POS.	OFF.	DEF.	HEAD	BODY	LEGS
QUB	Antrim	Dub	Sig F	09/01	0:14–06	0:1	LHF	6	5	7	4	5
Tyr U-21	W'Meath	Mullingar	HC	15/01	0:15–0:12	0:1	MF	7½	6½	7	8	7
QUB	Crossmaglen	Dub	Sig F	16/01	2:11–0:15	0:5	CHF	8	6	8	8	7½
QUB	Sligo IT	Dub	Sig Rd 1	26/01	2:10–1:10	1:2	CHF	7½	6½	8½	8	8
Tyr U-21	Leitrim	Irvinestown	HC (S-F)	29/01	0:12–0:6	0:2	CHB	7½	7	8	7½	7½
QUB	St Mary's	Dub	Sig L16	01/02	2:11–0:11	0:1	CHF	6½	7	7½	8	8
Tyr U-21	Down	Longford (Slashers)	HC (Finale)	05/02	0:11–1:7	0:1	MF	6½	8	7½	7½	8
Tyrone	Donegal	Ballybofey	TSL	13/02	0:10–0:10	0:0	MF	6½	7½	8	7	7½
QUB	MICE (Limerick)	Maree	Sig (QF)	25/02	1:9–1:4	0:0	CHF	6	7	7	8	6
QUB	UCC	Salthill	Sig (SF)	26/02	0:13–1:7	0:4	CHF	8½	6½	9	7½	9
QUB	UCD	Moycullen	Sig (Finale)	27/02	1:8–0:8 (AET)	0:0	CHF	6	8	7½	7½	8½

and upwards. He discovered a way during the following winter. It lay in the realm of sports psychology.

Nowadays, psychologists are part of the furniture for most top-level Gaelic teams; but in the late 1990s, sports psychology was pretty novel. Cormac's muse then was Dr John Kremer, a Reader in Queen's School of Psychology. Hailing from Cumbria and with no Irish links prior to moving to Belfast, John was invited to assist the Queen's and Tyrone Gaelic football teams in the early 1990s. That made him one of the very first professional psychologists in GAA-land.

One of John's basic methods was 'Eyes Off'. He'd ask teams to close their eyes and focus on their best past matches, recall how they had prepared, and pinpoint what had worked for them then. Some players didn't care for this mindfulness lark. Others gained a lot from it. For Enda McNulty at Queen's, it was an early pointer towards a career in sports psychology. Having taken first-year modules in psychology and enjoyed them, Cormac was all for it, ready to absorb anything that could enhance performance by even a fraction.

In an interview in spring '99, he explained that he drew on John Kremer's visualization techniques in preparation for big games: 'You try and imagine things going well, what it will be like coming out on to the field, that sort of thing. You try and picture everything so that whenever it happens you're already fairly used to it.'

At a Queen's team meeting the following winter, John floated the idea of players assessing their performance through isolating the different components of their play and marking each one out of ten. He had already adapted this model of 'performance profiling' or 'mirror-gazing' from the work of the English psychologist Richard Butler, and he advocated it in his own work with Irish Olympic athletes. In essence, self-assessment is intended to isolate the athlete from pats on the back, increase self-motivation, and turn him into his own sports psychologist. Or, as Cormac put it simply, 'The purpose is to see how you can do better the next day.'

John advised players to do a written self-assessment immediately after the game. The longer you leave it, the more the comments of coaches and others, together with your own selective memory, would contaminate the assessment. But Cormac worried that compiling such data in a crowded dressing room might draw adverse attention, so he waited till he got home.

I doubt any other Tyrone or Queen's player of that era followed up on the personal profiling. Indeed, if any other Gaelic team was doing that back then, I have yet to hear of it. Cormac, at the age of nineteen, made it his new-millennium resolution.

He identified five components of play to be marked: Offensive, Defensive, Head, Body and Legs. The first two were self-explanatory. The others need a bit of teasing out. John explains it along the following lines:

For Head, he meant:

How was my decision-making?

How good were my attentional styles and switching? – i.e., moving from a broad-sweep view of the pitch to a focus on narrow targets?

How well did I handle setbacks and manage mistakes?

For Body, he meant:

How comfortable did I feel?

Was I in my stress 'zone', allowing my body to work to its best advantage?

How well did I get stuck in?

For Legs, he meant:

How fit did I feel?

Did I really tire myself out physically?

Cormac wrote all his self-assessments in private, not to be discussed with anyone – he certainly never discussed his ratings for any match with me – and not for anyone else to pore over. Few people knew that he was doing it at all, though no one who knew him well was really surprised to learn of it in due course.

I asked John to put Cormac's evaluations in context:

Cormac was always very attentive; he didn't always ask a lot of questions or have long, deep conversations with me, but I could see he was taking it in and reflecting.

The way I would characterise him is as a filter-feeder. He would take ideas and constructs that were useful to him and then adapt them as he saw fit. If he could get just 1–2 per cent extra from something I'd said, then he'd use it.

Some players see personal profiling as a threat, as they think they already possess all it takes. You need a certain hardness of resolve to keep appraising your own failings. That's why some don't stick at the evaluations.

Cormac was exceptional in that he was such a decent guy despite having that constant desire to learn and improve. But at the same time, it was not all-consuming for him. Crucially, he was also very honest with himself. None of it works unless you have the honesty that underpins this approach. To do that self-assessment methodically, and with that level of diligence and thoroughness from such a young age, was truly exceptional.

On match days, Cormac made his first waking moments into private pep-talks. Once he had stirred in the morning, that was it; he couldn't go back to sleep. The first minutes awake were when his thinking was clearest, he said. That was when he could set his targets as to how he would improve on the previous day. He used to tell teammates to do likewise.

For all that, he also indulged in a bit of naked physicality to get psyched up for a big game. Sometimes he slapped himself repeatedly on the forehead. A programme on BBC Choice captured him doing this before the 1999 Sigerson semi-final. He'd throw hard shoulders too, of course. And before club games or during training he would invite me to punch him on the torso and be hit in return.

During the pre-match parades at Clones in 2001, while others talked or swaggered or swigged from a bottle, Cormac walked calmly in a straight line with two fingers pressed across the carotid artery on the left side of his neck. Instantly, John Kremer recognized one of his own tips being put into practice. Cormac was registering his pulse-rate. If it was too fast, he'd have to relax by closing his eyes and picturing somewhere peaceful; if too slow, he could think of something energizing.

His mind was now right. There was so much more to do.

*

Facing into 1999, many observers took it for granted that Cormac would be playing for the Tyrone senior team before the year was out.

Some of the hype came from the national media. In those early January days when papers rely on filler features, a piece by Colm Keys for the *Irish Mirror*, 'From Boys to Men', listed Cormac as one of the stars in waiting for the year ahead. There alongside him were Nicholas Murphy of Cork, 'Beano' McDonald of Laois, Nigel Crawford of Meath, John Donnellan of Galway, and a few more: 'With Tyrone's inherent midfield problems comes a knight in shining armour. Last year's All-Ireland minor captain may still be eighteen, but already there is talk of him filling of the anchor roles in the problematic Tyrone engine room.'

Cormac didn't accept the old canard that 'Tyrone have no midfield'. Followers had incanted it like a mantra since Plunkett Donaghy left the stage. Cormac saw it as a lazy, clichéd fallback analysis of every Tyrone defeat. It was also harsh on the middlemen for the Ulster triumphs in 1995–6. The detractors seemed to want Tyrone to have twin towers like Derry or Armagh had. But they ignored how midfield play had changed: with half-backs and half-forwards now congesting and contesting kick-outs, clean-catching was becoming rarer, and mobility and the ability to break ball were becoming more essential.

In March, another tabloid identified him as one of '5 Young Players to Watch'. Later, he wrote in his scrapbook: 'Premature at the time for where I was at, but confidence-building nonetheless.'

Danny Ball was in his third year as Tyrone senior manager. Having coached county sides to All-Ireland under-21 triumphs in 1991 and 1992, he had been widely expected to succeed with those same players as seniors in their prime. The fans were impatient. The agonies in Croke Park in 1995–6 convinced us all that Tyrone was nearly there.

The Ulster Championship, as ever, scoffed at such great notions. Tyrone had been dismantled by Derry in 1997, and lost with an injury-stricken team to a middling Down side in '98. The 1997–8 minor young bloods seemed vital to revive fortunes.

Ball went for it. Once university, county under-21 and National

League campaigns ended in late March, Cormac got the call-up, along with three more '98 minors: Hub, Stephen O'Neill and Michael McGee.

They were made welcome. Cormac knew Mattie McGleenan, Colin Holmes and Ciaran Gourley well already. His first run came in a challenge against Antrim at Cargin on 16 April. He started out as centre half-forward, and scored 2 points in a drawn match. Six weeks later, he held the same spot and scored 3 points in a friendly defeat by Clare.

As the Championship drew close, a rash of midfield injuries led to Cormac moving there for June challenges against Mayo (losing) and Dublin (winning). He marked himself eight out of ten for both games.

The team to play Fermanagh in the first round contained championship debutants, but there was only one big media story: McAnallen's Tyrone senior debut, straight in at midfield. Partnering him was Gerald Cavlan, who had played only in attack before. Ball explained to the waiting press that Cormac was a 'very mature footballer' who was fit for the task. Players, supporters and media concurred.

Journalists rang the family home, but he wasn't there. There was no answer in his student house in Belfast, as it was the last week of exams and other lads had left for the summer.

The journalists then called my student house, a mile away from his. I said I'd contact him for them; I'd never known him to snub the press. I tried to call, but no answer. I crossed the Lagan bridge to his door, but he was away. Nobody could say where he was. We began to worry that something was wrong. Even in peacetime, Belfast could have that effect on you.

Cormac resurfaced on the Friday. He had been lying low for a couple of days: he knew journalists would be on to him and the more the match previews became about him, the bigger burden he'd be under.

He didn't manage to escape entirely, however. Des Fahy tracked him down just in time for a feature in the *Sunday Times*, and Cormac agreed to an interview. The article revealed that the manager was also looking at him as an option for long-range free-kicks. There was almost a belief abroad that the boy could do no wrong.

Fermanagh weren't billed as the pushovers of the past, having beaten Monaghan in the preliminary round. Cormac was leaving nothing to chance anyhow. His first ploy for kick-outs was to punch the ball forward and let a forward pick it up. Once this worked and Tyrone sped ahead, he chanced some clean catches and made a few. On the verge of half-time, with Tyrone six points up, Cormac ventured forward. Peter Canavan had the ball in the corner and he picked the pass flawlessly; Cormac received it and opened his scoring account for Tyrone seniors. Later on, he returned the favour to Peter, setting him up for a point. It proved to be a handy victory, and both Hub and O'Neill were blooded as subs. The new generation was here to stay.

Newspaper columnists praised the new-look central pairing. Teammates predicted that Tyrone had found its answer – this was the midfield 'for the future'. The only really dissonant note was sounded by the Fermanagh manager (and former Tyrone player) Pat King. 'When their midfield comes up against a stronger one than ours,' he said, 'then questions will be asked.'

Over in Philadelphia around that time, three Tullysaran lads from school – Pierce Donnelly, Lenny Conlon and Ciaran Corrigan – were playing for the city's 'Tyrone' Gaelic club in their championship. Fermanagh's captain, Sean Breen, flew out as a guest player. In his team-talk, he told colleagues to do like Cormac McAnallen, 'putting himself in for balls that you wouldn't put a dog in for'. Pierce felt proud to hear a stranger extolling a former schoolmate, 3,000 miles from home, after he'd played just one senior game for Tyrone.

Before the Ulster semi-final, Cormac spoke warily in an interview of 'so much pressure to succeed' in a county that had such high hopes. Tyrone met Down at a packed Casement Park, Belfast. It was 'Twelfth' eve and a scorcher. Down had stuttered past Antrim and a walkout of several players made them appear threadbare. Observers underestimated Down's physique and ability, and the tactical nous of manager Peter McGrath.

Cormac hardly touched the ball and was hauled off in the 44th minute. Down tore Tyrone to shreds and romped to a 5-point win, pulling up. The midfield zone, and Cormac's ineffectiveness primarily, were held up as key factors in the collapse.

That wasn't really fair to him. Most of the damage happened in his absence. When his sub slip was written, Tyrone led by 0-10 to 0-7, having been in front throughout. When the substitution was relayed to the sideline officials, Ciaran McCabe had just danced along the endline, past four players, to score the equalizing goal. In the quarter-hour after Cormac's exit, Down added 1-5 while Tyrone mustered 2 points. A malaise affected every line of the Tyrone team that day, not simply midfield.

Still, it wasn't Cormac's best day. Danny Ball said afterwards that he was outmuscled and the referee gave him little protection. Mickey Harte, who watched from the stand, later wrote that predictable kick-outs and the weight of expectation undid him. 'The world was expected of Cormac.'

There were other factors. Long ball was king then and it pinballed up and down frenetically that day, often bypassing midfield. Down's No. 8 and No. 9, Brian Burns and Alan Molloy, were better known as backs, but both were bigger than Cormac and Calvo. Cormac had never jumped in a midfield moshpit like this.

Cormac summarized it in his scrapbook:

> THE worst day I've had in a Tyrone jersey. Nothing went right for me personally, even when the team was going well. Passes I ran for weren't given to me, kick-outs went away from me, and when I got on the ball there was no time to play it. Never got started at all.

He marked himself four out of ten. The comedown was sudden, hard and painful. His fallibility had been laid bare on a big stage. But he made sure to learn from the experience. Never again would he have to rate himself so low.

*

Our abject failure with the Eglish senior team was the biggest regret of Cormac's playing career, without doubt. We didn't even come close to achieving our potential.

Why didn't we? It's a complicated subject to revisit. The GAA club is stylized as an idyll of idealism. When you see one on TV, it's usually a county champion or else a romantic wee club surviving against all odds. County players speak of their club duty and glory, alongside neighbours and friends, as the acme of the sport.

For most clubs and adult players, the reality is less romantic: a huge amount of effort and angst, but only evanescent rewards, and grand, unfulfilled ambitions. Christy O'Connor's book *The Club* could have been written about Eglish or hundreds of other clubs as well as his own St Joseph's Doora-Barefield.

Cormac wanted the best for Eglish. He gave his best. He didn't always play his best but he nearly always played. Of our forty-eight senior league and championship games from 1998 to 2000, he played in forty-seven, every minute. No one else played so much. All of that while he was nearly ever-present for our minors and under-21s and for dozens of Tyrone games. Doing his shifts for Eglish often meant coming from a match or session with county or university and barely a breath in between.

Others made huge sacrifices too. Like Cathal Glackin and Paul 'Buzzer' Hughes shuttling to training from Dublin, even midweek. Like Declan McKeever, our own Belfast-to-the-Brantry ferryman and Man Utd diehard, missing the glory of Camp Nou just to run the lines on a filthy wet night in Eglish.

Still, few equalled Cormac's commitment or application. Throughout every training session, he held pure focus. 'I always thought a training session with Cormac present was worth twice one without him,' Anthony Daly says of that time. When our young county star was present, attitudes were generally more focused. When he was absent, the bad habits of some – to take the odd rest, cut a corner, showboat, or prank about – were a little more pronounced.

He wasn't game-faced all the time. When we won, he threw himself into the thick of celebrations. He saw this strictly as a reward for victory, however; and was not among those who went out after each weekend game – win, lose or draw. He couldn't grasp this mentality, and said so in team meetings. He wouldn't be in any form to go out after losing, and he'd be ashamed to be seen by neighbouring clubmen.

This was a bit hard on some of our teammates. It was not fair to expect lads who worked Monday–Saturday to stay in on a Sunday evening; unlike students, they couldn't get up whenever they liked during the week. But while some talked over defeat through the hazy hindsight of a pint glass, Cormac was at home, aching, checking results on Aertel to draw up a revised league table, and marking his own play through a microscope.

Playing in the top flight in 1998, we had our moments – including a victory over Errigal Ciaran, the best side in Ulster. For the first time in a generation, people started to take Eglish seriously as a force in Tyrone senior football. We looked the part too, wearing the new style of long shorts. They matched our jerseys, making us the All Blacks, the fearless MIBs of Tyrone.

In our fourth game, we slew Ardboe – county champions later that year. About then, an old failing of our senior teams re-emerged. Any big scalp seemed to inflate Eglish heads. Players dined out on beating Errigal and Ardboe, as grand notions grew in our minds.

They were soon shot down. In the senior championship, we lost a replay to Cookstown. In the league, we won some matches and lost several narrowly. Cormac went everywhere he was required: three games at centre half-forward, then four at centre half-back, two at full-forward, one at midfield, then one more at centre half-back. He did each job as tasked, no complaints.

Alas, he couldn't clean up every mess. A restructuring of the county leagues meant that the top flight was shrinking from sixteen teams to ten. We were stuck in eleventh spot and missed the cut.

Anthony Daly and Jim Fay stepped aside at the end of '98. We had made solid progress in their two-and-a-bit seasons, but they had heard on the grapevine that club aficionados had ambitions of recruiting an outside manager to bring us to the next level. This was a common mindset within clubs, that a stranger would work magic. In a club like ours, it tended not to work out that way.

Our next manager, Benny Haughey, came from Carrickmore, but he was entangled in Eglish through marriage, and with his roguish rustic charm he blended right in. He had tasted senior success with his club as a player and manager. Training was spartan. Pre-season, we waded into a sloped quagmire with only one set of goalposts, as our ground wasn't available. Those thrice-weekly sessions often descended into mud-wrestling, but they built up camaraderie. Benny chuckled.

Before our first league game, Benny put the senior captaincy to a vote. There was no dialogue, simply a straight secret ballot. The result: Cormac McAnallen. At nineteen years and two months, he was our youngest outfielder. Benny was staggered. He expected an old hand would be picked. Cormac was also quite surprised, I think. But for the pool of young players, this boy seemed a natural leader, and not just because he lifted cups for Tyrone minors.

It was the small things, too. The mere sight of him demanded a seriousness from others. With bags over their shoulders, JP and Jody Ogle met him on a Belfast street early one spring evening, on their way to the train to Portrush for a big night out. He might take a dim view of that. So they told him they were going to train in the gym.

After Greg O'Neill's cruciate operation that year, Cormac offered to go with him to the gym for rehab sessions. But Greg was a laid-back lad and thought that training with the team would suffice. He recollects Cormac saying to him, 'No, you need to be doing your own separate training. You need to build up the muscle by yourself. I don't want to see you falling by the wayside.' Greg made the excuse that he was working evenings and didn't have time. Cormac kept on his case, when others forgot about him. But 'I didn't listen to the man. That's a regret.' Greg would come back for a couple more seasons, but the knee was never the same again. Stiff and sore, he retired at twenty-three.

Our last-sixteen senior championship tie that season was against Dromore. Cormac had watched Dromore turf Errigal out in the preliminary round – one of the biggest shocks in Tyrone championship history. He rang home straight after the match, buoyant, to tell me the news. For Eglish, the Red Sea seemed to have parted suddenly. Dromore had good players, but no major titles to their name, and languished low in 1B, below us. We had hammered them away in the league the previous autumn.

We fielded a strange team, lost by a point and exited the

championship. That evening of June '99 turned out to be a crossroads moment for both sides.

Cormac was crestfallen. To make matters worse, several players skipped off to America for the summer. Once Tyrone's season ended in July, Cormac started getting calls from Chicago and the east coast. One club got an Eglish player to ring and promise him money, a job and a good time. Cormac wasn't persuaded. To him, the Eglish exodus represented a loss of faith in our dream. He dared to dream still. He stayed home and helped the club pick up the pieces.

We were lucky that he did. We could have plunged into the drop-zone. Instead, he led us from the front, and upward. Bit by bit that summer, Benny devolved an ever-greater role to Cormac at training, to set up drills and coach us through them. And from game to game, once again, he hopped from one line to another to fix problems. He joined me in midfield for crunch league victories over the Moy and Moortown. He returned to centre half-back against Dungannon, and somehow scored 1-3 of our 1-8 total, his fifty-yard kick riding the wind into the top corner to clinch victory. Then the county board did us a huge favour, deciding late in the year to revert to the old league format. Four teams would go up from 1B. Other clubs had lost interest in the league, but our late surge had pushed us up to fourth place. By a small miracle, we were promoted.

Cormac's commitment also salvaged our under-21 campaign. When we were badly depleted and facing a landmine opener away to Lough-macrory in mid-July, he asked to play full-back for the first time that year. He knew he had to plug the gaps in defence, despite his roaming instinct. The move worked and we scraped through by a point. Cormac rated himself nine out of ten for the only time in all of '99.

We careered through that under-21 championship to meet Errigal in the final. On average we were about a year older, inches taller and pounds heavier. We had been minor champions twice; some of them were still minors. Switching Cormac from centre-back to centre half-forward after five minutes was our main gambit. Yet we were outwitted by Mickey Harte's developing swarm-defence tactics. We caught so many kick-outs, only for an encircling pack to choke us. It went to a replay. In a rare lapse, Cormac let his man slip by for a goal.

Then he led our charge back and thundered their crossbar. But the rest of us lacked the cutting edge to break through.

That defeat really hurt. Our generation had picked up titles at every age-level, but no more. Some of us believed that if Paddy McIntosh had returned to guide us as under-21s, we could have won again. But that wasn't going to happen.

That defeat also exposed our Achilles heel: for all our big physiques, Eglish had too few nippy whippets. We were surely Tyrone's tallest team, with half our players at 6' 1" or more. We could out-muscle opponents without stooping to dirt. But any top senior side needs will-o'-the-wisp artists and trickster forwards; and their ilk were a rarity in our ranks.

*

At ambitious clubs, there are some familiar ways in which tension brews. A big-name outside manager is appointed. Under pressure to deliver, he puts on more training sessions and creates a more combative atmosphere. When things go well, all is fine. When they go wrong, rows blow up quickly.

Nowadays, that sort of dynamic is well known in lots of senior clubs. Even then, it wasn't unique to us. But for some of us younger players, Cormac included, who still held an idealistic view of club football, the year 2000 brought a loss of innocence.

Our new manager, Martin McElkennon, was unveiled to the team in the clubhouse on the second Sunday of the new millennium. He set out his plans, and made honesty his watchword. Cormac left that ice-breaker content and confident. He knew that Marty Mac was clued in to modern training methods and he liked his attitude. We needed more honesty of effort. McElkennon spoke with knowledge, conviction and swagger. And his message that Eglish had to do better in the league before talking about championships also was a point that Cormac had been making as captain.

He trained us furiously. Between long runs, hurdles and endless ear-popping sprints, he scolded and goaded us individually. He challenged our manhood and warned us to eff off if we hadn't got it. Cormac tended to escape such badgering. He was proven.

Into that explosive mix, we had just acquired a WMD. His name was Martin Toye. A seasoned Armagh veteran, he had come to live and play in Eglish. He was super-fit, fearsome and passionate. Instantly his legend grew. His (fake) Bebo profile – thanks, Rory McKillion – later stated that Marty didn't do push-ups; he pushed the world down. Marty had a knack of insulting each member of his team in turn to their faces, one by one, as an incentive to do great things.

We blazed into the league, with Cormac giving all he could. Consider the Sunday in April when he played a whole National League game at midfield for Tyrone against Armagh, suffered bad bruising to his hand, then presented for the Eglish v. Galbally league game at 7 p.m. He had ample excuse to rest and come on as a sub, but the thought never entered his mind. He lined out as our No. 6 against Galbally and earned the late free-kick that won the match. Two wins out of two, we dared to dream again.

But as the fields got firmer, we got back on a losing streak. McElkennon tried to fix problems in post-training meetings, reviewing clips on video and provoking clear-the-air debate past 10 p.m. These meetings didn't build team spirit; on the contrary, they were creating a culture of cheap-shot comments. In an interview after the All-Ireland under-21 final, in May, Cormac described his teammates as 'a great bunch of lads' and, more interestingly, added: 'In some teams you get bickering and rifts between players, but in this team, we're really like a family.' The 'bickering and rifts' reference arose directly from his experiences that spring with Eglish.

Once again, we were abysmal in the championship. Against a Dungannon side that was bottom of the league, we trailed by 4 points. We were misfiring completely up front, so Cormac was thrown up from centre half-back to full-forward as a last roll of the dice. Within moments, he was placing the ball on the penalty-spot. He kicked wide. But nil desperandum. In the last minute of the 60, he rounded the goalie and rattled the net. An even later free-kick drew it and saved us.

Subsequent events turned that season somewhat sour for Cormac and me. The first came on Saturday, 13 May, the day of Tyrone's All-Ireland under-21 final at Mullingar. A light training session was fixed for Eglish at 6 p.m. that evening, ahead of a league match the next day. Our senior players couldn't attend both. By the time the under-21 cup would be presented, hopefully to Cormac, it would be nearly 5 p.m., and home was two hours away. It was senseless. Players felt compelled to stay home, as this seemed like a test of loyalty in championship month, and minor infractions had already incurred an iron-fist response. And a sure-the-match-is-live-on-TV attitude pertained. Mad as it seems, I toed the line. I watched Cormac lift the cup on telly, then went to the Eglish session.

From that day on, I regretted my call. I didn't go to every under-21 match, I admit, but a national final was different. Cormac was still Eglish's only All-Ireland-winning captain. As his brother, I should've been there. I should have spoken up. I had let him down. I couldn't believe the club had let this be. I took the scheduling of the training session that evening as a snub, whether by accident or design. Cormac was quite stunned. He didn't cause a fuss, but the two of us saw that common sense had gone, and we agreed that if there were another aberration, we wouldn't hold back.

The second incident happened three weeks later, in our championship replay. We edged out Dungannon, but the two of us were seething at the introduction of a long-gone veteran who hadn't trained all year and had played just once in five years – in a bizarre championship cameo in '99, which we had written off as never-again. This kind of thing was unheard of in other senior clubs, and the talk of honesty turned to dust. After so many sacrifices to train since January – such as Cormac turning out night after night during his final exams – a stranger could just appear for our big day and get on.

A line had clearly been crossed. Once we got inside the dressing room, we didn't even need to look at each other. We both packed our bags to leave, quickly and quietly. But as I tried to turn the door-handle, I was blocked by a well-meaning clubman. Marty Toye shouted across, 'What's wrong, Dónal?' Bad call, Marty.

'I'll tell you what's wrong,' I exploded. Rather ineloquently, I called some spades. Cormac uttered a few words. Then we left, to a stunned silence.

I was gutted afterwards. I didn't regret my stance, but rather the furore of my Keano moment. Other players stayed silent. Some later expressed disgust at the double standards. A few, I think, viewed my protest as purely selfish and disruptive, arising from pique at having been taken off, and chose to believe that Cormac had sided with me out of brotherly loyalty.

The next Sunday, Eglish played against Strabane in the last sixteen. This was another big opportunity. Strabane hadn't won a senior championship match since World War II. With Cormac at midfield, and marking one of their county players, Eglish led at half-time. Then Cormac was switched to full-back to mark their other county man. Strabane became more assertive around the middle, gained forward momentum, and sealed victory. It was a diabolical defeat for Eglish. And I wasn't even there. I had started an MA at NUI Galway and played for the university in the Galway SFC that day. It was a hateful decision for me, but I felt like a bad smell after the row, and a conversation with McElkennon convinced me that my absence might defuse the tension. Cormac told me the bitter news as I stood in a phone-box on Eglinton Street. I had lost in two county championships on one afternoon.

Within days, Uncle Sam called again. This time Cormac was sorely tempted. For county men knocked out of championship at home, America was seen as the place to be. Talk of high jinks gave him itchy feet. On the phone one night, while I was in the Donegal Gaeltacht, he told me he was probably going for a few weeks. 'But we need you at home,' I begged him. 'You helped us to turn it around last summer. We can do it again.' After that emotive call, the *fear a' tí* tore into me for hogging his landline and blocking a call. I got upset. Why was I bothering, after all the recent events? Some other players didn't hesitate to take flight. But Cormac and I always wanted Eglish to achieve our potential.

He ended up staying. And with Cormac on board, we hauled our way up the table. McElkennon came into his own too, keeping us fit, keen and mean, and bygones were let be. On an August weekend, we beat Strabane on the Saturday evening and then had to travel to a fresh and second-in-table Trillick side on Sunday at 2.45 p.m. We were tired and aching, but our cunning plan was to send Cormac on another special mission: into the full-back line to mark their target-man, Damian Gormley. Problem solved. Ball after ball into the corner pinged right out, via Cormac's hands. To our half-time roar, our goalie, Mickey McCann, swung a fist and broke a dressing-room window. He had to be replaced; so did the glass. Yet, against all odds, we ground out victory.

We knew now we were a serious senior team. The manager had hardened our collective resolve and raised our game. He had taken us higher up the league than we had ever been, or ever would be; this made him much in demand with county teams, and that in turn is ultimately why he wouldn't stay with us.

But there was one more debacle in our penultimate game. We led Killyclogher away, ten minutes to go. We were going at it hammer and tongs. Then four subs came on for us at once, breeding chaos, and Killyclogher snailed through for a farcical equalizing goal. The match ended in a draw. We traipsed up the long steps, livid. Nine months of hectoring about honesty and sacrifices, and now this! Why had Dermot Donaghy bothered to fly back from Lancaster to play today? Why had Marty McCann nearly wrecked himself going for a ball? Why had Cormac emptied his tank again? In the dressing room, Marty Toye called it a disgrace, loud and clear. Cormac and I lifted our bags and walked out. No one stopped us this time.

8. 'You're going to lift three cups'

In their second year at Queen's, Cormac's posse of ex-Armagh pupils moved to 85 Fitzroy Avenue. They stayed there for their third year and moved down the street to No. 125 in their last year. Noisy, anarchic Fitzroy was the main artery of student Belfast; 85 was slap-bang in its middle, and sited on a corner, so they were badly exposed. And it was such a tip that Daddy came to Belfast to accompany Cormac and Co. to the estate agent, to make a complaint; their rent was reduced for the next year.

Front-door security was flimsy. Finding a homeless man in the kitchen was only shocking the first time. If you fancied an early-morning cheese toastie, as the nomadic McQuade brothers did, you could let yourself in, put on the grill, fall asleep on the sofa, go home, and let Cormac and OD get out of their beds to deal with the fire brigade. 'It can give you a few sleepless nights,' Cormac said in an interview at the time. 'It also detracts from your academic career as you can do no work in the house.'

That same core group of eight to ten lads stayed together throughout their student days. Cormac enjoyed being part of such a tight-knit bunch. They went out together as a wolfpack, always preceded by a dance-off, in which participation was compulsory and competition was fierce. They played as '85 & Hove Albion Football Club' in the Queen's Societies Cup soccer tournament, reaching the quarter-finals. They donned tuxes for their 'Annual Christmas Doo' [sic] (and still doo today). 'Christmas' parties took place as late as May; I can still see Cormac clasping air-headphones and belting out his desig-nated line from Band Aid, then lighting an imaginary pipe to 'Chestnuts Roasting on an Open Fire'.

Even as Cormac's star rose, the lads kept his feet firmly on the ground. They slagged him relentlessly: about his awful slice wide in the 1998 minor final; about any time he appeared on TV; about his clunking steps on the stairs. And Johnny just revelled in calling him 'too fat to play football'. (If you saw Johnny, you'd get the irony.)

Cormac's biggest weakness was an inability to refuse a challenge, no matter how gruesome. Like the time they challenged him to gobble up the leftover from the previous day's frying pan, cold.

'Right, let's go then!'

And he'd do it. He was ever determined to prove himself the hardest, the strongest-willed, the best.

His startling competitiveness and dedication set the tone for late afternoons. When back in the house by four, he watched *Fifteen to One* with notebook in hand to mark his personal score. This required a lot of concentration as questions came thick and fast, so he didn't call out all of his answers.

'You didn't get that one!' some of the other lads would taunt if they saw him mark one down without saying it.

'I knew it,' he'd retort.

Cormac had a way about him that endeared himself to people. 'He'd talk for long hours with you in the house,' recalls Johnny. 'And he always took an interest in you.' He could also make a compliment to a girl in a platonic way. 'That's a nice coat,' he might say casually in the middle of the day, politely and with no ulterior motive.

There was one obvious exception. They met on University Street one night in January '99, Cormac and Ashlene. He had been out with Leo when they crossed paths; she was walking home in a tracksuit with a friend. She didn't recognize him, and he didn't say he played football. The conversation flowed anyhow. Ashlene was bubbly and gave as good as she got. His open and genuine manner impressed her. She thought he had a lovely smile too. They parted on the street. She waited to see.

He phoned her the next day and they went to the cinema. They saw *Practical Magic*. His review? 'I'm never letting you choose again.' From that line she detected that something would develop.

Cormac was still eighteen when they met, but he knew she was the one that he wanted. Having had minimal interest from girls till he was a minor star, he then managed to elude the sudden advances of the jersey-grabbing sisterhood. Unlike many of his age, he was look-ing for a serious relationship. Ashlene was the one.

They were very similar. She played Gaelic football for Derry and was on the sports studies course at Jordanstown. She was competitive as well. They could play or watch any sport together. They loved exploring the great outdoors and rambling up mountains. They had a similar sense of humour. Being with her eased his inner anxieties and made him more confident. He was happy. She accepted his sin-gular devotion to training and games more than many other girls would. And with her supporting him and driving him on, he stayed on track and continued to improve as a player.

*

Cormac's second crack at the Sigerson Cup felt fated for success. Belfast was hosting the final weekend: quarter-finals, semi-finals and final in the space of three days. On the eve of it, he was interviewed live on BBC TV *Newsline* by Jackie Fullerton, the face of Ulster sportscasting.

Cormac was initially reluctant. He was just nineteen and had never done a live TV interview before. What about some of the older play-ers? But Jack Devaney, the Queen's club chairman, had asked him because he knew he'd do it well. Daddy persuaded him. On screen, he came across smoothly. 'What I wouldn't give to be nineteen again!' Jackie said in parting, with his post-box grin.

The occasion was a reception in the majestic City Hall, only the second big bash for Gaelic games there since 1968. During the Trou-bles, such an event was unthinkable. Jack Devaney and the key officers – Diarmuid Cahill, Aidan O'Rourke and the McMahon twins, Arlene and Loraine – were always looking to break new ground. Cormac tried to help out, attending club meetings in the chaplaincy, assisting me with PRO duties. Dinner-dances; fundrais-ers; a club exhibition opened by Mo Mowlam and President McAleese; the medal presentation at Áras an Uachtaráin; and the first-ever GAA-related function at Stormont, in 2001. Whatever big gig the Queen's club ran, Cormac attended, even when other first-teamers didn't.

Queen's opportunity to win Sigerson at home owed much to Cormac. In the two previous games – against the Garda College in the Ryan Cup league final, and the Sigerson first-rounder against UCD – his battling qualities had saved his team and marked his rise to stardom.

The game at Belfield epitomized Sigerson tradition. Soft, cratered turf. Two long lines of spectators leaning over pitch-side railings. Betwixt cheering students, a seasoned press corps and well-known managers, star-gazing and talent-spotting. At centre half-forward, Cormac was marked by John Divilly of the reigning All-Ireland champion Galway side. Undaunted, he scrapped, blocked, carried and harried. He kicked two clinker points, swooping and twirling in the wind, clipping post and nestling on top of the net. Columns on Queen's win predicted his imminent promotion to the Tyrone senior team. He marked himself seven.

That win lifted a heavy yoke from Queen's shoulders. We had dreaded the prospect of hosting the finals weekend as disinterested spectators. Now, everything was falling into place nicely. Our father's company, Ardmac, stepped in to sponsor a new set of black jerseys. We got the easiest quarter-final draw, against DIT, and strolled it.

In the Saturday semi, we ran into the Garda again, this time on home ground. When Barry Ward goaled in the second half, we led by 8 points and had a foot in the final. Suddenly, our back-unit froze. A long ball dropped lazily goalward and a Garda player punched it in, uncontested. Then a Garda '50' sailed straight to the net, unchallenged. They started to shoot on sight and hit the target every time. With a 10-point turnaround in twenty minutes, they stole victory – or Queen's threw it away. Operating up front, Cormac could do little about the rear implosion.

We sat in the temporary stand at the next day's final, under a bright sun but in a funereal atmosphere, staring blankly at a beatable Tralee side running around a spent Garda force. Queen's men could only wallow in self-pity, pondering their best shot at Sigerson glory wasted. Stalwart players said a sad goodbye.

Cormac shared the general belief that Queen's would be weaker in his third year. More than half of the previous season's team had gone. Early league defeats bore out initial fears.

University sport is unpredictable, however. In Dessie, they had the ideal man-manager to concoct a serious team. His Wednesday-afternoon and Saturday-morning training sessions could last most of three hours, but they didn't drag, even in bitter cold. He devised the tactical ploy of having a midfielder retreat to cover the full-back line – a proto-blanket defence, perhaps. Queen's were blessed with skilful and strong players all over the pitch, so route one – long ball or high – was usually in favour. Cormac tended to thrive in this catch-and-kick game.

That Queen's team began to turn the corner in December '99. A victory over an Ulster select on the weekend before Christmas, and suddenly the parts made a great sum. Training got tougher. When they won a January friendly against Crossmaglen, the All-Ireland club champions, they sensed their possibilities. Cormac was on fire too, notching 0-5 against Cross. In the Sigerson prelim at the Dub, he scored one of two Queen's goals to pip IT Sligo. He quarried well against St Mary's in the next round to help send Queen's on the road to Galway.

Sigerson weekend 2000 proved to be a saga of attrition. In marshy Maree, Queen's made hard work of ousting Mary Immaculate. Cormac scored one free-kick but misfired a few into the swirling wind.

In the next day's semi, when it was really needed, he put in one of the performances of his life. UCC, the Munster club champions, hared ahead at the Prairie, Salthill. Cormac notched a good early point but his man, All-Star Anthony Lynch, slipped away to score a better one. UCC went 5 up in the last quarter. Daddy shouted from the wet grassy knoll. It's faint on the video. '. . . For God's sake, get into the game!' Was it at Cormac or the team? He can't recall.

Queen's kicked high up-field; commentator Garry Mac Donncha exclaimed, '*Breathnaigh ar an bháisteach!*' No matter, Cormac caught it high on its descent, about the '21'. Quick hand-pass out to Philip Oldham, who spun around and slung a dodgy return to sender. Cormac balanced the ball on the tips of his left glove and *ciotóg*-ed it low over the bar in an instant. 0-6/1-7.

Dessie then sent on two subs and Cormac moved to midfield. Tom

Brewster scored from free and play: 0-8/1-7. Cormac ran on to a long Diarmaid Marsden ball forward, picked it up outside the 21, shimmied as if to go right, then hooked it over again with his left. 0-9/1-7. Brewster free, yes! 0-10/1-7. Level.

Daddy shouted again. 'Cormac, watch those kick-outs!' Queen's gathered and Barry Ward passed to Cormac, ghosting up the left wing, some 40 yards out. Without breaking stride, he let fly off the outside of his right boot. It was a 100–1 shot, the sort you'd try for a bet after training. Factor in the mud, wind, rain and fatigue too. The ball headed wide on the near side, as it ought to do. But at the last moment, it curled to the right, crept inside the left post and plopped over. Cormac's perfect point. 0-11/1-7.

A drenched huddle of Queen's fans let roar. 'This is it!' thought their players. That score was worth much more than a point in the referee's notebook. It was a precious moment to inspire Queen's and demoralize Cork. Ward tagged on two stellar points at the end and Queen's won, incredibly, by 0-13 to 1-7.

Two tired teams took to the field for the Sunday final, the swamp at the end of the assault course. An overnight downpour had saturated the Moycullen park, and no end of graiping could drain the gluepot. Health and safety officials would have scratched the match. But this was Sigerson, and it was meant to be gruelling. The show had to go on and live on TG4.

After a Queen's goal at the start, UCD owned the ball for most of the hour, but shot carelessly. Cormac foraged at centre half-forward, then toiled with Joe Quinn at midfield in the second half. As the clock ticked 60, UCD led by a point. Paddy McKeever won a soft free in the left corner. Last-chance saloon. It suited a right-footer. Some thought Cormac might kick it. But Brewster lifted the leather and lobbed it over nonchalantly with his left.

Extra-time loomed. Dessie didn't know how to rouse the exhausted troops. Then he heard a rumour that UCD were unhappy. 'Get up!' he told them. 'They don't want to play on!' UCD would never have forfeited the game, but from that moment, Queen's had the psychological edge. A brace of Marsden points knocked the stuffing out of UCD. The final whistle spelled victory for Queen's, 1-8 to 0-8.

Shoulders chaired Dessie. Marsden and Enda McNulty received the cup. 'We lifted her!' resounded. Queen's female fans sang out 'Amazing Grace'. I rushed into the ruckus and hailed the Eglish trio: Cormac, Conall and Joe Daly. And Cormac seized his chance. He leaped head-long into the muddy puddles like Daddy Pig on a world-record bid. He was at one with the puddles. Everyone was at one with the puddles.

★

When Cormac first got the call to play for Tyrone under-21s, in 1998, he was still seventeen and had half a dozen teams already on the go. He felt he couldn't handle any more. 'I have started to feel a few muscle strains,' he wrote in his diary, 'undoubtedly from the excesses of running in the deep mud of this time of year.' The 'fear of straining myself too much' already occupied his mind.

Eventually, after some arm-twisting and a pledge that he wouldn't have to do most of the training, he gave in. But he was far from impressed by the set-up, describing one training session – a week before the championship – as a 'mess-about'. Tyrone limped lamely past Antrim with a 1-point win, then were easily beaten by Armagh.

Mickey Harte took over the under-21 reins for 1999, and his players were confident of adding to their recent minor triumphs. A year older, wiser and more developed, Cormac felt more up for it. By picking Cormac at midfield and as captain, Harte made continuity his theme. Eleven of his first team were 1997–8 minors.

Brian McGuigan stayed away, however. It was suggested in the media that his disgruntlement over the '98 minor captaincy issue hadn't been entirely resolved. Such a response would be only human. In fairness to Brian, it never caused an issue between him and Cormac.

February friendly victories over Donegal and Mayo away augured well. Maybe that's why Harte lost faith in friendlies, for Derry ambushed Tyrone in the first round at Omagh. Cormac hit his side's first score from play in the second half to narrow the gap to 2 points, but they got no closer. Over and out before St Patrick's Day. The county secretary's report faulted Tyrone for appearing 'totally lacking in commitment and ideas' for most of the game.

In December, Mickey copied that document and handed it to the incoming team, marked '*Keep safe for 2000 Campaign!!' They were under pressure to deliver this time. Entering the Hastings Cup enabled them to focus and play competitive games earlier – pre-Christmas, in fact. They took a while to hit top gear. Each of their four Hastings games was a battle. They didn't hit the net once. Leading from midfield again, Cormac was averaging a point per game. That was their margin of victory over Down in the final.

If ever a Tyrone skipper looked dirtier when lifting a cup, I've yet to see it. In Cormac's relieved smile, posing for the camera, I see him saying, *This trophy mightn't mean much to an outsider, but we know we won it the hard way. And we're better for that.*

Only going all the way now would please Mickey. His sheet of notes to players started, 'From Jan. 31st 2000, we have 10 weeks to championship.' It concluded, 'So there is 10 weeks to prepare for the All Ireland and 10 more to win it!'

The sense that this was a special team struck Cormac again as the championship got under way. He knew he could depend on his colleagues, and that liberated him as captain.

> When you come into this camp you don't have to worry about building team morale from scratch or knowing each other's style of play. A lot of that work was done when we were at minor age together. Team spirit has never been a problem for this group of players. It's basically like a club set-up. There is a great buzz at the moment . . .

They proceeded to atomize Armagh, 3-12 to 0-3. The hype machine cracked into motion again.

In the Ulster semi, Monaghan were reigning champions and fearless. Tyrone were stretched through injuries. Cormac saw the contest becoming tighter, close to half-time. He pushed on, notching a lovely point from out on the right. Then three minutes after the interval, he shot low to the net. The Tyrone press had their hero again: 'McAnallen Plays Captain's Part in Securing Victory'.

Tyrone mauled Donegal in the Ulster decider at Clones, by 14 points. Captain Cormac controlled the middle. His appetite remained as ravenous as ever. 'Each title could be your last,' he said in an inter-view afterwards. 'You just never know, so you have to keep going.'

Cormac was one of seven members of that team who were playing for the Tyrone seniors. 'You come up against stronger fellas at senior level and you have less time on the ball,' he noted. 'It all makes you sharper when you come to play under-21s.' And there was his mentor mastering the craft. 'Mickey Harte is an innovative trainer, he keeps us all interested.'

The respect was mutual. On the day of the All-Ireland semi-final against Galway, Harte had a quiet word to tell him he was on course for a trio of All-Ireland triumphs. 'You're going to lift three cups', he said. 'You've lifted the minor, you will lift the under-21 and you'll lift the senior.'

That prediction lay in jeopardy two-thirds of the way through that semi at sodden Carrick-on-Shannon. Galway led and should've been further ahead. Cormac had wided three far-out free-kicks. Worrying times. Yet, ever unflinching, he helped to turn the game in an unexpected way. Marking tightly, he put his arms out to shepherd his man. In return he took a whack in the guts, off the ball. The red card was brandished and Tyrone surged forward, scoring 1-6 without reply. 1-10 to 0-6 it finished. That was no mean feat. Cormac wasn't elated, though. His misses could have cost his side. Despite his strong defensive showing and late power-burst, he awarded himself his low-est personal rating for a game in 2000.

*

On the Sunday before the final, the under-21 squad went on team-building exercises in Pomeroy Forest Park, then watched two club championship games at Carrickmore. As Cormac stood in his T-shirt, a very hot day cooled into a chilly evening.

A sore throat turned into a heavy cold by Monday. Feeling steadily worse, he decided to skip Belfast for the week. As captain, he couldn't bear to think of missing out on the final. Only one person could attend to him properly.

Our mother was always helping Cormac along the way. She didn't go to all his games, unlike Daddy, but between matches she was his aide-de-camp. Beyond washing clothes, making feasts of healthy, herb-loaded food, taxiing him about, videoing his matches, and fielding the phone calls that came to him at home, she was constantly counselling. If the landline rang in his student house, Cormac would race upstairs to get it, knowing there was a 50/50 chance it was her, calling to advise or warn him to keep safe.

For years, Mummy had tried to ply us with natural medicines: Bach flower remedies and Jan de Vries recipes. At the hint of a cold or exam-stress, she'd dispense drops from the wee brown bottles. She'd hand the bottles to us for our travels, but we rarely used them. Now, trying to get Cormac right for the final, Mummy prescribed echinicea and elderberry syrup. She didn't expect him to recover in time as he was still 'flued up' in bed for most of Thursday. But the magic tonics kicked in and he improved rapidly on the Friday. He got just three hours' sleep that night, but, as he told me, 'that was as much due to nerves as anything else'. When Saturday came, he felt up to it.

He knew that Limerick in the final would not be the cakewalk that some expected. He was aware of their size – seven starting players 6' 2" or taller, all bigger than him. He joked nervously to me that he had been studying Jonathan Swift's philosophy for his final exams and could empathize with the Lilliputians when he pondered his opposite numbers, Jason Stokes and John Galvin. He recalled playing schools basketball against the 6' 4" Galvin and knew him to be a ready-made sporting titan.

On the road to Mullingar, Cormac supplied a video of *Rocky IV* for the team bus to get everyone in the right mood. The *Rocky* films had always pumped him up; even just watching in the sitting room at home, that theme tune would have him on the floor doing sit-ups. Then, as they came through Newtownbutler, it dawned on him that *IV* was about the triumph of the underdogs, and Tyrone were runaway favourites.

He was mildly miffed at Tyrone fans' attitude to the game. On one hand, their expectations had grown to the point where the attitude was: All-Ireland or failure. Yet, few of them were bothered to follow the team to Mullingar. There was a shade of 'Sure it's only the under-21' in their heads. You'd think the county had won it more than twice before. Of the crowd of 7,366, at least three-quarters were Limerick supporters. Cormac saw that they looked 'all set-up for a shock'.

That danger increased as a real contest developed in the second quarter. The cheers for some long-range Limerick points dwarfed the meek applause for Tyrone scores. One particular roar shook right through Cormac. He was pushing himself to the limit, having come from his sick-bed. His work-rate concealed the fact that he wasn't at a hundred per cent. Plus, he had friction blisters on his feet, which he had tried to dress that morning; cousin Anne Kelly, who had dropped by, persuaded him to ask for micropore tape, though he didn't want Mickey to know.

There was a clue when he hit a ball badly wide. Marty Morrissey commentated, 'Cormac McAnallen, not renowned for his scoring accuracy.'

Darn you, Marty! I said to myself, watching TV. *He's scored 1-6 in four matches.* Marty still comes out with that line about players today.

You need the lucky bounces. Limerick hit the crossbar shortly after the restart. Tyrone counter-attacked for Richard Thornton to score his second goal, and Brian McGuigan kicked another to clinch the title for Tyrone. The winning margin of 8 points was generous.

Cormac's joy was pierced slightly by his late substitution, being replaced by Enda McGinley. Harte had never taken him off in a big match, so he was surprised. But the manager knew of his illness and had intended to rest him. 'We got far more out of him than we expected,' said Fr McAleer. 'In fact he could have stayed on a bit longer, but we thought it would be a good idea if we sent in fresh feet.'

Cormac thought he had done well against Limerick's leading line. He marked himself at least seven for each aspect of play and, crucially, seven and a half for Legs and eight and a half for Body. Clearly he believed he was fit for the hour, and he was embarrassed to have been replaced as a winning captain. One tabloid took it as a cue to comment that he was 'a big disappointment', making 'no impact'. He couldn't really gripe, though; in so many good times, he had been treated royally by the press.

Cormac became only the second captain to lift both the minor and under-21 All-Ireland football trophies. The second part of Harte's prophecy had come true. Cormac dropped his guard in a post-match interview with Mark Gallagher of *The Examiner* and said aloud what the players had begun to think: 'This team has won the minors, [and] we have now won at under-21 level. This is the second leg of a three-leg success. All that we have left now is the senior All-Ireland.'

The scene at Aughnacloy that evening could not have been more different from the hoopla of September 1998. About 300 people turned out to welcome the Tyrone team. The Westmeath under-21s' homecoming in 1999 had drawn 10,000. It was clear that under-21 success did not register on the same scale as minor success for Tyrone, let alone senior.

Cormac took the mike and said his bit on the stage. He went out of his way to apologize for his 'tetchy' form at home during the previous week. Above all, he paid tribute to our mother, without whom he might not have been there.

★

When people speak today of Cormac and his Tyrone senior exploits, they naturally focus on what he achieved under Mickey Harte. It's easy to forget that Cormac played at senior level under Art McRory and Eugene McKenna for more than twice as long as he played under Harte, and that six months before his death they were the most successful men in the county's Gaelic football history.

'Big Art' was the godfather of modern Tyrone football. The first qualified P.E. teacher and certified coach to manage a team in the county, he could claim four Ulster and one All-Ireland minor football championships in the 1970s. In two periods as senior manager, 1980–87 and 1993–6, he had guided Tyrone to four Ulster titles and two All-Ireland finals. He was the quintessential Tyrone man: no airs or graces; a reserved manner that hid his learning; an old-fashioned honesty bordering on bluntness; and a dry wit, used against anyone who deserved it.

Eugene was a generation younger and had captained Art's Ulster-winning teams of 1984 and 1986. He exuded style and grace as a player with his high leap and effortless stride. He was seen as a leader and a deep thinker. He had been Art's assistant during the 1993–6 phase. Next to plain-speaking Art, Eugene came across to some players as more cryptic, posing a random question and letting it hang in the air, leaving them to scratch their heads.

Their previous tenure ended after the Meath massacre at Croke Park in 1996. On that day, sixteen-year-old Cormac looked on in horror from Hill 16. By the time they came back in autumn 1999, he was already supposed to be one of Tyrone's saviours.

Cormac had great respect for Art and Eugene. They had filled trophy cabinets before and could again. They knew their stuff. For years Art had been ahead of the game in embracing sports science, psychology and nutrition. This was not universally recognized: he was of a certain age and dodged PR (he let Eugene do most interviews). But Cormac saw it and benefited from it. They were also cool customers: no ranting or referee-confronting. They didn't dollop praise on young lads, either. If you made a genuine effort, they'd appreciate you. Cormac was already on a pedestal in their minds before they started, and they never felt the need to knock him off it.

Their first instinct was to place him at centre half-back, where his county minor days began. He donned No. 6 on his league debut, at home to Dublin in October 1999. It went a dream. When Tyrone clicked on days like this, each attack sparked spontaneous applause, amplified by the old corrugated roof of the O'Neill Park stand. Cormac rounded off a flowing movement by kicking a fine point late on, and Tyrone coasted to victory.

The bubble burst quickly: first a 14-point tanking by Kerry at Tralee, then an unexpected home defeat by Roscommon. Away at Ballybofey in February, Tyrone trailed Donegal by 5 points at the three-quarter mark. Cormac set up a half-back roadblock against any further scores, and Tyrone made a late rally up front to eke out a draw.

Cormac moved to midfield for the last three rounds. He would have three different partners: Paul McLaughlin, in the narrow home defeat by Galway; Pascal Canavan, for the away win over Cork, recent All-Ireland finalists; and Terry McKenna, in the home defeat to Armagh. Cormac was holding his own, and Tyrone staved off relegation.

Injuries were stacking up, and the pre-season pact with Mickey Harte to let the under-21 stars train away from the senior team was coming back to haunt Art and Eugene. Tyrone lost all their games in the run-in to the Ulster Championship derby versus Armagh. No one really knew Tyrone's best team.

In a last-ditch bid to find a winning formula, the managers had placed Cormac at left half-forward in a challenge match against Kerry, and he coped well. While he skipped the last Thursday training for exam preparations, a dummy selection was announced for the Ulster Championship opener against Armagh. Cormac and Pascal Canavan were named as the midfield duo, A. N. Other as No. 12, and Peter the Great at 14.

On the big day at Clones, the line-up was very different. Cormac moved to left half-forward, Ciaran McRory came in at midfield, and Peter was out, injured. The sight of Peter in a tracksuit turned the outnumbered Tyrone fans – but a third of the 30,000 crowd – white with dread.

Armagh imposed their will from the off and stayed in front. The *Irish Times* said it was 'about as physical as the game gets, with man-to-man mauling for every ball, often spilling to the ground, and few periods of flowing football'. Tyrone went scoreless from the fourteenth minute till half-time. Seeing little ball at his end, Cormac struggled to make an impact. A switch to midfield at the interval brought him more into the fray.

The defining moment came nine minutes from time, when Tyrone trailed by 4, and the ball rebounded off the post. It dropped delightfully into Cormac's arms, completely unmarked. This was a gilt-edged goal chance at last. He had to go for it. He didn't dither or try anything fancy. He right-footed it with power.

He didn't know that Armagh goalie Brendan Tierney was injured and likely to be taken off. Tierney, for his part, didn't even see who had the ball. He just saw a figure, picked a side and dived that way. He saved. No sooner had the summer begun, than Tyrone's campaign was over.

Cormac set aside his dejection to grant interview requests.

I'm naturally disappointed about the result and missing the goal chance. I was half expecting it to come back off the post and reacted accordingly . . . Tierney's experience as a goalkeeper was more effective than mine as a forward . . . [F]or the team it was a case of the interrupted preparations and the injuries taking their toll.

Armagh . . . will improve. Knowing so many of them, I would love to see them going on and win Ulster and perhaps even the All-Ireland title as well.

He replayed that shot in his head many times, and knew he should've tried to dummy or place it. His initial switch out of midfield was also a cause of private regret. Having established himself as the first-choice midfielder, he had earned the chance to start there, though his relocation probably wasn't the winning or losing of the game.

He equated the defeat to a loss of dignity. The next day, we were labouring for Daddy in Armagh. On other days like these, if Moloko played on the radio, twenty minutes later Daddy would say, 'Aye sing it back, if ya don't mind!' and Cormac would mimic him by adding 'if ya don't mind' to every remark for the rest of the day. But there was no singing back or mimicking on this day. I tried to console him. 'Don't be so downhearted. You won the under-21s and you'll have many more senior seasons ahead. The rest of us might never win anything.' It was futile. I was taken aback by how hurt he was.

Eight days after the match, the Tyrone players were summoned to a meeting to watch it on video and confront their demons. The message from the managers rang clear: be prepared for our return in September, for it will be tough.

Armagh retained the Ulster title and Cormac was happy for them. He handled the teasing by Orchard fans at close quarters all summer. But while watching them push Kerry to the brink in the All-Ireland semi-final, he resiled; an Armagh victory suddenly became a frightening prospect, like Scott watching Amundsen reach the South Pole first. As he put it: 'Perhaps it is the sort of insane jealousy or selfishness that one needs to win in sport: to be motivated by the fear of being outdone by one's neighbours.'

Armagh lost the replay. Privately, he confessed to a slight relief not to have to face their gloating supporters for the next eight months.

*

Art set out his stall as the autumn leaves fell. For 2001, the Tyrone side would be bigger and stronger. Since June, the image lingered of strong Armagh arms shoving Tyrone players aside. If Armagh could pump iron, so could they. Weight-training would begin in earnest. In previous years, gym-work was viewed as a way of keeping fit during the dark nights. Now they would lift weights specifically to build upper-body strength. Twice-weekly sessions were ordered. Players had to record the details and hand them in.

That winter, Cormac frequented the gym at Queen's with lads like Ciaran Gourley and Stephen O'Neill as partners and spotters. The shift in emphasis was timely for him. He had eased back on the skipping that year, having built up his stamina and jump; any more leg-pounding then would be counter-productive, he thought. But to survive in the midfield bear-pit of modern inter-county football, against greater men, he'd need a well-toned upper half.

The other element of the strengthening regime was creatine. The Armagh side were renowned exponents of the supplement. When the McNulty brothers wore figure-hugging T-shirts outside the Bot, we all saw. Some of the Tyrone squad had taken it in the mid-1990s, but by 2000 it was what you had to do to keep up with the Joneses. It wasn't just a Gaelic football thing. 'Every athlete right down to the table-tennis players were taking creatine at the Sydney Olympics,' Art recalls.

So when Art held up a tub and told his charges to start taking it, they understood and weren't surprised. Art had already given it to his greyhounds and found that it put a couple of lengths on them. 'If it's good enough for my dogs, it's good enough for you boys,' he told the team.

Cormac did as advised. He'd do whatever he could to improve himself, provided there were no ethical issues. Creatine was over-the-counter stuff, full stop. It might make you bloat or fart, but it was legit: a naturally occurring amino acid. He took the recommended daily teaspoon. He thought it helped him; on one occasion, he encouraged me to try it. Of course, for all he knew, he might've been the same without it. Aged twenty and doing heavy reps in the gym, he was bound to develop physically as he entered his prime, supplements or no.

The creatine craze would pass. Some Tyrone players took it for a while, some not at all. Stephen O'Neill was a creatine-free phenomenon. It seems that Cormac stopped taking it after 2002, as the next management team said nothing about it. Tubs remained unopened in his room.

Cormac was modifying his diet, too. Having eaten ever more carefully for three years, now he wanted to eat like a champion. He was impressed by the muscle-testing that the kinesiologist James Meyler demonstrated on Hub at one session. He went for a consultation with a nutritionist, Sharon Madigan, in Belfast. He began to scour every food product before him to ward off the enemy, high-fat content. At times, he took natural supplements like whey protein and cod liver oil tablets. All-Bran became his daily breakfast of choice.

There was another thing to work on. In late 2000, probably at Art's prompting, he underwent a battery of fitness tests at Queen's. They were monitored by Dr Harry Brennan, the Queen's sports science officer who had worked with the Ulster rugby side that won the 1999 European Cup. 'He came back and he was absolutely devastated that his short-sprint speed was below average,' Art recalls. Art wasn't surprised, having seen speed over 25 yards as his natural weak spot. So Cormac went for SAQ sessions – speed, agility and quickness – with Brennan in early 2001. His persistence paid off, as Art could see:

He went at it. And he worked and worked and worked on his short-sprint speed. I was aware he was doing it because I could see the improvement. He had all of the skills: use of the ball, fielding, natural ability, strength. But by God, he was going to work so hard on the things he needed to improve.

And just one more thing.

★

In midfield you have a bit more freedom to play your game. Maybe the pressure comes because some people think we're not up to it. I don't really mind where I play, as long as I have the freedom to run. I don't like to be held to one spot, like full-forward or full-back . . . There's usually not much clean possession nowadays, it's as much to do with the half-backs and half-forwards. You could nearly say that all three lines are the midfield now. [Interview with Kenny Archer for the *Irish News*, 2 June 2000]

For the National League campaign starting in October, half the Tyrone team were twenty-one or younger. The kids injected confidence and pace. At the first session, erstwhile fringe players Declan McCrossan and Ryan McMenamin zipped around ten laps of O'Neill Park much quicker than the regulars.

Tyrone began to flourish. They plundered Dublin at Parnell Park, scoring a tidy 19 points in one afternoon despite an early sending-off. Cormac, now restored to midfield, was partnered by Peter Campbell.

But the next game brought disaster. It was a home tie against Kerry, the new All-Ireland champions, at Dungannon in November. Cormac was motoring well. Near half-time, he crouched to pick up the ball, but took a kick from a Kerry hard man and retaliated with his fist. That may be the only time he ever punched an opponent deliberately and, typical Cormac, it wasn't sneaky. Both of them were sent off. Three late Tyrone goals raised the roof and inflated a 14-point win, but Cormac could hardly celebrate.

He accepted his automatic four-week suspension, no appealing to anywhere. His absence almost certainly cost Eglish the county under-21 semi-final against Errigal a week later. Moreover, due to a recent

GAA rule-change, December and January did not count for suspension purposes. Not until mid-February 2001, almost three months after the incident, did he get the all-clear.

He returned to the side on his twenty-first birthday for a home victory over Donegal, albeit a mediocre showing on his part. He was much improved in the next game, a gallant defeat in Galway. Happily, Tyrone held second place in Division 1A and had winnable matches left. Qualification for the semis seemed certain.

The Foot & Mouth outbreak scuttled such hopes. First, a frustrating month of scratching heels as all NFL fixtures were called off. Then, in early April, Tyrone got two free league points, as Louth were not allowed to field. It was free passage to the semis. Three days later, a recent 'hot suspect' at Ardboe was declared negative.

Friday the 13th upset everything. The Ardboe find was suddenly deemed positive. Tyrone were thrown out of all inter-county competitions then in process. Daily life and work continued, and the likes of Dungannon Rugby Club played on, but Tyrone kicking Gaelic football would derail the Irish economy. He felt that the county board had been somewhat meek in accepting this ruling.

By then, Cormac was carrying an injury: he cracked his left cheekbone in a club league match at Aghyaran. It happened on April Fool's Day, and he was supposed to be out for a month. After missing the Ulster semi-final a week later, he hoped, somehow, to play in the final against Fermanagh the week after that. But no one offered him a Gazza-style facemask for protection.

I had an idea. How about a hurling helmet with a facial visor? If a hurler could wear one against bareheaded opponents without hurting anyone, why not a footballer? I saw no bar in the GAA *Official Guide* or the football playing rules.

Cormac wavered. He was afraid of looking daft, charging about like the first helmeted footballer east of New England. Would the referee even allow it?

Well, ring him, I suggested.

But the ref mightn't like a player calling him, he thought.

OK, I said, I'll ring him.

He was Jimmy White of Donegal and he knew his stuff. He picked out a passage in an obscure manual for referees, stating that a helmet couldn't be worn in a football game.

It didn't sound much like a hard-and-fast rule, but Cormac accepted it. That was that. Cormac would miss the final.

The Foot & Mouth ban was announced a couple of days before the final. Tyrone were out. The Fermanagh manager rushed in with an offer that his county would represent Ulster in the All-Ireland series and the Ulster final could be played off at a later date. How kind!

Cormac didn't lose hope. Instinctively, he knew Mickey wouldn't let this one lie. He had a fair measure of the man by now. He saw in him a reflection of himself: someone who would always fight his corner, whatever the odds. Mickey didn't disappoint, driving a media onslaught against the decision, arguing for the Ulster final to be postponed until the Foot & Mouth crisis was over. His persistence, coupled with Cork's noble offer to wait (as Munster champions) for the Ulster final to be played, saved the day. Tyrone were reinstated, and the competition was pushed back. Cormac would get to captain his county in another Ulster final. And his admiration for Mickey grew further.

The FMD restriction was lifted, and Fermanagh met their doom in late May. Cormac shook Jimmy White's hand. And for the seventh time, he lifted a trophy in the name of the O'Neill County.

*

When Tyrone seniors crept into Clones for the big Ulster Championship derby in May, a lot of their fans in the 30,000 crowd were a little nervous. It had been twelve weeks since their last match.

And Armagh were seeking a third Ulster title in a row, on their farourite ground. Cormac had a personal quest: to prove himself as a top-level midfielder. Some people doubted he had the height or aerodynamism to control the sector.

He was ready. He caught from the throw-in, burst straight through the middle, soloed on his right, then raked the ball low with his left in behind the defence. Skinhead Mulligan slid full length along the front of the square to side-foot past Tierney to the net. Ten seconds in, 3 points up, and possibly the quickest-ever Ulster Championship goal. Cormac had fifteen clean possessions in that first half. Armagh stormed back to lead after the break, but Cormac kept busy and kicked an inspiring equalizer. Tyrone never looked back. Stephen O'Neill kept pinging over points until Finbarr McConnell played his imaginary violin.

Cormac and Hub were reunited, now as the senior midfield duo. While not terribly tall, they were both rugged, dogged and dynamic. They were also looking mean, both shorn of their old crops of hair. Theirs was very much a union of equals, with no offensive/defensive division of labour. From experience, they had developed a sixth sense for each other's play. Cormac was the more solidly consistent, though Hub arguably had more style. Cormac couldn't leap like Hub, but he had mastered how to handle taller, higher-catching midfield opponents – so he tended to mark the bigger name. Intense concentration, shoulders and timing were key. He'd glue himself to his man, muscle to ball-side of him and use his upper-body strength to make himself awkward. Then he'd time his own jump bang-on. His old basketball backboard work was making the difference.

To appreciate how tightly Cormac was marking up, consider a passage of play at 0-4 all. Paul McGrane gave him the slip and bore down on goal from an angle. Cormac gave valiant chase and caught up to block his path, only to be bumped forward by the Armagh man, who then steadied to fist the ball over for a point. Yet at the last moment, Cormac pivoted back and threw his arm across to block the ball, out for a '50'. A masterclass in pursuing a lost cause.

Everyone wanted a bit of Cormac now. On our doorstep landed the biggest box of stuff I had ever seen. It contained every conceivable item of Fila sportswear, in multiple – over £1,000 worth of gear, easily. The company rep had asked Peter Canavan which Tyrone players were going to really shine that year. *Thanks, Peter.* Then Cormac was pursued to give political endorsements ahead of the June general election. *Thanks, but no way.*

Out of the frying-pan . . . and into a semi-final against Derry and Anthony Tohill: Derry captain, Ireland captain, and, as Cormac said, 'one of the best players ever'. Tohill dwarfed Cormac and Hub in stature and reputation. Cormac steeled himself for total focus, no matter what might happen: 'If he does get a big ball and catches one twelve feet over your head what am I going to do? Or if he does kick one from sixty yards, am I going to drop the head or am I gonna get up?'

For most kick-outs, Cormac got in front, made a screen of his body in front of Tohill, jumped late, and got a hand on the ball somehow; or, if caught behind, he made sure to get an arm over his man's shoulder and at least spoil the big catch. At other times, Hub flew in from behind or the side to break it. One way or another, Tyrone won sixty per cent of first-half kick-outs and broke even in the second.

The game was fractious, with all that old Tyrone–Derry bitterness still simmering. At the three-quarter mark, Cormac got a pass on the run about 35 metres out and, without looking, kicked it over his shoulder for a point. Tyrone held on to win, 3-7 to 0-14. By common consensus, Cormac had trumped Tohill, and that earned him the RTÉ 'Man of the Match' crystal. Again, he batted away bouquets. 'I probably got it because I was marking Tohill. Sure there was talk he broke his toe anyway.'

*

When Adrian Logan of UTV called for an interview to reflect on the big win, Cormac told him to catch him at work. And Cormac's workplace, in the summer of 2001, was Daddy's shop.

Cormac [*handing two plastic bags of groceries to Mrs Eva Nelson*]: Thanks very much again.
Mrs Nelson: Thanks very much, Cormac.
Mrs Sarah Ann Daly: Could I get two pastries, please?
Cormac: Aye, no problem, yeah.
Mrs Nelson: You played well at the match yesterday.
Cormac: [*reaching into paper bag*] Aye, it was . . . well, winning it was the main thing. We were dodgy enough in the end. We nearly threw it away, but . . . [*reaching across with tongs to lift pastries, with a Cheshire cat grin*] . . . there you go.

It was staged and a bit cheesy, but he was in great form and didn't mind. Mrs Nelson was the home-help for Mrs Daly, who was nearly ninety then and is no longer of this world. They were just two regular customers, obliging a request to be captured on camera.

Daddy had bought the Benburb Spar shop and post office in November '99. He was supposed to be semi-retired but, true to form, he made himself busier than ever with his new project. Making a quick buck wasn't his motive; the village was too far off the main roads. Rather, he liked to champion rural regeneration through local enterprise, and saw here a potential heritage village. If the shop hadn't been in an eighteenth-century building, he wouldn't have bothered.

To get Benburb Village Stores off on the right footing, he needed family to muck in. Cormac was a useful man for him to have about. He was a hard worker, a safe pair of hands, and he had a way with people. After a few odd weekend and holiday shifts in the early months, he became a daily figure about the shop in summer 2000. Many of the customers already knew him to see from football, as Benburb sat on the Tyrone–Armagh border. Some were slightly shocked to see him working there at first, as he was more likely to be seen in the media than around the village. Now here he was, arriving with Daddy at 7.30 on many a morning to lift in the daily deliveries. Then he'd stack the shelves with newspapers and magazines – a couple of which had him as a cover star.

'I'm a retail wizard,' he used to joke to me. 'I just put things on the shelves and people buy them.'

One morning he arrived to find the delivery from the bakery had been pecked to bits. He went behind to write in the logbook for wasted goods. 'X loaves of bread,' he recorded, 'Ravaged by crows.'

From the neighbouring areas of Armagh came a steady string of customers that summer. Cormac noted how many of them wanted to talk football with him. When he was at the till, a queue could pile up quickly.

Daddy was proud to have Cormac working there, thinking he gave a wee boost to business. Sometimes Cormac thought him a little too keen, given his own busy schedule. The worst thing about working for Daddy was that if you did one job for him, he'd reward you by handing you nine more.

★

Tyrone entered the Ulster final as raging hot favourites, but once more Cormac faced one of the toughest personal battles. Dermot McCabe was the lionheart of the Cavan team; when he attacked, he did damage.

Midway through the first half, Brian Dooher thumped the ball in high. It ricocheted about till Mugsy gathered near the endline. His hand-pass dummy fooled his man rotten. A selfish forward would have taken a pot-shot from an acute angle, but Mugsy spotted Cormac, arm raised and rushing through the middle, ten yards out. He fist-passed across to him, on the money. Our boy threw himself at the ball, full stretch on the edge of the square.

Freeze.

Of all images of Cormac's career, that's my favourite. The one showing him airborne, eyes fixed on the ball he has just pawed two-handed. It's milliseconds from the net, and a few more before the 10,000 or more heads in the distance realize its destiny – except for one Tyrone fan in the top right already raising his arms. The photo captures a perfect moment – Cormac's only senior championship goal for Tyrone.

Up off the goal-line immediately, he turned, ran out with his head down and back to the middle. For Cavan were steely and he was needed. Ten minutes later, he caught clean from a kick-out, only to be penalized for pushing. Cormac shook his head at that ropey decision, but plonked the ball straight on to the ground and retreated; no firing it away or holding on to obstruct. Within seconds, McCabe lashed the free-kick downfield to the goal-machine, Jason Reilly, who did his duty. The ground erupted as the Cavan team dashed for the tunnel, leading by 3 points and waving fists. Tyrone were in trouble.

Once Tyrone started using their bench, however, their greater class told. Subs Eoin Gormley and Brian McGuigan scored wonder-points to add to O'Neill's while Cavan hit wide after wide. Tyrone prevailed by 1-13 to 1-11.

In a game of few standout displays, some papers named Cormac Man of the Match. One prize begot another. Seeing off the three billboard Ulster midfielders in successive games landed him the 'Player of the Ulster Championship' award. The presentation was made at the Donn Carragh Hotel, Lisnaskea, and broadcast on BBC NI's *The Championship*:

Dominic McCaughey: On behalf of the BBC and on behalf of the whole Tyrone panel, I am pleased to present you with the Player of the Championship award, Cormac.

[*Cormac receives crystal bowl, with head slightly bowed, smiling gingerly*]

Players: Yeoooooh!

Seán Teague: Speech! Speech! Speech! Speech!

Mark 'Sidey' Sidebottom: You look a bit shocked. Are you shocked?

Cormac: I am indeed. Everyone thought Ryan McMenamin was going to get it!

[*Players laugh*]

Voice: Damn right!

Cormac: Himself and Stephen O'Neill . . . would certainly have been in the running, and I'll just accept this as a team award. I think the team have worked extremely hard in all three games and in training in the meantime. And well, again, I accept this on behalf of the twenty-four – the thirty-two – men on the panel.

Sidey: You're holding on pretty tightly to it.

Cormac: Well, it's nice to get it!

Sidey: Well . . . you held on to the ball for most of this summer campaign. Let me bring in a man who had absolute confidence with you, being part of the joint management. Art McRory, I take it, no more deserving man for this award?

Art: Well, I would have to congratulate Martin and Jarlath on their choice, on this occasion. [*Pregnant pause, with knowing stare*]

[*Eruption of laughter from players*]

Then, Tyrone's rotten luck with fixtures returned. The National League fiasco was bad enough. Now, under the new qualifier system, they had to face up to an All-Ireland quarter-final. Under the old format, Tyrone would have been straight into an All-Ireland semi-final against Roscommon and a final against a flakey Meath team. Instead, the Croke Park bingo balls threw the two Ulster teams together – and the two Connacht teams and the two Leinster final teams. What were the chances?

Like all of Tyrone, Cormac groaned at the draw from hell. Bloody Derry! That was the one team who knew Tyrone inside out and had an axe to grind. And grind it they did. Within two minutes, they had a brace of bookings for off-the-ball fouls. 'Private, spiteful duels broke out in every corner of the pitch,' the *Ulster Herald* reported. 'The whereabouts of the football was almost irrelevant.' Playacting abounded. The game was disrupted to the point of boredom. Nothing was going Tyrone's way. Hub, still suffering from a recent car accident, made way at half-time. Wee Peter didn't even get that far, being red-carded for retaliation.

While all this chaos curdled around him, Cormac was Tyrone's pillar of strength. He scored an excellent point in the first half. He won a lot of dirty ball and rode heavy tackles. He served passes on clean plates to the attack. He shuttled back and forth, never giving up. For that, he got what little praise his team accrued that day, but it wasn't enough. Derry won that horrible game by 1-9 to 0-7. There was no second chance for Tyrone.

9. 'Hit him, sir!'

The long-postponed All-Ireland under-21 semi-final was finally played on 9 September 2001. At half-time, the scores on the board were Tír Eoghain 0-5, Corcaigh 0-0. Most of the team were satisfied, but Cormac not so much. On a wide count, it was 5 against 9. If Cork had taken their chances, he said in the dressing room, it would be a different story. He felt his team had sat back on their early lead, inviting trouble. They'd have to be more positive all over the field. 'Drive on if you get a chance to get forward,' he said to Philip Jordan, a wing-back but not yet a rampager. 'Don't just play safe.'

Cormac always had a gun drawn against complacency. Tyrone went on to win by 0-14 to 1-2 – and the goal was a late one. Cormac was imperious that day. He marked himself 42½ in total for the game: Off 7½, Def 8½, Head 9, Body 9, Legs 8½. He wouldn't score higher in a Tyrone jersey. He had Mickey Harte in raptures afterwards. 'Cormac is just an amazing player,' the manager said in a post-match interview. 'In the second half he just took that game by the scruff of the neck. His performance was just incredible. There's good players about who can do it when you don't need it, then there's great players who can do it when you need it. Cormac McAnallen is a great player . . .'

That was no mean Cork team; five of them would go on to be All-Ireland senior medallists. Their sporting offer to wait for Tyrone after the Foot & Mouth episode had come back to bite them.

The final, on Saturday, 6 October, was against Mayo. It had been six months since their semi. So high had Cormac leaped in that six-month period, it seemed almost wrong that he should still be playing in a young lads' game. He was now an international, packing for departure.

Bundling in suitcases and kitbag, the two of us made haste.

Torrents thumped the windscreen in our race to Quinn's Corner. Bang on time. No bus, though. Anxious minutes later, we twigged that it might be gone early. We beat it up the greasy A4, Ireland's deadliest single carriageway, and caught up with the bus at the Ballygawley roundabout.

Tyrone were favourites. Just look at that forward line now: Mellon, McGuigan, O'Neill, McGinley, Hughes, Mulligan. Future All-Ireland senior stars, the lot. But Mayo weren't scared. Eight months earlier, in an epic Hastings Cup final, they had beaten Tyrone after extra time.

Cormac saw the danger. He jabbed his gloved finger vigorously to direct colleagues, and pointed to play with the screeching wind. Tyrone tramped through the churned-up earth to lead by 4 at the turn. Wary, he called for men to prove their character.

Facing into the monsoon, Cormac came to the fore. He took control of the central corridor and cauterized incisions. He slogged and hustled and bustled. He dived on spilt ball, desperately. He shipped hit after hit, burst out of parcels of Mayo tacklers, and won frees. He stayed calm, kept possession, and distributed cleverly.

Tyrone won by 3. Cormac thus equalled Peter Canavan's record as captain of two Clarke Cup-winning teams, and set a new standard as the first player to skipper three underage teams to All-Ireland success. He also had a third All-Ireland match-ball for the sideboard. But, as before, he was considerate and dignified in his victory speech, sympathizing with Kevin McStay, the opposition manager, on the death of his father, days before.

Then it was time to go. He scurried inside to collect his stuff. There was no time even to change. Shouldering heavy bags as he crossed Markiewicz Park, he said happy goodbyes to us all. He had a plane to catch.

*

Getting on that plane to Australia surpassed anything he could have expected from 2001.

Cormac suspected his direct style would suit the International

To keep his options open, he spent the 2000–2001 session at Queen's on the PG Diploma in Computer-Based Learning. Multimedia programming, courseware engineering and web-authoring were useful skills to have, and the hours weren't taxing – Monday and Tuesday evenings, 5–8 p.m. 'You might see him coming in with one bag, and out with another,' recalls Conor Judge of those days. He was vice-captain of the Sigerson team that year, but their title-defence fell to St Mary's at the first hurdle. It was time to sort out his career now.

He got back in touch with Coleraine, pleading that football duties and illness during his final degree exams had cost him the 2:1 and wondering if they could accommodate him. Coleraine said no: there was serious pressure for places, and too many candidates had scored higher. He went to the Queen's careers office and rang the UU to discuss other teaching options – like English – but all the places were gone.

The experience left a bitter taste. He thought the restricted access to teaching in the North, with its narrow focus on BA results, was at odds with the end-goal of providing a holistic education. He deplored how males were becoming a minority species in teaching. From UU graduation lists in July he calculated that seventy-three per cent of new secondary teachers were female, and eighty-eight per cent of the primary teachers. He drafted a letter to the press, citing these figures and arguing for more gender balance in the vocation; this would help to mitigate juvenile crime, when so many boys were growing up without a father figure. He decided against sending the letter. Better to bite his lip and sort out his own situation.

To become a secondary teacher, he would have to leave the North. To enrol at an English university, like some of his peers, came with substantial funding but the requirement to spend a post-qualification year in Albion as well. That would take him up to summer 2003. He didn't want that, nor did the family. We implored him not to go.

Luckily, another pathway opened up for him – one he hadn't planned for. The H.Dip.Ed. course in the South was never mentioned by Northern careers advisers. So-called experts in education acted as if looking across the border would turn you to stone.

I had been at NUI Galway in November 2000 when the university Gaelic football club chairman, Mick Dermody, mentioned the next week's deadline for the course. 'What's your Cormac doing next year?'

Knowing that Cormac's teaching prospects were few in the North, I persuaded him to apply for the H.Dip. and make Galway his number one choice. He wasn't too pushed at first, as he'd have to pay fees, unlike the British course. When he came round, though, we had no idea how many hurdles there'd be to beat the deadline. The biggest one was that Department of Education didn't identify Queen's qualifications as standard for the H.Dip.

We didn't have mobiles just yet, and I couldn't get him on the landline. So I emailed him on the Tuesday evening. I listed five hoops to be jumped through. The good news was that his 2:2 should qualify him.

Cue three days of furious faxing and messaging between Belfast, Galway and Athlone. Only for the national H.Dip. office being in Galway, we'd have run out of time. I handed in the application with less than an hour to spare and sauntered off, relieved and satisfied.

We thought nothing more of it until spring. Cormac's pocket-diary note of 2 May 2001 reveals his state of mind: 'Don't know what I'm doing next year – need to know soon! or going to crack up.'

Then the H.Dip. letter slipped through the letterbox. He was offered a place at UCD, his number two choice.

He was surprised; he hadn't seen Dublin as his next staging post, and he wasn't sure what to do. Who better to sell the idea than Dave Billings, the UCD Gaelic games development officer? I rang him, told him of Cormac's offer, and got them talking. By the end of that call, Dave had offered to secure his teaching practice at a local school, and a potential sports scholarship. That was how he operated, with phone in one hand and elastic band in the other, using his vast network and charm to help out young players. No other man in Ireland nurtured as many county stars in those years as Dave did.

Seán Mulvihill, a former UCD footballer from Longford, was contacted. He gladly obliged to accommodate Cormac at his school, St Benildus' College, Stillorgan.

Dave had delivered. Cormac packed his bags for Dublin.

★

UCD was going to be very different from the preceding four years. Out of the jolly claustrophobia of student Belfast, into a campus where he knew no one.

After sheltering that first week with a nearby cousin, Brian McAnallen, waiting for the accommodation office to get their act together, he moved into the Belgrove halls on campus. He shared with a vet from Tipp and an architect from Wexford – two quiet lads, serious about their studies. No harm: making friends and socializing were off the priority list. The TV signal carried only two stations, Fuzzy 1 and Fuzzwork 2. This was his *Rocky IV*, his log-lifting in Trasnogourbinsk.

He studied as hard as he had ever done. The H.Dip. was intensive, no course for slacking. He thrived in this climate and became more regimented. He smartened himself up to meet the shirt-and-tie code. While his attendance at afternoon lectures was interrupted by the three weeks in Australia and various early-evening matches when he returned, he managed to keep up. Most evenings he sat at his desk, under the lamp, sorting notes, writing reflections and planning lessons, with the FM104 late-night phone-in on a low hum.

Ashlene, then in her final year studying in Belfast, set aside her Fridays to come down to him. A real romantic at heart, he took her out for surprises, like shows at the Gaiety. Or they swam. Her arrival had him doing cartwheels – literally. Early one autumn evening on the campus green, he was trying to copy her handstands. Along breezed Dave on his bike, giggling. Cormac was rightly scundered.

St Benildus' was a large secondary school of about 750 boys. He took five classes of first and second years – three for history and two for maths – and made an immediate impression on his principal. Mr Mulvihill recalls:

> a very unassuming, gentle kind of giant. For a young guy of his stature – though he didn't look as big in his civvies as out on the pitch – he was remarkably modest and self-effacing. He was much more controlled, curtailed and careful as a trainee teacher than on the field. He'd sit in the corner and would never, ever talk aloud about himself as a player. You'd nearly have to push him to talk about that.

And yet, he had a real presence about him, in the staffroom and in the classroom. Without ever looking for attention, he got attention.

All 150 first-year boys crammed into the library on an October morning to watch his international debut. At one point he was in a fray, fending off an Aussie fist. 'Hit him, sir!' they roared.

Eamonn Cosgrove, a fellow history teacher and football coach from Monaghan, eight years Cormac's senior, once asked him what sort of training Tyrone were doing. Three days later he was stunned to receive an old Armagh school exercise-book with four pages of hand-drawn diagrams, signed *Cormac*.

He made a mark on fellow H-Dippers too, mainly the rural GAA folk. 'Cormac was a brilliant teacher who had a wonderful presence in the classroom and a fantastic knowledge of his subject,' Aisling Kelly of Athenry wrote later. 'He was always the measuring stick for me when it came to judging my own teaching.' When she felt homesick for Tipperary, his 'sunny outlook' always cheered her up.

Personal evaluation was an integral part of lesson reports, and the honesty of his self-appraisals stands out in education as it did in sport. The shortcomings of one history lesson, he said, were 'partly my fault, as I did tend to lecture at times'. Another time, he confessed to misinterpreting a couple of illustrations, due to a lack of prior research; 'the boys got great mirth out of this'. During a game of 'Stone Age Who Wants to Be a Millionaire', the inner cavemen of class 1.26 emerged. Despite repeated warnings, 'the boys proceeded to shout and whoop, and crash tables and chairs', so he stopped the game.

As far as possible, he avoided punitive measures and inculcated good discipline instead. Some of his class reports are virtual mirrors of how he coaxed teams on the park.

The inclination of 2.20 to sell itself short was very apparent early on as several boys, being careless with their work, made mistakes and went looking for another page. I stopped the lesson, gave them a short word on planning work and being careful and meticulous. After this reprimand the work produced was of a much higher standard, as boys took more time and made sure the symmetry they were meant to be illustrating was shown on the pages. Work produced was encouraging – we now have something positive to show as encouragement.

As a reward for improved effort, Cormac treated one class with showings of *Hoop Dreams*. South Dublin was a far remove from inner-city Chicago, but this was how he encouraged lads to defy low expectations in life and reach higher.

He graduated with first-class honours. He was also offered a job at St Benildus'. He declined, politely, in a handwritten letter of thanks to the principal. He had another course plotted already.

★

Three days, three provinces, three teams, three matches, three positions.

The Eglish players knew of his six-hour trip back from Kerry for our relegation play-off. Did any realize he'd be back in action the next day in Dublin? I doubt it.

The UCD crew knew that trying to dissuade him would be futile. A fortnight earlier, he'd joined in training at Belfield on the day of his return from Oz. 'You don't need to train, Cor-muck,' said Dave Billings, pronouncing the name just as Daddy intended. 'You should get some rest.'

'It's OK,' Cormac replied, 'I could do with a stretch of the legs after the long flight.'

That was it, end of conversation. He trained.

Similarly, that November league match against DIT was no big shakes. But there was a football to be kicked, so he was there. This would be his debut in the sky blue, navy and saffron. He also felt an obligation to play as a sports scholarship recipient, though no one would have minded if he'd missed this one, least of all Dave and coach Brendan Dardis, who always prioritized player welfare. They picked him at wing-forward with instructions to stay up front and not tire himself out.

Dave had introduced Cormac to his new teammates in his usual bubbly way.

TEAM	OPPONENTS	VENUE	DATE	SCORE	PERS.	POS.	OFF.	DEF.	HEAD	BODY	LEGS
Ulster	Connacht	Killarney	10/11	1:10—0:15	0:1	MF	7	6½	7	7	6½
Eglish	E. Ciaran	Dunmoyle	11/11	2:8—2:12	2:1	CF	8½	7½	8½	9	8
U.C.D.	D.I.T.	Belfield	12/11	1:14—0:9	0:2	R.HF	7½	7	7	6	6

'Ya might recognize this fella, lads. Cormac McAnallen's coming from Queen's. He took a Sigerson off us, the f*****! And he's joining our team!'

They were a talented bunch from around the country. There were household names: Nigel Crawford, already an All-Ireland medallist with Meath; Ciaran McManus, Offaly and Ireland veteran; Brian 'Beano' McDonald, minor marvel with Laois; Stephen Lucey, emerging dual star with Limerick. And there were hardy yet unheralded university players: Gerry McGill of Donegal between the sticks; Conor Evans of Offaly, Noel McGuire of Sligo, Ronan Kelly of Meath, and captain Breandán Ó hAnnaidh of Wicklow at the back; and J. P. Casey of Westmeath and Ray Ronaghan of Monaghan up front. With Cormac jumping between the lines, they reached the Ryan Cup league final, but lost to UUJ after extra time in the replay.

In January, he felt pain in his right groin. On examination his left leg was found to be 1.5 cm longer than his right, and he had orthotic heels fitted by a podiatrist. Now he began to feel pain below his right kneecap, increasing during games and more severely afterwards. Patellar tendonitis, or 'jumper's knee' was diagnosed. It was a classic overuse injury.

Something had to give, you might well say in hindsight. He hadn't really taken a prolonged break from training and games since early teenage years, almost a decade before. Considering his all-action style and catalogue of hard knocks, it's a miracle he'd stayed largely injury-free for so long.

He kept playing – five friendlies in three weeks, with UCD and Tyrone – in spite of the pain. Managers weren't pressurizing him; that's just how keen he was. The impact of the injury became more obvious in Sigerson Cup games in February. He was noticeably under par when UCD beat GMIT at Belfield, and scarcely much better in the shock quarter-final defeat by Athlone IT at Sligo.

UCD would also be competing in the Dublin club championships. Undoubtedly it was slightly unfair that students at certain colleges had a dispensation to play for clubs in two counties in one year. But Cormac was delighted to have a shot at any club senior title, especially as Eglish wasn't shaping that way and Tyrone's season had ended abruptly in July. Still, it seemed like a long shot. UCD hadn't won it since 1974. And in recent years, college clubs seemed to land bum draws and myopic referees as tacit payback for their special privilege.

This year, however, the ball seemed to bounce nicely for UCD. And Dave went into overdrive. No one had more persuasive skills to summon the troops. He was ringing around the country, cajoling, confirming and counting his numbers. At times like this, his emails and letters to players were uppercase calls to arms.

THIS VITAL VITAL VITAL VITAL MATCH IS FIXED FOR THE ABOVE DATE . . .

YOU MAY HAVE TO PLAY TWO MATCHES THAT WEEKEND WITH YOUR HOME/COUNTY COMMIT-MENTS BUT **YOU** ARE NEEDED . . .

OUR STRENGTH IS IN OUR NUMBERS, OUR STRENGTH IS IN OUR CAMARADERIE AND KNOW-ING THAT **YOU ARE HELPING YOUR COLLEGE FRIENDS. DON'T TAKE THE EASY WAY OUT. YOU ARE ONLY YOUNG ONCE.**

Stirred to action, UCD fielded a strong side that year and Cormac was pivotal to its progress. Partnering Ciaran McManus at midfield, he scored two crucial points as the college came from behind to beat Ballyboden in a crunch first-round tie, 1-9 to 1-8. He switched to centre half-forward the next day, a stroll against St Sylvester's. Cormac missed the quarter-final against Kilmacud as it clashed with a play-off for Eglish, but two last-minute goals pinched an unlikely victory for UCD.

No one minded the students too much if they got knocked out early. But once they beat the big boys, everyone else cared. Cormac was one of thirty-four players fielded by UCD, from sixteen counties. The college's permit to pick players for a year after graduation really raised heckles. The gloves came off. Kilmacud objected to a college player as far as the Leinster Council, unsuccessfully. UCD survived but didn't learn their opponents until forty-eight hours before their semi. Na Fianna, chucked out for using six subs in their quarter-final, had gone to the High Court to salvage their four-in-a-row hopes. On the Friday, the judge threw out the case.

In this blown-open field, suddenly UCD looked like title contenders. As the championship dragged on to November, well into term-time, the student players were welded together by more regular training and the complaints against them. Cormac, now teaching in the North, met up with them only on match days. He saw the gathering momentum, and relished playing alongside skilful peers, under no burden of expectation.

When that semi eventually came off, it was UCD v. Raheny. Cormac and Nigel marshalled Ciaran Whelan tightly, and the college did the needful in workmanlike fashion. That left them as favourites to beat a dark-horse St Vincent's side in the final at Parnell Park.

From the throw-in, postponed by twenty-four hours due to a midweek deluge, Cormac man-marked Pat Gilroy, the towering former All-Ireland winner. Nearly every Vincent's kick-out was aimed at Gilroy. With Cormac spoiling from behind, Stephen Lucey – his third midfield partner of the campaign – to his side, and McManus helping out in the cockpit, UCD hoarded possession. Yet, going into the last quarter, their advantage was only 2 points. Cormac struck the second of 6 late UCD points to clinch the matter.

Seldom was a Dublin senior-title triumph greeted with such a muted response. The players' cheers were accompanied by the modest acclaim of their meagre band of family members and friends on the pitch. The McAnallens embraced Cormac. Delighted, he could now strike out another line on his GAA bucket-list. Winning any county championship was a big deal, and Dublin was as hard as they came.

Once college sides escape from county confines, they tend to prosper. Dave made no secret of their ambitions now: Leinster and All-Ireland titles. But UCD could hardly have got a grittier draw. Away to Rathnew, the reigning Leinster champions, at Aughrim, that toughest of county grounds to visit, or even find. Cormac drove over three hours from Tyrone to south Wicklow through lashing rain, only for the match to be called off twenty-five minutes from throw-in time. His mood was still as foul as the weather when he got home. Each day was precious to him, and that one was wasted.

The next Sunday, 1 December, was similarly soggy, but the match went ahead at Newbridge. Scores were at a premium and bruises were going cheap. Cormac led the UCD charge. Close to half-time, he shot a low piledriver to the net and fired over a long-range free to put his side 1-3 to 0-2 ahead. After the break, all changed. McManus hobbled off, and UCD lost their thrust. Rathnew crept back to equalize. Deep into injury time, the Wicklow side were awarded a soft free. Tommy Gill's kick seemed to tail wide. Up went the white flag. UCD players surrounded the umpire, irate. The final whistle sounded within seconds. *Good enough for the college*, thought everyone else.

The UCD side smarted, hurt, more than outsiders realized. Of course it's not quite the same as playing for your home club. But players are all selfish to some extent, and Cormac was no different. This defeat ended his one shot at major club titles, and his college football experience.

★

Cormac's other big drama that autumn was the home International Rules series. He was one of a dozen players retained from the previous year's squad. Whereas that squad got good time to bond and gel as a touring party, the 2002 model was less cohesive as the players met up only at weekends. Playing at home appeared to have become a handicap in this series. But that wasn't all. This time the Aussies brought a more skilful team, more adept with the round ball.

Despite surging into a half-time lead of 38–19 in the first Test, Ireland lost, 58–65. Or 1-13 to 2-13, as Cormac noted the score would have been in a Gaelic match. He came on as an interchange player once again in that opening match and did reasonably.

He started the second Test. A record-breaking crowd of 71,552 came along, but the conditions were horrible: howling wind, bucketing rain, freezing, dark. A temporary power-cut made it almost apocalyptic. He thrived anyhow, straight into the thick of the action. Just on the brink of the quarter-time hooter, Joyce put him through on goal. Was this really happening? Better be quick, no time to dither in this game. His rushed shot was blocked by a defender.

Next time, he would make no mistake. It came five minutes into the second half at the Canal End goal. 'You are always told to follow in chances like that . . . I stuck my toe on it and the next thing it was in the back of the net.' A glorious moment for him personally, though no time to gloat or showboat. Wind at their backs, Ireland needed to pile points on the board. They went on to win that quarter, 20–0, and lead by 19 points. Even after conceding an early goal in the last segment, Cormac believed Ireland would hold on.

But this was the imperfect storm. The Aussies kicked a couple of quick overs. The Irish relapsed into old failings. Kicking low bounce-passes, lovely in Gaelic but awful for this game. Getting caught in possession. Panicking under pressure. There were also fisticuff sideshows. Meanwhile, the Aussie ref made a series of big calls that upset the home side, and crowd. 'I wouldn't like to comment,' Cormac said afterwards, damning the official with silence.

The Test ended in a draw, 42–42. Cormac's goal and behind made him joint top-scorer for Ireland. But primarily he was disappointed that Australia won the series and claimed back the cup. Yes, that cup with no name.

He had no idea his name would be part of every Compromise Rules series ever after.

10. Role Model

On 10 December 2001, Cormac made an entry in his pocket-diary:

> Send Xmas cards to:
> F & R McGirr / Fr. McAleer /
> M. Harte

To those who mattered to him, and to anyone who had done him a good turn, Cormac was a faithful correspondent. He penned letters of thanks to aunts and uncles who gave birthday presents and to others who helped him along. When abroad, he always sent postcards home, and anyone who wrote seeking a favour was sure to receive a detailed response. The greetings flagged in the diary were to reciprocate for some recent messages congratulating him on winning the GAA Young Footballer of the Year award.

The card from Francie and Rita McGirr meant a lot. They were facing into their fifth Christmas without Paul, their second boy. Their grief had receded from view as the world moved on, but assuredly they still bore it in private. They could easily have turned away from Tyrone football and all the sad memories it elicited. And yet, here they were, going out of their way to salute Paul's former comrade; to wish happy Christmas to him and his family, and continued success in his football career and personal life.

Fr McAleer and Mickey Harte had sent separate congrats, both with the subtext that they had reached a chapter-ending. After five golden years, they wouldn't be managing Cormac in 2002. 'We have been lucky to have had such a capable, dignified and unassuming leader,' wrote McAleer. 'I am tempted to look into the future but I resist that temptation . . .'

Mickey thought Cormac had been somewhat hard done by: 'Another well deserved award, Cormac. Many including myself feel you should also have been selected on the "ALL STAR" team. I know it will only serve to make you more determined to get one in the not too distant future. I have no doubt you will.'

Cormac wasn't aggrieved about the All-Star XV. He had a fair idea beforehand. Tyrone, as Ulster champions, would have a shout for one or two awards, max. Stephen O'Neill slotted neatly into the No. 11 spot. Midfield was a tighter call, and the nod went to Kevin Walsh and Rory O'Connell, as totems of landmark campaigns for Galway and Westmeath. Cormac couldn't complain. He knew well the vagaries of awards, having lately taken a few by a whisker. The Young Footballer trophy could just as easily have been given to Stephen O'Neill, it was a rarer honour and, in the circumstances, it seemed to equate to a sixteenth All-Star anyhow. His smile showed his delight to win that national honour – the capstone on an excellent 2001.

By this stage he had bought his own tux, a cheaper option than hiring out for so many dinners. Earlier that autumn, he was selected as a midfielder on the *Irish News* Ulster GAA All-Stars team. Also in November '01, he picked up the Ulster GAA Writers' Footballer of the Year award.

There was one more big award to come before the new season. In January, Cormac attended the *Belfast Telegraph* Sports Awards dinner.

★

Seán McCague [mid vigorous handshake]: Well done, Cormac, well done.

Suzanne Dando: Congratulations, Caw-mack. Now it's turning into some night for Tyrone, isn't it?

Cormac: It is, that's the second award for the Gaelic footballers, and, eh, David [Humphreys] there picked up the rugby award – well, he's playing for Dungannon anyway, so we can claim him anyway.

Suzanne: Now it's been a fantastic year, many awards. But from your point of view it's also been a very good year on a personal note, hasn't it?

Cormac: It has, yeah. Em . . . I mean, whenever the team's

going well, eh, players pick up individual awards, but I don't mean to be clichéd when I say this, but I mean, if the team wasn't winning anything, em, it wouldn't matter how good a season you had, you wouldn't win individual awards. So everything does reflect on the team. But personally, yeah, it's been a great season.

Suzanne: Just very quickly . . . Seán, of course. It's young men, isn't it, like Caw-mack here, that maintain the very high standard that we see in Ulster football, isn't it?

Seán: Yes, Cormac is typical of all the great young players in every sport. And his commitment, his dedication, his skill and his great role as an ambassador for his club and his county mark him out as a guy who's gonna be about for a long time. And hopefully he'll stay injury-free and we'll see a lot of Cormac McAnallen for the next ten years.

Suzanne: I'm sure we will . . .

The stage was glittering with Norn Iron stars that night. George Best, Martin O'Neill, Dennis Taylor, Barry McGuigan and a young Tony McCoy, to name a few. All pausing their postprandial patter to watch Cormac win the GAA Personality of the Year award. This new award came hotfoot after the repeal of Rule 21 – the ban on police members – two months earlier. It seemed to symbolize a fresh acceptance of Gaelic games in unionist quarters.

Cormac had toyed with staying upstairs in his room. He knew hardly anyone there and felt a bit out of his depth. Would anyone notice him missing? But he knew he was privileged to be there, so he dressed up and went in, alone. Only then did he find out. '*Big award for you tonight, boy,*' came a voice from the side.

The interview was typical Cormac, deflecting praise instinctively. And yet, the more he deflected, the more he received.

Cormac had become a Role Model. His appeal extended beyond football success, captaincy and speaking ability. It lay in the way he 'carried' himself. How he exuded experience and wide-eyed innocence at the one time. How he could still pass for a teetotal Irish-speaker, without ever claiming so. How he flashed a wide-open smile for every picture. How, despite all else, he didn't take himself too seriously. When DJ Patsy V shouted out for volunteers for a Riverdance sequence at Eglish dinner dance – cringe! – Cormac was the first up.

He was rubbing shoulders with a lot of GAA officials too. The Ulster ones were most impressed. President Seán McCague pencilled him down as thirteenth man for the new Players' Committee, thinking him just a bit young to appoint first time. Aogán Ó Fearghail gave him a lift back from Killarney and still recalls their deep conversation with gladness. Páraic Duffy drove him back from Ireland training, heard of a budding history teacher, and wondered about recruiting him for his school in Monaghan.

He was becoming public property. Requests came for special-guest roles at club functions: Augher, Clogher, Castlederg, Edendork, Moortown, Maghery, Muff, Faughanvale, An Port Mór, and others. All were accepted, big or small. He hit the right notes for audiences of all ages – a joke to lighten the mood, a local reference, a nugget of advice or praise. He scribbled bullet-points on a beer-mat, a napkin, anything to hand, but with practice he hardly needed to look at them. Ashlene teased that she could go up and make a speech for him, as she knew his formula so well.

There were also star turns coaching children. From a packed summer camp at Bray to a barren pitch at Buncrana, he acceded to requests. He had experience coaching kids, going back to summer youth camps in Tyrone. Some big-name players, when asked to coach kids, would just turn up, take the children for a penalty contest, and collect their few pounds at the end. Cormac was different altogether, recalls Mickey Donnelly, the camps co-ordinator:

He was highly organized. He always brought along a sheet of plans he had prepared as to what he was going to do. He'd come to me at the start and ask, *What do you think of that? Do I need to tweak it at all?*

And what he had was all fine. He didn't need guidance, just affirmation. He was going to do it to the best of his ability, properly. He was not just trying to help the youngsters improve individually, but he also wanted to improve himself as a coach.

Whatever he was doing, he tried to act as an ambassador. Hello-ing to the Ederney under-14 hurlers who sat in the dugout while Tyrone trained, and not noticing their surprise. Teaching Eugene McKenna's children – Fionnuala, Niall, Peter – card games during a Tyrone team holiday. Greeting eleven-year-old Lorcan McGrath with the line, 'I've heard about you. You're some player!' Talking away – as he always did – to the nine-year-old team mascot, Barry Dardis, at the front of the UCD team-bus, while other players celebrated county final glory at the back. Always greeting young Michael Daly and any other ball-boys at Eglish training sessions.

Within him still burned memories of county players talking to him as a child. He hoped to pass on that magical feeling to young lads who looked up to him. One day they might go on to achieve, and they in turn would act as role models for the next lot.

Cormac rarely declined an interview request. While he admitted a fondness for (positive) publicity, that wasn't his main motive. Rather, it was his desire to help people out, be they journos or joiners. Why slam a door in someone's face if you'd hate it done to yourself? Often he went far out of his way to accommodate media folk. Returning a missed call. Changing schedule. Waiting for them to finish other duties. Hunting out a tree or riverbank or haystack or old building to pose for features photographers. Giving honest, considered answers.

No manager he played under imposed outright media bans, and certainly not on Cormac. Indeed, sometimes when a knock sounded on the Tyrone dressing-room door, he'd be put forward as a designated spokesman. As a family, we didn't buffer him either. The bulk of media calls came via the landline and we always sought to put him on the phone or relay the message. There was no call-screening, no false leads about his whereabouts. Even if he was pressed for time, we'd remind him, 'I told yer man you'd get back to him.' We didn't see papers as the enemy. They piled high in our house: northern, southern, Tyrone, Armagh and Monaghan papers, and a few from further afield.

The calls kept coming in the off-season. In one interview, his love of wildlife programmes became the headline subject. He became a reliable B-lister for filler features. A tabloid surveyed him – along with the singer Brian Kennedy and the actress Lisa Riley – about what they wanted for Christmas. His answer: a brand new left leg (because his was 'useless') and a declaration from Santa that all college fees had been abolished.

The press augmented his image as a role model and leader. One picture of him as master and commander against Derry adorned many *Irish News* back pages and sports supplements: he's standing tall with brow furrowed, eyes glaring, mouth pursed upwards, and left arm and index finger outstretched at forty-five degrees, like the Tyrone team traffic-corps directing bad drivers in rush-hour. That was Daddy's favourite picture of Cormac – his boy, in control.

The journalists sensed that while his status grew, his ego shrank. He was always grateful. If a journalist wrote kindly of him once, and encountered him even in the steam of a post-match corridor, he said thanks. When he met supporters outside faraway grounds like Killarney, he thanked them personally for coming to watch his team. He took no goodwill for granted. Colin Mackle, a Tyrone fanatic who interviewed him first back in '97 and many times afterwards, put it simply: 'Although I looked up to him, he never once looked down on me.'

★

I didn't take up GAA to play for the money. When I started out all those years ago, it was for other reasons. If the likes of me started getting paid, the role of the volunteer would slowly disappear from the Association. The guy who washed the jersey would start looking for a few bob.

When I'm finished college and go home for the weekends, I look around and see all the local GAA fields and complexes that have been built over the years, which are outlets for young people. If an amateur association can do this, it's got to fill you with pride. I don't want that to change. [Interview with Damian Lawlor, *The Star*, recorded on 13 December 2001]

As Cormac rose to GAA stardom, the association was changing in many ways. The backdoor system shook up the championships. Rule

21 disappeared. The Croke Park redevelopment was near completion. Headquarters became commercially minded. More money entered circulation. Media coverage intensified. The amateurism question reared its head again.

In his outlook on the GAA, Cormac was far from old-fashioned. In a newspaper survey in 2002, he said he'd agree to soccer and rugby in Croke Park in certain circumstances. He'd welcome technological advances. He considered all things on their merits.

On some matters, though, he was old school. The GAA was about much more than personal glory for him. It was bound up with his national identity. It was a collective cultural conduit. He took time to fill out the lengthy GAA strategic review questionnaire, for he believed in the 'enhancing community identity' message from the top of the association. But he wondered about the corporate direction and the long-term good.

As for the GPA, Cormac wasn't a fan. He saw the creation of an elite inter-county players' body as driving an unnecessary wedge in the playing ranks. He laughed to see the sudden flush of GPA track-suits about, the new status symbol. When he received a perk or prize, he'd joke privately, 'I'm an elite athlete, byyyye!' – mimicking Daddy's pronunciation of 'boy' at the end of emphatic statements.

He didn't identify with the GPA's policies, either. Its cash demands left him cold. He scorned the €127-a-week quote for a county player's lost income – a magic mushroom figure. Making financial reward a concrete part of the experience would queer the pitch. Once payment became the norm, the figures would only increase, and the pressures. He looked at the professionalization of rugby and other sports and felt that structure and participation were skewed in the process.

If a club compensated his travel to a function, he'd accept. And when the Ireland players got $100 a day in Australia, he spent it and banked the rest. But if asked 'How much?' for an appearance, he demurred. Pieces of crystal, turf-craft, and inscribed plaques were his lot more often than not. One night he was gifted a small ceremonial clock. It was a special clock that seemed to forget to keep the time.

For most of the way home from that dinner-dance, Ashlene dangled that clock out of her window, while Cormac begged her not to.

Perhaps if he had been in a county where players had a big beef with the board, he'd have had a different view. But inasmuch as the GPA impacted on him, indirectly, he saw it as divisive; not just between county players and the rest, but within county squads. In those early years, peer pressure to sign up was a spectral presence in dressing rooms. When an established player like him declined to fill out the form, the county GPA reps would mutter, 'Why won't he join?' There was no ostracism. But if you held out, you felt a little like a black sheep, if not a blackleg.

*

In January 2002, Art and Eugene asked Cormac to take up the captaincy. They saw it as a logical step-up after his four years of leading underage teams. They had noted the universal respect he commanded among peers, and agreed that he was their natural leader. Now that this young group formed the mainstream of the senior team, the time was ripe for him. Hard to ignore his lucky streak, or his Midas touch either.

Cormac didn't need long to think it over. He passed it up. He felt not quite ready or free to commit properly to the role. Studying in Dublin till championship season, he couldn't attend all the training sessions. A half-absent captain would be no good. Much more than parade-fronting or cup-lifting, captaincy was about leading by example. So he had shown before. With veterans like Peter and Chris Lawn plugging away and hanging on, he couldn't short-change their quest for deliverance.

For most of an hour, Daddy sat in the car outside Art McRory's house in Dungannon. Art didn't know he was there. Cormac had come to explain why, reluctantly, he had to say no. Art understood. He appreciated Cormac's earnest evaluation. And, of course, he had someone else to turn to; one who had captained Tyrone to an Ulster title six years earlier and remained the beacon of the team.

Peter Canavan became skipper again, as he was entitled to be. He, like Cormac, had turned down the captaincy in other years for the sake of the team.

The Tyrone players returned to training in January after a longer rest than most. With many of them having had club and county under-21 commitments into the tail end of 2001, they needed a break.

Cormac's stated desire for league success wasn't quite matched by Art. 'If we really wanted to win the league, we would have started back training two months ago,' the manager said with customary caution in February. 'I still maintain you can't win the league and then the championship,' he asserted after a hard-fought away victory over Galway, the All-Ireland champions. Throughout Art's career, league triumphs had set teams up for summer defeats.

Cormac still preferred to see the smaller amount of evidence to the contrary. 'What we have to realize is that a lot of high-quality teams have used the league as a springboard to further success during the past few years,' he commented in March. 'Winning it isn't some kind of curse, and the likes of Kerry, Meath and Galway have all proven that.'

These questions recurred as Tyrone's spring flowered like never before. At home to Dublin at O'Neill Park – before 9,000 people, a monstrous league crowd – Cormac fired over 3 points and made two brilliant catches from injury-time kick-outs to set up winning scores. He earned more superlatives in the third game, scoring 1-1 in a 15-point romp over Roscommon.

The talent at Tyrone's disposal was the key factor in driving the team forward. Brian Robinson, Conor Gormley, Ciaran Meenagh and Jarlath Quinn were all blooded. The rearguard tightened up, competition for places increased. Quinn and Jody Gormley did shifts as midfield anchor for Cormac. The new compacted league format, with weekly matches from February to April, added to their momentum.

They went on to top their group. Only Donegal at Fortress Ballybofey got the better of them in the first six games. Anything went in that foul-fest, which was defined by a picture of a midfield scuffle. There's the hapless referee pulling Cormac's jersey as he grimaced and grappled with Jimmy McGuinness.

By late March, the right knee was really bothering Cormac. The pain worsened near the end of matches and sessions, and it endured for a couple of days. Despite a flurry of physio treatment, he missed the last league game against Cork, and a few Eglish matches. He went to Dr Pat O'Neill, who diagnosed the jumper's knee and a tear of the medial meniscus (a band of cartilage). A modified training schedule and more physio work were recommended.

Up to the eve of the league semi-final at Enniskillen, he was an injury doubt. Art warned him about the danger of tendonitis, but he was more afraid of atrophy on the bench, and chose to play. He fared well enough, though Tyrone's 10-point tanking of Mayo and the goal scored by his new midfield colleague, Collie Holmes, masked his personal struggle.

On league final day, a new black knee-strap helped Cormac to cope much better. After an early nosebleed forced him off for repairs, he returned seamlessly to catch the slipstream of Storm Peter. Scorching through the middle, he had a goal on, but chose to fist a point to make it 0-9 to 0-1. The rest was a cakewalk, Tyrone beating Cavan by 0-16 to 0-7.

Considering that it was the county's maiden national title in senior football, the joy was strangely muted. Complacency about beating Cavan, the procession that transpired, and the Clones venue all dampened Tyrone fans' ardour. But those close to the players knew how much this milestone meant. Behind the Gerry Arthurs Stand, we shook Cormac's hand, hugged and backslapped him. We all foresaw a happy Ulster Championship.

Art remained apprehensive.

*

Cormac couldn't see where Tyrone would get a goal from. Armagh were funnelling men back so quickly that chipping over three points seemed more feasible. Even when Seán Cavanagh caught the ball, no goal seemed on. Yet his shot squirted under three or four men to the net. For a nineteen-year-old greenhorn to have the nerve to do that in the cauldron of Clones was startling.

Well Cormac could recall Teddy Cavanagh bossing the square and dumping men in the dung-piles of the Moy field in the late '80s. He had seen the son who gambolled through college and minor games in 2000–2001, but he was only getting to know him now. Clearly he was different. When he took a bag of sweets and fizzy drinks in the car to an early training session, Cormac tutted to the Moy lads. The rookie busted himself to win every sprint that evening. Until out came the sweets, retched on to the grass.

That giddy enthusiasm saved Tyrone the first day. They were a tad fortunate to escape with a draw. When Cormac led Tyrone out for the replay, the hearts of his own supporters in the 30,000-plus crowd sank. The rumours were true: Peter wasn't playing. Victory prospects receded. Cormac tried his best to rouse the troops. He scored 2 points and contributed to several more. Tyrone were in contention to the end but couldn't find the net, whereas Barry Duffy's late poke pinched victory for Armagh.

Ironically for one who reviewed himself so stringently, Cormac came to detest player-ratings in the papers. Once earning 7s and 8s for marking big names, he was now a big name being marked with 6s and even the odd 5. By consensus, he and Collie were outplayed by McGrane and Toal in the midfield minefield twice over. Here we go again, Cormac thought, the old 'bad midfield' bogeyman being wheeled out as usual. As he elaborated months later: 'It didn't matter how well the midfield played, it was a bad midfield because we didn't look big enough. Simple as that. It didn't matter if I had twenty good games, the first bad game Tyrone would be told they had no midfield.'

The new backdoor system offered redemption, but Cormac soon tired of it. Saturday after Saturday out on the road, driving through puddles of qualifiers, held little appeal. They skidded around Wexford Park, narrowly avoiding defeat. They aquaplaned about Carrick-on-Shannon for thirteen minutes till the ref shouted stop. They skimmed back to Carrick a week on and liquidated Leitrim by 18 points.

Art and Eugene experimented. They placed Cormac at centre half-forward against Leitrim. They had loaned him there late in the Armagh replay, but this was his first start outside midfield since 2000.

They thought the attack needed more thrust, and wanted to give a run to other hopefuls in midfield, to see if they could cut it.

He stayed as No. 11 for the next-round match: Tyrone v. Derry at Casement Park. Cries of a fixed draw echoed around Ulster again. Assault and battery were talked up. Tyrone folk worried, but Cormac not so much. He saw no easy teams left, 'and no matter who you got, it was going to be a sharp intake of breath and let's get on with it'. Despite the number on his back, his own game remained familiar: foraging, defending, intercepting, linking, charging forward. He flew through the air to punch a crucial point six minutes from time, sending his team towards a 5-point win.

Doubts circulated in some minds, all the same. This summer, he was blending in more than standing out. The sight of that knee-strap came to signify a man who was not quite at ease.

*

> At the start of this year I set targets for myself that I wanted to achieve in 2002 and one of them was to get to play in Croke Park. That won't be happening in the league because of the redevelopment, so it's going to have to be in the championship. [Interview with the *Tyrone Times*, 22 March 2002]

So his wish was granted. After four busy years waiting, he returned to the revamped arena. It was six years since the Tyrone seniors had played there.

Now in the final round of qualifiers, a quarter-final place at stake, Tyrone faced a Sligo team that was quietly ascending the ladder. In their friendly five weeks earlier – played before the championship draw pitted them as opposition – Cormac's goal had spared Tyrone from defeat.

Now Tyrone were weaker. Half of the first-choice forwards were out through injury. Some others played on in spite of niggles. And some came into the match sleep-deprived, having been kept awake by the noise of flights above their Dublin airport hotel. Still, there was no sign of much wrong in the early stages. Cormac tapped over

Tyrone's sixth point from play and by twenty minutes it was 0-8 to 0-2. Coasting.

What happened next *still* baffles Tyrone people. Sligo started shoving our lads aside, frolicking freely and kicking cloudbursting points that nestled neatly on the goal-nets. All Tyrone systems broke down. To Cormac fell a last, nigh-hopeless chance. Receiving from a short free-kick, he swung anxiously for goal. His shot was blocked, his misery complete.

The comedown was heavy, hard and horrific. The Tyrone public, nay the GAA nation, demanded scapegoats for the crime of losing to Sligo. They blamed a statuesque backline, an infertile attack, and a midfield against whom the evidence seemed damning: O'Hara's lightning runs and three scores from play; Paul Durcan pointing and breaking.

The assumption that Tyrone underestimated Sligo held some truth, but there was much more to it. People forget now how injury-riddled the squad was. And just as a buoyant Tyrone took the foot off the pedal in the second quarter, some thought the referee let Sligo tackle that little bit tougher, carry that couple of steps further. Ultimately though, Cormac accepted the facts: this was their Miracle Day, our Macedonia. 'I thought [the stick] was unfair to us and insulting to Sligo because they were a good side . . . I was in no way ashamed or anything like that. But a lot of people seemed to make us want to feel ashamed of it.'

Opinions varied on Cormac's culpability. The *Irish Independent* rated him 7, one of Tyrone's best. The local misery-sheets stooped lower: one said 6, and another gave 5 for his 'nightmare' game. All agreed he wasn't the forceful presence of last season. If this knee problem was going to persist, some critics queried, would he be better deployed in defence?

★

The Eglish football team had come to resemble the English football team in more ways than spelling. We had won one big championship forty-something years earlier, and our people constantly reminded us of it. We had a pack of big personalities who could put it together to take any scalp in league stages. Route One was our natural style. Before each summer knockout campaign we believed we'd do big things. And every time we flopped horribly.

Cormac's diary account of a training run in January 2003 tells a story about him – but also about the club:

Eglish training, running 6 laps (3000 m)
Finished 1 min in front of anyone else 10.45 – closest was 11.30
Feeling flying fit

Granted, mid-January was early pre-season, and we'd train hard till reasonably fit, ten weeks later. But we didn't push for personal improvement like he did. And it didn't really dawn on us that we'd have to speed up year on year.

For club football was changing, getting faster. Tyrone clubs were coming down with young talent. As bucket-loads of All-Ireland schools, minor and under-21 medals entered the county either side of 2000, the senior club game was rocketing in standard. Competition between clubs was as fierce and as even as in any county in Ireland. We needed Cormac on the field to beat the best.

At the end of 2001, the club chairman, Conor Daly, presented him with a large framed picture of him in action, as recognition of his various deeds. The caption read: '*Cormac, your success is our success.*' Of course, it meant '*We're proud of all you've done, as one of our own, and we're with you all the way*'. And it was true. The club was so proud of all the new honours Cormac brought to Eglish. Members could also see his pride in the club, evident in his loyal playing service, his face at AGMs and functions, and his readiness to join in a youth practice or summer camp on request.

With that picture hanging on my wall today, I see in hindsight another, unintended, meaning to that caption: '*Cormac, we depend on you to bring us to the top*'.

From 2001 onwards, we saw less of him. Tyrone campaigns and injuries deprived us of him for long stretches. His presence was great, his absence huge. When he was away, we didn't really, truly believe we should win.

His playing, and our believing, wasn't enough. In 2001, with

Anthony Daly back as manager and Stephen Rice as trainer, we started poorly but seemed to come right just in time. Five days before the championship opener, we drubbed Donaghmore – a serious outfit – by 13 points. Cormac's screamer from the '21' capped his midfield dominance and our joy.

For 120 hours, we felt really good. Confidence soared. Coalisland were beatable and we liked the O'Neill Park venue. Our golden generation were twenty-two, twenty-three years old. This could be the year.

Then the whole house came down, again. It was gruesome to watch the same stupid failings, in multiple. Kicking balls over the sideline. Corkscrewing passes. Fumbling. Touching on the grass, time after bloody time. Missing easy frees. And above all, taking too much out of the ball. For all our possession around the middle, Cormac and cohort tried to carry the ball through, only to hit brick walls of blue jerseys. Game over: 0-6 to 2-4.

Knocked out as May was budding, team morale withered, and discipline too. We tumbled down the league. The whole club seemed to lose heart, and players didn't give or sacrifice as they had the previous year. Many had got hooked on the thrill of outside managers, and couldn't adapt to home rule once again. Being Cormac-less for most of the season made it even tougher.

Our reliance on him came to a head in the end-of-league play-offs. The bottom eight had to play each other. Cormac was the only Tyrone player on the Ireland tour of Australia, and Eglish officials dug their heels in: no games without him. (They didn't often do hard-ball; our under-21s had had to play and lose without him.) Other clubs started the play-offs, while we waited. When he returned, we won our last two games, and stayed up. Cynics carped that Cormac kept Eglish up by default, as we got cheap points after the delay. But I maintain we'd have won whenever he played.

When Tony Scullion came in as our manager in 2002, he relit our fire. We all knew his face as a Derry legend. Cormac and the '97 minors had risen to his rousing rhetoric. Soon that roaring passion resounded in all our ears. Training numbers soared to fifty-plus, our

1. In our yard, summer 1983. Daddy is holding baby Fergus, Cormac's in the middle, and I'm crouching below Mummy.

2. St Patrick's, Armagh, under-13½ basketball team, October 1992. They became Ulster champions that year, and the same group of players went on to win four more Ulster titles. Five of them were future All-Ireland football champions. *Back (L–R)*: Patrick McGuigan, Lorcan Vallely, Gareth Lavery, Francis Rushe, Cormac McAnallen, Aidan Donnelly. *Front*: Paul McCormack, Kevin McElvanna, Philip Jordan, Declan McAuley, Karol McQuade, Thomas Clarke, Paddy McKeever. (*Damian Woods / St Patrick's G.S. Armagh archive*)

3. Cormac's first time competing in a Tyrone jersey, for St Patrick's, Armagh, on *Blackboard Jungle*, summer 1995. Next time out, the team had to wear school uniforms. (*RTÉ*)

4. Returning to Derrylatinee, autumn 1996, as captain of Eglish's latest under-16 success. *L–R*: Patsy Jordan (coach), Patsy Jones (club chairman), Mrs Eileen Donaghy (principal and Cormac's teacher right through primary level); Cormac; Gary Daly; and Conor Daly (coach).

5. (*top*) Celebrating Eglish's Intermediate Championship final victory, 10 August 1997. Cormac and I are both at the back right. We thought it would be the forerunner to many senior successes. (*Pat McSorley*)

6. (*bottom*) Holding on to the ball, and rejoicing as captain with the Tyrone minors on Croke Park, September 1998. His three All-Ireland footballs are still at home, with everyone's name written on them. (*Billy Stickland/Inpho*)

7. Bringing the Tom Markham Cup to Paul McGirr's grave with former teammate Kevin O'Brien, February 1999. (*O'Brien family*)

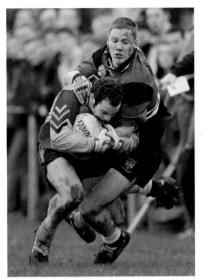

8. Getting tangled up with John Divilly, Queen's v. UCD at Belfield, 10 February 1999. A year later, he won his Sigerson medal with Queen's; and in 2002 he was on UCD's Dublin SFC team. (*Matt Browne / Sportsfile*)

9. His only championship goal for Tyrone, in the Ulster final, 8 July 2001. (*Pat McSorley*)

10. All-Ireland final, 28 September 2003. A goal-saving tackle on Diarmaid Marsden. (*Morgan Treacy / Inpho*)

11. The pinnacle: lifting the Sam Maguire Cup. (*Patrick Bolger / Inpho*)

12. St Catherine's first sponsored football jerseys, autumn 2003. *L–R*: Mrs Margaret Martin (principal), Lisa McQuaid, Daddy (as sponsor), Mrs Fionnuala McGrath (coach), Eimear McKenna, Cormac (coach). (*Mary Kilpatrick / St Catherine's College archive*)

13. With Ashlene on the Dubai sand, 3 January 2004 – a fortnight after their engagement.

14 Four generations of the O'Neills at the Moy, 13 January 2004. Gandy, at eighty-seven, entertaining his daughter, Marie Burns, grandson Cormac, and great-grandsons Max (*in cup*) and Caolan. Gandy made it to ninety-seven, more than four times Cormac's life, before he died in 2013.

15. (*above left*) The Tyrone captain leads his team out for a league match against Longford, 15 February 2004. (*Matt Browne/Sportsfile*)

16. (*above right*) *Irish News* page 1, 3 March 2004. The paper had used the same cover-picture in September 2003, with the headline 'CHAMPIONS' – its top-selling issue ever. (*Irish News*)

17. (*below*) 'Shoulder-high we bring you home': 5 March 2004. (*David Conachy/Sunday Independent*)

18. Mickey Harte and Professor William McKenna join Mummy and Daddy at the launch of the Cormac Trust website, Belfast, 31 May 2006. (*Oliver McVeigh / Sportsfile*)

19. The family at the opening of Páirc Chormaic, Eglish, 27 May 2012. (*Damian McAnespie*)

February standard, and held up as months passed. We whacked Carrickmore, the county champions, in June. Old heads believed again. Come the crunch, against Killyclogher in the first round of the championship, we leaked two early goals and lost by 6 points. The dream died for another year.

Cormac loathed our underachievement. He regretted his enforced absences from club training, but something had to give, and it shouldn't be his body. He wished that others would do that bit more when he couldn't. He longed for more level-headedness. After every big league win, he warned us to stay grounded and focused; yet time after time we puffed up with imagined greatness till we got punctured the next day out.

Privately, Cormac felt a bit taken-for-granted at times. Like when the Moy asked to bring forward our league derby from Saturday 4 p.m. to 1 p.m., and he said 'yes' as he had a Dublin SFC tie with UCD at 6 p.m., and he'd like to play in both. Yet some players kicked up as to the Moy's motives and resisted. Cormac, astounded by this blinkered-ness, went to play for UCD; both his teams won that day anyhow. But a month later, when we really needed him, he chose an Eglish game over UCD's quarter-final; and his sublime display edged out Coalisland.

For all of our failings and frustrations, Cormac remained rightly proud of his team. He could look at our squad and see hardly a nasty streak. People often said, 'Eglish are too nice,' or 'Yiz aren't cute enough.' They had a point. We had physical strength and used it – our disciplinary record wasn't perfect but we weren't known for hatchet-men, play-actors, cheaters, sledgers, stampers, or cramping timewasters. When we ran into experts of the 'dark arts', we were outfoxed – so the theory went, and not entirely without foundation.

*

The embers of Sligo-gate singed the skin of Tyrone football. Only a few weeks had passed when Art resigned his position, for personal reasons. He didn't say publicly what they were, but anyone close to him knew they were real, valid and unconnected to football. That didn't stop speculation about other factors. Second time around, some observed, the managerial double-act had struggled to recapture their old magic. They whispered: Art just wanted out.

Cormac took Art at his word, as ever. But just in case there *was* some other issue, he felt it his duty to get involved. Like nearly everyone, he had presumed Art and Eugene would remain in charge for another year. He believed they could achieve more yet, and if he could do anything to keep their show on the road, he would.

Peter Canavan and Cormac, as captain and vice-captain, arranged to meet Art at his house. They talked things through for most of an hour, but nothing changed. Art explained why he had to take a step back from football. That was that.

Eugene would be in charge then – so the players assumed, and accepted. He was the man in situ, and he had begun to plan for the next season. It came as a shock when the county board declared the position vacant. Confusion and controversy ensued, stoked by press reports. Applicants were interviewed, including Eugene, but the ground had shifted.

Mickey Harte was announced as the new manager.

Cormac was sad and surprised to see things end the way did for Eugene, as for Art. Be that as it may, neither he nor his colleagues would be sticking their noses into board decisions. And when the dust settled, Cormac was happy to have Harte at the helm. He had expected this day to come, albeit not so soon, and he knew they would stay on the right path now.

*

St Catherine's College popped up at just the right time for Cormac, and vice versa.

Summer 2002 had started with a couple of applications turned down flat, no interview. That vexed him, as he thought he had plenty to offer, and he was a stranger to rejection.

What was for him didn't pass him by. St Catherine's invited him to interview and, though he undersold himself a bit on the day, made him an offer. A week before the start of term, he passed the driving test and promptly bought a car. No more scrounging lifts! School was a modest fifteen-minute drive away. Buttoning up a new shirt and tidying himself up rightly, Mr McAnallen felt like a real professional now.

The principal, Mrs Margaret Martin, could see he'd fit perfectly into her plans for the school. Once an Eglish resident herself, she had seen him grow from an infant at playgroup to a senior club-mate of her sons.

He took up a wide portfolio of subjects and duties. He had ten junior groups for History, and one for French, and a Year 11 IT class. There was also Social Education with his form-group, 11M, and the attendant pastoral responsibilities. That's 283 different pupils in his classes; add in his extracurricular roles, and he was getting to know about one-third of the school on first-name terms. The two blocks in which he was teaching were a ten-minute walk apart, and even when he drove between them, it was a mad rush on the bell.

He even had a PE class, though 8I was no ordinary group. St Catherine's, hitherto a girls-only all-ability school (or comprehensive), was embarking on a radical educational experiment as the first Northern secondary to offer a fully bilingual curriculum. The admission of boys – albeit just five at first – to the new Irish-medium unit transformed 'the Convent' further. Among a thousand female faces, this tiny herd of green-blazered *buachaillí* needed their own pen, their own shepherds.

Mr McAnallen was an ideal figure to steer them and make the school more 'boy-friendly'. As a sportsman with whom they identified (as most of them were from Tyrone), his presence reduced any stigma about going to a girls' school. He was the obvious candidate to assist Mrs Fionnuala McGrath, Head of PE, in team-teaching PE through Irish.

His profile helped him command the classroom with the girls too. Mention of Mr McAnallen caused a ripple of excitement in the younger classes. Some girls scrambled through the door to nab the seats in front of his desk. 'It was the only class I was never late for,' recalls Niamh McGirr. His 'Classroom Contract' told them he wasn't messing. Each student signed it, committing to be on time, in uniform, and to behave; he countersigned, pledging to teach and praise and penalize as appropriate. He referred back to this covenant often, and did his best to live up to it.

Having taught only grammar boys before, he wrote in his end-of-year report, 'I was now confronted with the full spectrum of abilities.' He had to come to terms with the wide range of learning styles and teaching approaches that were needed. 'Enjoyability' was a post-millennial buzzword in teaching, not least for all-ability schools. It was to the benefit of pupils, but it also increased teachers' workloads. Mr McAnallen captured youthful imaginations with innovative teaching methods. He brought in artefacts to enliven history lessons and excelled at using kinaesthetic learning activities to engage everyone's attention. 'In class he would do the weirdest things to help us learn,' the 9G history class wrote in a tribute afterwards. 'He had eye stares with us to show how Roman soldiers used eye contact. He split us up into the four corners of the room and we had to act as peasants . . . He sprayed Lynx all around the room to let us get the scent of the Roman baths.'

9G had plenty of fun with him, even at his expense:

> He always wore cool ties, a different one every day. He was too tall for his trousers, which led us to see his Bart Simpson socks . . . His drawings were never that good but he always said that he wasn't an artist. In class he used to try and make us laugh at his jokes but he was the only one laughing . . . He took about four stairs at a time . . .

Pupils appreciated how Sir talked to them personally. How he asked them what they thought during class. How he never passed them without saying hello, inside or outside school. How he remembered their names. How he talked to them not as mere children but as individual people. How his positive words and praise spurred them on. How his smiling approval was due reward. How he tried to be fair to everyone and not have favourites.

Teaching colleagues were equally impressed. Mr Kieran Gallagher, a Maths teacher, first encountered him at interview. 'Coming from Down, I despised Tyrone,' he jokes. 'I didn't know Cormac. I had heard of his name from under-21s and that, but nothing more. I was waiting for this cocky fella to swan in, full of "I'm a county star, here I am" attitude. He was the total opposite.'

Mrs Martin was struck by his regular requests for feedback on his performance. It was unlike many new teachers, who would shy away from evaluation from a principal.

Mr McAnallen's arrival was a boon for sport at St Catherine's. Traditionally, the school had taken part in various codes, with modest returns. Girls' Gaelic football had been a real minority interest, with Mrs McGrath juggling all the teams by herself. Then from 2002, under Coach McAnallen, it surged in popularity at the school. Attendance at the after-school joint practice sessions of the under-14, under-16 and under-19 teams easily doubled, scaling ninety. More coaches came forward too, meaning each team was well catered for.

Aside from his profile, he brought infectious enthusiasm to coaching. 'At football training he was always supportive and encouraging,' wrote one young recruit. 'If you didn't get something the first time he would just stick with it and make a joke about it.' The girls were really struck, and flattered, by the attention he gave to their teams and their individual improvement. Colette McSorley, a natural left-footer, was routinely blocked by Cormac at practices. 'Kick with your right foot [also],' he coaxed her. When he stood in goals to even out the numbers, he gave the practice games an extra level of interest. And in competitive matches, his loud cheers echoed from empty, windy sidelines, willing them on.

His personal example also inspired imitation. 'It became easier for me to encourage health and fitness among the girls,' Mrs McGrath says, 'because he was there and living that lifestyle, and they could see what effort he put in.'

The under-14s and under-16s won the county schools junior and intermediate titles in his first season.

His promotion of sport at St Catherine's went far beyond football. A few months in, the new role of Youth Sport co-ordinator for the school was advertised. This was an education board scheme for pupils of the college and feeder primary schools to enjoy a range of sports in a fun, relaxed setting. Cormac asked Peter Canavan about his time as a co-ordinator in Cookstown, applied and was appointed. It would be more useful experience of sports leadership for one with ambitions.

The role kept him busy, booking coaches and facilities for sessions of athletics, camogie, football, netball, basketball, tag-rugby, volleyball, hockey, badminton, dance, kick-boxing, tae bo – you name it. Calling up teachers in the various schools. Liaising with the scheme administrators. Processing payments. Organizing a fun day for 160 primary pupils at the end of the year. The family had no idea of the extent of this workload until we saw his diary.

All this activity made him a familiar face on the city's sporting scene. Borderlines on a map wouldn't stop him promoting sport anywhere. While Armagh football was swinging and Tyrone men were supposedly the enemy, he patrolled Sherry's Field and collaborated with local elders of the game like Adrian Clarke, Ger Houlahan and John Morrison. He bought his apples and oranges from Brendan Oliver's greengrocers, an orchard of GAA talk.

For he was partly *of* Armagh, and fond of it yet. He was in Croke Park for the '02 All-Ireland, and when they won he was glad for his former teammates and many friends in Armagh. He waited till the stadium was nearly empty, so as to take in the enormity of the outcome.

The ribbing started at school next day, but he did something that people didn't expect.

The victory parade was coming to Armagh – closer to home than any homecoming before. Might he look like a sad gatecrasher? 'What do you think? Should I go in?' Daddy advised him to go – which, as usual, clinched things.

He went with Ashlene to see Sam in the city. As he stood among the crowd, envy grew inside him. Armagh had beaten Tyrone by a hair's breadth and were now All-Ireland champions. That really could've been his team celebrating up on stage.

He made a quiet exit. Any doubts about whether Tyrone could win the All-Ireland were now eradicated. *That has to be us soon*, he said. Their reputations depended on it.

11.   Cormac's Brother

Happy Birthday Dónal
Good luck in the next
year, keep working hard
(But not too hard, you
Workaholic!)
From Cormac

[His card for my twenty-fourth birthday, July 2002]

I was blessed to be Cormac's brother. He was as good as they came. I never said that to him in so many words; it's not how young brothers tend to greet each other. I saw him simply as what a brother should be. But on some level I sensed that he was a deeper and more decent lad than almost anyone else I knew.

Defining my relationship in words with Cormac from teenage to twenties is one of the hardest things for me to write. It's about a side of Cormac that most people who knew him rarely saw. It's replete with fond memories to be thankful for, but also tinged with regret – lots of regret. Thinking of fun times, never to be repeated. Reflecting on how Cormac shaped my life, and how I affected his. Ruing my thoughts and words, what I did and what I failed to do. It's about the art of brotherhood and what I hadn't learned in time.

For twenty years or so, we had been two of a kind, peas in a pod. Almost twins. That's how others saw us, unsurprisingly, because we did the same things in the same places around the same time.

After he caught up with me in height and thinned out, people also remarked all the time on how similar we looked. I didn't see a striking resemblance, but some mixed us up. There was the beardy librarian who started teasing about Armagh's victory over Tyrone and 'your brother' . . . until Cormac coolly replied that he was returning a book for Dónal. When people spoke about Cormac as a teetotal fluent *Gaeilgeoir*, they might have been conflating him with me. There was even the *Hogan Stand* calendar which captioned 'Dónal McAnallen' lifting the All-Ireland Under-21 cup. *Thanks, fellas*. I was a winning captain at last.

We had broadly the same interests and ideals. We were both readers and writers, hoarders and recorders, workers and worriers, compulsive and competitive, strait-laced and straight-talkers. We paced pavements and ran roads in tandem. We marched together against the Iraq War. We prayed on the one pew. We sounded similar. We still played pointless target-games at home, like trying to kick an empty orange-juice carton over a fireguard and into the fireplace, for an hour if necessary. We shared the same sense of humour yet. He teed up my silly jokes. We still called each other daft nicknames at home and babbled on in our own baby-talk that we'd have been mortified to let anyone else hear. After hearing him parrot my phrases, Ashlene nicknamed him 'Dormac'.

Perhaps he had always heeded and looked up to me more than I ever realized. The clues are more obvious to me in hindsight. Starting to drive, he confessed, 'Now I know why you shouted at us to stand in years ago on the road home from school. There's times I could easily have hit a child walking.' I had never really relinquished that role of protector.

Trouble was, I put too much pressure on him: to support me, to agree with me, to do the right thing (as I saw it). I didn't tame my temper with him. When he startled me with a 'Boo!' as I somnambulated back from the toilet in the dark, I thumped him on instinct. It wasn't all one way; he narked at me too. But I was harder on him, downright mean at times. And I hectored him pedantically about petty points. If he said, 'There was a ball of people there,' I'd interject, 'You can't say "ball of people" – that's not proper English!' Why did I do that? I couldn't help myself.

Nonetheless, my hunger for his attention and approval never diminished. Hearing his footsteps beat along the landing, and hoping he'd hover at my bedroom door – to share a story, to tell me someone was asking for me, to pose a question, to talk music. Blasting *Pet*

Sounds and Dexys vinyl at obscene volumes up the corridor to try to impress him; succeeding, despite yells to turn it down. Answering a call and feeling heartened to catch his slim voice, half-aspirating my name to 'Dhonal'. Running across him on a night out, hearing the 'Jitterbug' finger-snap of 'Wake Me Up Before You Go-Go', and scurrying to face off in our Wham! sideways shimmy.

Cormac still looked out for our younger brother, more so than I did. Fergus still navigated a different way through life. What we gave to football, he rendered to rallying, from a safe distance. He documented the differential-locking underworld on videotape. The success of 'Test Your Diff' led to TYD 2, TYD 3 and TYD Retro, and a *Belfast Telegraph* cover splash – 'ULSTER'S MOTOR MADMEN COMING YOUR WAY!', illustrated by some of the Brantry boy-racers hanging out of a car window, mid-doughnut. When Fergus went overground, he wrote for a rallying newspaper, *Pace Notes*, as well as working in Daddy's shop.

In sport, which we had done so much together, now Cormac and I forked apart ever more. It has often been said of GAA county stars, 'Sure his brother at home is twice as good.' People didn't say that about me. While he soared on the sports field, I plateaued. And I became ever more Cormac's Brother. In those years of pre-maturity, of self-discovery, I winced to see my identity diluted. I was like Ant without Dec, Zig minus Zag, Daphne bereft of Celeste. I felt a bit occluded and excluded.

I remained so proud of Cormac's sporting success. I scalded the bald scalp of Peter Canavan afore me with my blather about My Brother and much besides at the '98 minor final. I scaled the roof later to put up a Tyrone flag, and got scolded for breaking two slates. I scoped him out from the Hill of Clones while Eglish players like Euge and Eddie Daly screamed, 'That man's a tank! He's a machine!' and I felt pride. I scrapbooked his career in lever-arch files full of plastic pockets. I scooped a magazine interview with him and ghost-wrote articles for him. I stuck him on my first cover as editor of *High Ball* magazine, merely seconding the designer's choice of a midfield action-shot from Tyrone v. Cavan.

At the same time, I kept a certain distance. I didn't tag along to his award ceremonies. I never wore his Tyrone gear at training sessions or his jerseys at county matches. One night when I wore an Ireland polo shirt he gave me, several lads came up to 'congratulate' me on my 'selection'. Never again. I tried to evade odious comparison.

The Cormac I knew well was hardly any less nerdish or eccentric than me. Here was a boy who gnawed the chocolate off a Twix bar before taking the biscuit. A lad who for many years ate yoghurt with a big spoon and cereal with a wee spoon, just as an act of kitchen anarchy. A teenager who popped bubble-wrap for hours on end. A young man of twenty who ran into the next field full of sheep, kicked ball high and chased until Mrs Ewing – real name – landed to chase him for scaring her pregnant ewes. A uni student who'd still sit down with each exam paper, hours later, and colour in each a, b, d, e, g, o, p, q and capital R; and who upon seeing the words 'Blank Page', graffitied 'Not Anymore'. A fella who bought a reject jersey from a factory shop to laugh at the mis-spelt 'Ballinasole' crest. A man who'd complain, 'Why do they call every big event "historic" on TV?! Sure anything that happens is historic once it's over.'

In company, however, he conformed and contained himself more than I did. My football socks stayed up, his went down. But if I seemed too highly strung about football, and life – even Fr Breslan told me to start drinking – my role model at home was scarcely less uptight. No one dared call him too serious. And club football in Tyrone had become a very serious business.

I let down Cormac in one way: I missed a lot of his Tyrone senior games, National League etc. Wrapped up in my own exigencies, I wasn't always about, or thought I hadn't the time, and what odds if I attended? He never grumbled over my absence, but today I can't expunge that grain of guilt for not going when I should have. To see Andy Murray pointing to Jamie where to sit courtside is to learn the value of brotherly support, of the comfort of having kith and kin by your side in that arena. I wish I'd seen it years earlier.

Cormac would have been there for me. He always wanted the best for me. He would never give up on me. And he wouldn't let me give up on myself either.

★

At nineteen, as a member of the Queen's senior squad when Cormac was making his breakthrough on to the team, I still harboured ambitions of great feats on the field, and thought I wasn't too far off the standard. I had the impression that Cormac believed in me and my potential more than anyone else, and his diary bears it out:

17 January 1998
Unfortunately Donal did not get on. I feel very sorry for him, he just doesn't seem to get the same opportunities or breaks as me. His luck is sure to change soon.

31 January 1998
The team was read out with me at Centre half-forward. Unluckily, Donal didn't make those able to tog out, hopefully he will not take this as too much of a blow.

Perhaps brotherhood blinded him to my weaknesses. It had in our younger years. Back in August '92, after we met silver-draped Wayne McCullough at the Drumsill Hotel, he said to me, 'Sure you could beat him in a boxing match. You're a lot bigger and heavier than him.' I was fourteen, had never boxed and had to tell him to wise up.

Still, I'd like to think his faith in me for football wasn't entirely misplaced. In '97 I was a fresher team midfielder, then a worker wing-forward on Eglish's Intermediate winning side. In spring '98 I was blossoming with the team. I was all action when we beat Errigal, goaled the winner against Ardboe, and walked on air. Then I crashed down on the crossbar of football reality. Quad-tears, concussions, a fractured scapula, and pain enough to murder my mojo for that season.

Someone else held out a light for me. That autumn, Dessie Ryan told Cormac that my form at Queen's training might earn a run in the big league derby, against Jordanstown. 'But don't tell Dónal.' Why not, he didn't say. Cormac told me anyway. He was excited, for he knew this would be a big deal for me. I resolved to show well in the preceding seconds match. Attacking up the left flank, I took a whack in the guts. I crouched down, hurt, but got no free or sympathy. I played on, but the stuffing had been knocked out of me, physically and mentally. The senior game passed, and I watched it pass me by.

On other days, I got on in friendlies against county teams. But in big games, I just didn't figure. No shame there. The team that won the Ryan Cup that year had sometime county minors and under-21s littering the touchline. I came to accept that my main role was on that line, as Dessie's notepad sidekick, the team 'statto'. As PRO, writer of match-reports. As a cheerleader for the team, and for Cormac.

My sole county trial came with the under-21s at the end of '98. Amongst 40-odd lads with All-Ireland minor final experience, I was a rank outsider. There came no call-back. Cormac didn't even have to trial. He was appointed team captain.

The penny was dropping. My sporting dreams would probably never come true.

I had been partly in denial. At club level, I wasn't meeting my own standards. Slaving away at wing-forward – possibly out of position, but we were a skyscraper team with maybe seven midfield candidates – I failed to sparkle often enough. I had become an accountant of a footballer: following procedure, fearing to take a risk, forgoing self-interest, and feeling satisfied just to contribute to team success. But a bookkeeper auditing a loss doesn't receive plaudits. And we lost every other game.

Cormac's very presence at training drove me on more than anything else. He set the benchmark. I paired with him for stretches, jumps and passing drills. If picked on opposing sides in practice games, I took him, stuck to him like a clag, and tackled him good and hard – at times, too heftily for his liking. I stayed late with him to kick points after others had gone.

Now I can see these things more clearly. I was quite fit but not at Cormac's level. Had I focused like him on self-evaluation and improvement, I would have seen my need to train more, major on speed-training, eat more carefully, and somehow score more. I made excuses for myself, and blamed outside factors for my failings. In my own cycle of delusion, I listened out for trusted opinions that would reinforce my own.

Whereas Daddy dissected with a big blunt knife, Cormac sugarcoated criticisms of me. He appreciated my team ethic, and didn't want to hurt my feelings. He couldn't be as tough on me as he was on himself. He advised me in gentler ways: to make more selfish runs down the central channel to demand more of the ball. To think positively to make good things happen, not meet trouble halfway. To be hungrier, more ruthless in my better games, not relax after well-done deeds; to make hay while the sun shone on me.

One moment typified the difference between us. The Moy, Monday, 27 July 1998. Eglish v. Coalisland in the under-21 championship. I was up for it. I slid a Depeche Mode CD into my bedroom sound-system and boomed 'I Just Can't Get Enough'. Again and again. Before it was retro-chic. Cormac walked by, grinning like the Cheese Standards Agency on a tour of Tuscany.

I drove us to Páirc Thír na nÓg and hit the firm ground running. In this safari of open football, I lolloped o'er the lush grass like a lissom antelope, gobbling up ball, gliding into attack. But in a manic 6-goal second half, we became endangered.

The moment came in the last quarter. The ball was in midfield, and I was a distance away on the right. I cut in behind the Coalisland defence, in hope more than anticipation. Then it came: the most perfect Gaelic pass I had ever seen. From the middle, Cormac had lasered the leather diagonally, unspinning, into the path of my outstretched palms, my stride unchecked. So beautiful was the pass, I had to check later that he had meant it. (He had.) I caught and ran. Ahead of me lay a great green furlong and a stranded goalkeeper. I had time to pick my spot or round him. In haste, I blasted it over the bar. We lost. I just couldn't get enough.

One shot. I had panicked where Cormac would have planted it. Maybe my frailer nerve was the reason for Dessie's secret.

*

Being Cormac's Brother about Belfast was an odd experience. It took me a while to adjust.

I had looked forward to his coming. Through fresher year I half-wished I was still at school, playing alongside him on the same teams (as I was still eligible to do). When he came to Belfast, we were bussing and balling together again.

Sometimes, bumping into him wasn't enough for me. During his first year, I got it in my head that he was snubbing me, that he had time for everyone but not to visit *chez moi*. For a few weeks that winter, relations were frosty. It was my petulant and immature fault. Cormac was merely enjoying student life. Only now when I look – guiltily – at his diary of that time do I see how unfair I was and how deeply he cared.

> Dónal was in very bad form, and did not speak to me. Not knowing what to do, I decided to head down to the chapel and pray, and talk to the chaplain. This definitely did help matters, although I did not get any solutions.

He had just returned from the rip with the fresher football team in Dublin when I caused this downer. Well-meaning to the last, he wanted to resolve rows, no festering. Days later, he gave me a silver tin of toiletries as a peace offering. After further petitions, we made up.

Cormac proved remarkably independent of me. In his second year, he opted for a single-honours History degree, as I was doing. Yet, in the time we walked those narrow, creaky corridors and winding stairways of No. 18 University Square, he sought no academic favours from me. He could have taken the same modules and copied my lecture-notes. Shortcutting wasn't his style, though. He picked almost entirely different topics, and harder ones too.

My wings spread beyond football and Cormac. Hanging with Hist. Soc. and *An Cumann Gaelach*, sitting on student council and its cultural affairs committee. Symposium, Super Furry Animals, Bentley Rhythm Ace and any other multi-syllabled concert act in the company of Cathal Scullion. By third year, I buzzed about like the centre of the student solar system, all of matter orbiting my personal universe. Still, I yearned for another galaxy.

I shuttled off to Galway as a postgrad, filled with Pearsean romanticism. To research history. To improve my Irish. To see new scenery. To meet new people. And, a little bit also, to be me – out on my own, away from the parochial North, beyond the prism of Cormac.

I did those things, happily. And football brought more of the same old. In Galway I remained a college club official and a Sigerson sub, liberated from the sideline only when bets were off. I dreamed a dream of coming on to mark Cormac in the final; winning it was secondary. But reality laughed in my face. With or without Cormac, my light would not turn green.

For chunks of my time in the west, we saw each other less, though we kept in touch. From afar I watched his league debut, Tyrone v. Dublin, on RTÉ. Housemates hadn't a clue about football. 'That's my brother playing,' I said, for the first time ever. All around me had always known him. This was a new, proud feeling. Here he was giving me identity, in another place.

His glories uplifted me. I wanted a piece of them. When Queen's won Sigerson in Galway, I waded in to embrace him. I hosted – and body-counted – fifty-one revellers in my house that night, but no Cormac.

I followed the bash up to Belfast. Midnight on Monday, the Bot was bouncing. *QUB, la la la*. I chanted and cheered as one of them. Then 'Angels' played aloud. I felt detached and demoted, and contemplated my fate as a Queen's émigré who'd fled too soon. Cormac left his jolly company to console me. Ashlene was looking on; now we met for the first time. And I looked pathetic. But Cormac helped pull me out of my conflicted state. Two hours on, we were standing on a sideboard in 90 Malone Avenue, singing a duet of 'Sloop John B'.

Dublin brought us close together again. While he studied at UCD, I was working in the city and kipped on his sofa. We shared trains, space, ideas, and joys and anxieties of young manhood. Cormac shared some of my *High Ball* magazine workload too, rowing in during a few busy production weeks in that dingy office on Camden Place. He sorted pictures. He interviewed Tyrone's new kid, Ryan McMenamin, and wrote up the feature anonymously, using the alias of Stephen Grew. But his idea for a cartoon strip based on a Rastafarian GAA coach – 'Selecta' – didn't make it.

*

During 2001, I benefited from his fame and success. It went beyond the feast of boots and freebies.

Ordering a suit from a shop off Grafton Street in June, far from the Ulster GAA heartlands, the man asked:

'What's the name?'

McAnallen.

'Anything to the Tyrone footballer?'

Yes, he's my brother.

'You can have a fiver off there.'

The oddest such episode occurred on a balmy night in July, driving home by myself from Galway. Past midnight, a few miles out of Sligo, I realized I was heading for Ballyshannon, not Enniskillen. I swung, impulsively, on to the next by-road to the right. My addled head-compass convinced me this would connect to my intended route, somewhere. Miles onward, the road was ascending, narrowing and turning into dirt-track. Still, belligerently, I persevered; easier to go on than turn back. Finally, the car got stuck in a rut and couldn't move. About the foot of Ben Bulben, it transpired.

I ran for help, more than a mile, to the next house. Luckily, the knock on the door was answered. The man was cagey at first. In this rugged wilderness, and at this unearthly hour, a young Nordie's voice out of nowhere carried a hint of danger. The householder called the cops and put me on the phone. I related my sorry tale to a sceptical constable. He had a fleet of rescue vehicles ready to launch, but he wasn't sure.

'So what's your name, then?' asked Garda Conway.

'Dónal McAnallen.'

'Where are you from?'

'Tyrone.'

'Anything to the footballer?'

'He's my brother.'

'I sent him off in the National League against Kerry.'

He believed me then.

★

In August 2001, a few days after the painful defeat to Derry, Cormac was in foul form. For once, he had said yes to an offer to play in America – just for one game, mind. It would relieve some of the pain. That was until he was turned away at Dublin Airport. Don't ask. I can't tell.

I mentioned my own match on Sunday in Galway, but didn't expect him to come along – he had enough on his plate. But he jumped in, selflessly. For distraction, he started a game of name-the-next-song-on-the-radio. We played till we were thrown by the Divinyls.

On a Tuam treatment table, he worked at my tight hamstring. Then he slipped out quietly. To head for the cramped but dry stand, you'd expect. But this was the county championship and he wanted to be useful to a uni team that had hardly any support. Alone he stood on the empty side terrace, a rainswept hooded man, shouting his heart out for a college he had never been to, and shouting for *me*.

Along the N17, and the right road out of Sligo, I felt elated and grateful – to have won, and to have a brother like Cormac, who would go anywhere to be there for me. Coming up towards Glencar, the dreamy tones of A Camp's 'I Can Buy You' were almost entrancing that evening. I couldn't buy that high, or his ilk.

And I had many good times in club football. Through long years with Eglish seniors, there were many Sundays when all the personal sacrifices and graft seemed worthwhile. Days of heroic team-triumph when I won a crucial possession, made a key assist or a vital tackle. Days when I bundled in an odd goal – from a tight angle, a deflection, or even an accidental header. Days when prior defeats and difficulties appeared to make sense, as a necessary prelude to success. Days when celebratory clutches and back-slaps gave ample reward and cemented friendships. Days when the McAnallen Bros, Eglish, did the business together. Days like in summer '99, when we were midfield partners, dragging the season out of the mire, confounding adversity as brothers-in-arms.

Those days didn't last long enough. Too often the team, and I, didn't make things happen. We brothers analysed every loss, forensically – on homeward journeys, over dinner, tea and afters in the kitchen. We'd get so het up in ferocious debate, we mightn't know we were making the same point. Ashlene feared to interrupt. And just when we thought we had the matter settled, Daddy would walk in and say the most incendiary thing to set us off again.

I was less considerate of Cormac's feelings than he of mine. I gave out when he missed club sessions and even some league games in

2002. With studies in Dublin and training for Tyrone and a knee to mind and his girl to meet, he had a lot to balance. Having not missed a league game in five years, I had my blinkers on.

'We need to see your face for the sake of the team,' I pleaded.

'I can't. I've too much on, and if I'm not allowed to play I won't make any difference,' he protested.

'Oh, just cos you're a county player you don't have to go,' I rasped back at him.

I hurt him more than I intended. He hit back with a harsh truth.

'You shouldn't be worrying yourself, rushing to catch trains home to train. Come championship, will your efforts be appreciated?'

That wasn't like him, the doyen of positive thinking. He wanted to protect me, for he knew I was enjoying it less and less. The sacrifices. The monotony of training. Ladders and cones. Forwards having to defend deep. The guilt of kicking a wide. My dropped head being (mis)taken for a drooping spirit. Reacting to shouting, swearing and backbiting. Spotting someone warming up. Being subbed again. Resenting the immunity of onetime county players. Taking football too seriously. Thinking – knowing – some weren't serious enough for us to win big.

Come championship, it happened. I had felt silent vibes from the manager. Cormac said stay positive, I'd be fine. But no: I was dropped, and shattered. Perhaps I had it coming, after middling displays in championships before. But I had started this season well and I seethed with grievance. Cormac smarted too. He took it almost personally and told people, home and away, that it wasn't fair.

He sensed that being Cormac's Brother didn't help me here. Part of it was in my head – but not all of it. Mutterers muttered. One player, in a rant, accused us of passing too much to each other. It was off radar, but it landed. I took it as a slight, depicting me as Cormac's chosen charity. Dammit, of course we had a fraternal rapport. Yes, we looked out for each other's runs, and passed; and sometimes we shouted pidgin Irish to each other – 'ar dheis', 'ar chlé' – just to confuse opponents. But we weren't mé-féiners, and our joint wavelength wasn't causing us to lose games. At least we thought and talked tactics between games. Did others?

I hit a new low. Back problems benched me for two months. I returned to find myself down the ranks. One day I didn't get on, I fumed home and tore down every All-Stars poster from 1979 to 1996 off my bedroom wall; well, OK, I took them off gently, lest they rip on the Blu-Tac. But I was no longer in love with the game.

Still, I persevered. One man wouldn't hear of anything else.

★

The last GAA medal we won together was not on a field, but in a hall in Coalisland in March 2003. It's one of the best memories that I – and others who were there – have of Cormac.

It was the county Scór Sinsear final, and Eglish were going for our third senior quiz title. Being on a Scór stage with Cormac always filled me with pride. The third man changed – Gerard Jones, Cathal Murtagh – but our team was invariably a certified minimum sixty-seven per cent McAnallen product.

As usual, a football clash meant a race across the country for us to get there. On '99 final night, we'd had to rush back to Sigerson in Belfast without collecting our prizes. In 2001, Daddy drove us from the Tyrone–Galway game in Ballinasloe to reach Strabane, three and a half hours away, just in time to win our second title. This time, I was the one in the breakneck hurry – on the 5.30 p.m. from Cork, with Fergus rallying me home from Dublin. In the semi-final that evening, Ashlene sat in for me; she wasn't eligible for Eglish, but who'd dare object to Cormac's team bending this wee rule? I was lucky to make it for the final.

Cormac stole the show that night, in the last individual round. With the scores tied, Siobhán McQuillan asked:

'Which Cork town is well known for its carpets?'

I could think of Navan and Des Kelly carpets, but it was take your pick of twenty Cork towns. *He'll never get it.*

On about the ninth second, as the timekeeper moved to ting-a-ling, he leaned in to answer, 'Youghal?'

'Correct. *Sé mharc.*'

Ashlene confronted him in the car afterwards. 'You're a freak!' she shrieked. He pleaded guilty.

How did he get it? 'I don't know. I think I'd just heard it somewhere.'

Constantly, to the end, he amazed me with stuff like that. Pub-quizzing, or competing in *University Challenge* at home, oftimes I saw him pluck the most esoteric answers about romantic poets and impressionist art from the remote cloud-storage of his outer brain – even while balancing frozen peas on his knees and peeling an orange. How?

'I dunno. It was a guess. I'm just a good guesser.'

In truth, from years of practice, he could read the structures and patterns of questions – the sixth sense of quiz buffs – well enough to pull up anything from his knowledge-bank in an instant.

Cormac's passion for quizzes never ebbed. If he saw one advertised anywhere, and could go, he'd gather a team. Mummy, Ashlene or me – if he could persuade me.

Wherever life would take us, the one thing I was sure of was that we'd be quizzing together for the rest of our lives.

Cormac wouldn't have had it any other way.

12. Reaching the Pinnacle

The opening match of 2003, against a fired-up Fermanagh in the McKenna Cup, gave Cormac many reasons to be pleased. Tyrone came back from 6 down to win, and Cormac stood in as captain, with Peter Canavan on club duty. Afterwards, he noted in his diary, Mickey Harte was full of praise: 'Good man, Cormac, you've never let me down!'

With that statement, their good understanding was immediately re-established.

Mickey's new set-up was enhanced by the addition of Paddy Tally as team trainer. Paddy's sports-science knowledge and enthusiasm were immediately evident to Cormac. Overall, the regime was up there with any he had experienced before. He expounded on this in an interview around that time:

> What impresses me most is the level of detail in terms of diet, what type of training you are doing and the reasons for it, the skills and the structures in place if players get injured. Nothing is left to chance and I think that's reflected in the performances on the field.

Cormac was also cheered to have come through the Fermanagh game uninjured. That knee problem had stayed with him through 2002, but a winter's rest and careful treatment might just have worked the trick.

Something wasn't quite right, though. The signs are there from the start of his 2003 diary. 'Didn't feel in great form for it,' he had written of the first training session at Augher, three days before the Fermanagh game. And his account of the next four weeks reveals growing anxiety.

Tuesday, 14 January
Back in gym, really hitting it hard today
Tired after yesterday, but pushed it out

Thursday, 16 January

Fitness test, Galbally – Did well in fat test (v. well), abdominal strength, and bleep test (joint top), not so good in speed test. May have pushed too hard, feeling exhausted and knee feels stiff too.

Friday, 17 January

Log: Now feel that I've trained too hard this week. Two problems – Patellar tendonitis has flared again, and feel very run down. Shouldn't be trying to do too much too early.

Sunday, 19 January

McKenna Cup ¼ final v. Antrim

Log: Knee was hurting, but thought I'd give it a go just to see how it would go. Got really pissed off in first half, we were winning well, I was running to support loads of attacks but no one was giving me any passes in attack. Remember remarking to Seán Cav towards end of 1st half – We had both run for a short free and were standing free in front of goal – that 'There's no point, get used to it, it doesn't get much better as we go on.' Anyway, came off at ½ time and iced knee – didn't feel great . . .

Thursday, 23 January

Log: Going to training and watching – it's hard.

Cold night, dragging yourself out, watching lads tog out, making contact but strangely not feeling part of it, struggling to keep warm; feeling yourself get more unfit as the lads get fitter. Still, good motivation.

Sunday, 26 January

Log: McKenna Cup match v. Cavan

Hard watching the lads play without me, I should be out there amongst them. Long enough day to pass, meeting up early with the team yet knowing that you won't get playing all day. Team played OK, but if we didn't have Peter we'd struggle up front. Ryan Mellon played well at midfield . . .

Thursday, 30 January

Log: Bombshell! After lecturing on need for discipline, commitment, etc., Mickey & Peter have decided that Errigal boys are pulling out of matches until after All-Ireland club. Fair enough, but they weren't at training tonight (and probably won't be until after AI Club) – If it was any other club there'd be uproar.

Got treatment . . . deep friction . . . about 40 minutes of it. Set my knee back about 2 weeks, really inflamed. Rippin'!

Friday, 31 January

Log: Got new orthoptics [sic] fitted. Sick and tired of explaining leg length difference that underpins any other injuries that I may have. Maybe these will make a good difference, the last ones did until they collapsed.

Sunday, 2 February

Log: Beaten by 1 point in Roscommon. Dirty, wet, windy day in Hyde Park, missing Errigal boys & myself. We played OK in first half, but no one (except Ryan Mellon) wanted to know in the 2nd half. We were constantly turned back in the tackle, we let them win the hard 50/50 balls, forwards showed lack of ideas. Mickey remarked to me afterwards on bus: 'If we'd had you out there we'd have won that match.' Thanks Mick, that's exactly how I felt, but didn't know if he thought so. With Tracker bars, Jaffa cakes, Bananas & Oranges aplenty in dressing room, never mind at team dinner, a non-playing member could easily become a fat boy in this set-up.

Thursday, 6 February

Turned up for training tonight at Augher. No one there. No one informed me. Found out later it had been moved to Dunmoyle – 'Oh Cormac, we never even thought of you.' Thanks lads. Am I out of the loop?

Sunday, 9 February
National League v. Galway, Pomeroy, 2.30
Watching the boys get changed, warm up and play today, felt

very detached from the whole thing. It was as if I wasn't there, you're not acknowledged at all. Boys played well all through, easily beat a decent Galway line-up. Much different performance from last week.

His narrative notes end there, and that's all for the next six months.

How strange and unnerving it was for him to sit on a county bench. How acutely distressed he was to miss a wintertime training-session or league match. How hyperconscious he was of falling behind in fitness. How quickly he felt disconnected from the group. How emotionally brittle he could be, more than anyone realized.

Weighing down his mind was the big dilemma. Dr Pat O'Neill had given a stark prognosis in December: go for an operation to remove the scar tissue and miss perhaps six months; or try to manage the injury, resting for a long time – up to 120 days, preferably – before returning to play, with the risk of recurrence. Two examples were swaying him against the knife. Brian Dooher told of having similar surgery that seemed of little benefit. Then there was Michael Bridges, the Leeds United striker whom Cormac Yahooed online: a doctor in Colorado had recently advised that his patellar condition could be rectified without surgery.

Still, Cormac agonized. Long hours were spent on the phone to Ashlene. Gradually, he came to the decision to fend off an operation for the time being.

You see, Cormac really believed this could be *the* year. And if this was going to be *the* year, he simply had to be playing.

But even the non-op route to recovery entailed a lay-off from action for several weeks. That recovery would require a huge effort. Heading up the M1 to the podiatrist to see if the feet were still an issue. Getting frequent treatment from county physio Siobhán McGuinness, to whom he was very grateful. Working hard on flexibility exercises. Constantly icing with a bag of peas. Swapping that clunky black knee-strap for a subtler white bandage that didn't restrict movement or shout 'I'm a bit injured' quite so loudly.

While Cormac was away, Sean Cavanagh was at play. The young turk made his midfield debut against Donegal, played a blinder, and told the TV cameras afterwards that he wanted to play there regularly for the county. His all-out-attack style opened up defences, and new possibilities for his own team: midfield could become the wind-tunnel for a fast running game. Cormac could see that if the team dynamic was about to change, his role might alter too.

It was 9 March when Cormac graced the county jersey again. The day's derby against All-Ireland champions Armagh was a real four-pointer. Cormac's priorities were more basic: getting game-time and avoiding injury. His introduction with ten minutes left raised a cheer. He got stuck in, escaped unscathed, and Tyrone claimed Armagh's first defeat in almost a year. But he was in no mood for wild celebration. Worries about his fitness permeated his personal ratings:

OFF.	DEF.	HEAD	BODY	LEGS
8	6½	7	7½	4

Six days later, that cloud lifted. He played the full hour for Eglish in our first league game, an away victory over Trillick.

OFF.	DEF.	HEAD	BODY	LEGS
8½	7	8½	8	9

Both he and Mickey saw he was ready to return to the county line-up. They agreed that he should sit out the next day's McKenna Cup final against Monaghan, however, lest he push himself too hard.

The following week would provide the supreme test for him and the team: away to Kerry. Tyrone hadn't won there in an aeon, but the new breed overflowed with the talent and confidence to do it. The combined energy of Cormac and Cavanagh, midfield partners for the day, propelled the team. Cormac's first shot rebounded to Wee Peter to pilfer a goal, and his second notched a point. Later on he dashed back to cover the goal and make a vital interception that secured victory. He awarded himself another 9 for Legs. He wasn't ecstatic – Darragh Ó Sé had out-fielded him; the Kerryman was his toughest midfield opponent yet, he concluded – but felt good all the same.

He thought he was over the worst. Tyrone club football had other thoughts.

The Eglish–Clann na nGael match seven days later seemed harmless on paper: we had won our past battles well and they had to trek fifty miles to our citadel. Complacency seeped in. The Clanns raided for early scores and retreated. We fired slingshots and sent in cavalry, but in every way we were repelled. Fifty frustrating minutes passed.

Cormac charged across midfield at full steam towards a Clannsman, reached a stiff forearm to body-tackle and dispossess in one go. An instant before impact, however, his target twisted and ducked, making the connection resemble a clothesline. Caught off-balance, the Clannsman toppled back and his head banged the turf. Mentors ran on and uttered, 'Stay down!' while the mob bayed for blood. It was a clumsy high tackle and bookable, but obviously accidental; anyone familiar with Cormac's play knew that he didn't do dangerous or malicious. The referee raised red. Cormac shook his head in shock.

Eglish lost the match there and then, and Cormac had more whammies coming his way. For a third time, bizarrely, he was sent off just as the GAA disciplinary rules were changing; had it happened a week later, his suspension would have applied to club games only. But this four-week ban put him out of Tyrone's next two big matches. No inter-county player would again suffer such a penalty. Yet, strange to relate, no appeal was made. Back in those days, the referee's report was taken as final, and Cormac didn't ask anyone to pull strings or look for loopholes for him.

If that wasn't bad enough, a local pressman stirred the pot further. 'Hughes' Views' in the *Tyrone Times* thrived on spicy asides about the county set-up. This time he wrote to 'applaud' the referee who sent off Cormac for showing the courage of his convictions, unlike others who had let off county players in the past. Hughes hadn't even seen the game, and Daddy was so incensed that he rang in to complain.

The next week's column alluded to the caller and kept the story going.

Cormac was enraged but stayed silent. He adopted a new policy instead: no more interviews to the *Tyrone Times*. It was his first-ever media ban and he stuck to it.

At least Cormac knew Mickey stood by him.

When his suspension ran out, Mickey put him straight back into midfield for the National League final. It was a big call. Cormac had played one full league game. He displaced Hub, who had been there for most of the matches and was in situ for the victories over Cork and Fermanagh that got them to the final. Mickey wanted him on his team for the championship, however, and this would be the last outing before then.

Cormac tailored his game-plan to exert but not break himself. Tyrone's absolute dominance over Laois that day afforded him the latitude that he needed. He took a holding role in the middle while Cavanagh cut loose. He broke kick-outs rather than try to out-fetch his taller opponents. And once the game was sewn up, he dandered forward and stroked over a fine point. Not dazzling, but effective. He lasted the distance, relished his first victory at Croke Park in five years, and earned his second league medal.

Plain sailing.

★

Cormac was very wary of Derry. The year 2002 had taught that league titles set you up for a first-round fall. He could almost visualize Derry, plan in hand, lying in wait for another Clones ambush.

Right he was to be wary. Derry came back from 5 points down to score 1-6 without reply. Cormac rescued the cause by earning an injury-time free-kick for the equalizing point, but little kudos came his way. The media marked him a flat six out of ten; full circle from 2001, Tyrone were now expected to rule midfield, and breaking even was deemed failure. He rated himself a 7.2 average, and wondered again where all the love had gone.

For the replay the next Saturday, Mickey assigned him to hold a defensive position while Cavanagh attacked. He would become the first undersheet of many Tyrone blanket defences.

So it was for seven minutes at Casement Park, until his season took its next unexpected, unfortunate twist. A fist caught him in the face, and while he lay prostrate under bucketing rain, he took a boot to the face. Result: busted lip and bruised nose.

Dazed and tattered, he was subbed and escorted straight to the dressing room. Daddy called in and had him at the city hospital before half-time. As he was being stitched up, news filtered through of Tyrone's easy victory. He headed home with instructions to take a few days' rest.

As if. The next evening, he packed for the Eglish–Kildress league game. He threw his bag in the boot. No one expected or pressurized him to play, but he wanted to be ready – just in case. He and Ashlene sang duets in the front, and I laughed in the back. We got to Pomeroy and he lifted out the bag – just in case. Inside, he put on his gear and tracksuit. Just in case.

The game hung in the balance in the second half when he asked to come on. Not ten minutes later, when he dived to block a shot, the kicker's follow-through thwacked into the side of his fragile face.

Lying in the back of Daddy's car, his head pounded more with every bump on the road to Craigavon Hospital. He doddered into A&E, where Cavanagh was already sitting with a freshly chipped anklebone. And who treated him but Dr Peter Campbell, a former teammate for Queen's and county! Three Tyrone midfielders in one casualty department, when people said there were none anywhere.

He stayed overnight. The hospital record says 'Thinks he may have passed out for . . . 3-4 minutes'. Two X-rays showed no clear evidence of facial fracture, but the swelling and loose tooth and episodes of head trauma warranted caution. No games for one month, he was advised. This time he'd follow doctors' orders.

Every other day for the next fortnight he was being seen to.

Tuesday: facial surgeon, Ulster Hospital, Dundonald.

Wednesday: dentist's, to get his tooth fixed.

Friday: doctor's surgery, to have stitches removed and blood-test.

Saturday: oxygen-tank appointment.

Thursday: back to dentist's, to have a new gumshield fitted.

Friday: outpatients', Craigavon.

The whole family was feeling his pain after his recent jinxed run. The achy, drowsy feeling in his head would last for weeks, causing a lot of anxiety, which small things amplified into semi-paranoia. The back pages led with Cavanagh's injury, while his own smashed mug was a footnote. He worried: *Am I yesterday's man or something?*

★

Cormac's comeback match was big for him, but for several of the Eglish team it was now or never.

Nobody said it straight out, though it was plain to see. We had several 30-somethings hanging on in hope. At twenty-three, Cormac was our second-youngest starter. New blood would be needed shortly.

Errigal were our opponents in the first round of the county championship, in late June. It was the toughest of draws. They were the reigning Ulster club champions. They had a full cast of sorcerers and a midsummer's eve to weave another reverie.

Still, we believed we could win. Cormac saw reasons as much as anyone. We were close behind them in the league. We knew all about them and might catch them cold. We had messed up so many championships that we were due a good day. All we had to do was focus a bit better, try a bit harder.

We talked. We swam in the pool. We loaded up on crates of fruit from McCann's shop. We decamped to the Brantry BARD for a steak barbecue to hear the team named and collect our new shorts and socks and watch Tony D'Amato's 'Inches' speech on a telly on a trolley. We told each other we'd win. We shouted it.

Oh, we shouted, and roared, and banged tables, and beat walls, and bounced our studs on the floor in a tribal rhythm. Noise-making wasn't really Cormac's style, but you can't very well be a conscientious objector in those circumstances. Problem was, nearly an hour before throw-in Peter Canavan could hear the din through the thin, tired walls of the cavernous O'Neill Park changing rooms. The Errigal lads had already figured how to beat the bigger Eglish team:

pass quickly and keep out of the tackle. Now they looked at each other and said coolly, *These guys are up for it. But they're psyched out of it.*

There was a barbecue that evening too. Only this time, we were the beef. We stood like fourteen Freezy McFreezefaces, dangling from meat-hooks. Errigal slung out their cleavers and vivisected us individually, like Itchy & Scratchy in kaleidoscope. Then they ate our raw livers with some fava beans and a nice chianti, leaving our carcasses to rot.

Or, in orthodox football terms, by the time we got the ball past halfway, about fifteen minutes had gone, two goals were in, and the game was effectively over.

Well, one among us wasn't a McFreezeface. As the second half played out against a surreal silence, Cormac put up a one-man fight-back, even stealing forward to kick a goal that reduced our losing margin to 18 points.

Exeunt the rest of us, staring downward: we had demeaned ourselves and our club, and embarrassed our families. Cormac kept his head high, greeting passers-by on the way out. He had done what he could; no point in moping. We weren't going to win a senior championship any time soon. We'd just have to live with that.

Typical Eglish, we achieved two brilliant league victories the following weekend. Cormac scored the goal that beat Donaghmore and made his most positive self-appraisal ever − 43½ out of 50 − for the second match, against Carrickmore:

OFF.	DEF.	HEAD	BODY	LEGS
9	8½	9	8	9

He was back. It was good to be back.

*

Cormac should never have doubted his centrality to Mickey's plan. Hub and Gerald Cavlan had deputized excellently at midfield in the semi-final victory over Antrim. Indeed, Cavlan had sailed and slinked his way to the Man of the Match award. Cormac's hyperactive mind went to work again. *Will I get my place back?*

But Mickey trusted his first-choice pairing. Once Cormac and Cavanagh returned from injury, he restored them to the centre without hesitation.

Cormac calmed down, and rewarded the manager's confidence. In the first half of the Ulster final, he caught three kick-outs. He held his own in the middle, even as his team was caving in to a Down onslaught. Four goals conceded in forty-five minutes, Tyrone trailed by nine points.

Somehow, he felt, they had it in them to recover. They did, and equalized, against all odds. Then McMenamin missed a last-chance kick to win it, and covered his face in despair. Cormac ran right up to him, tapped his midriff, and told him to forget it and move on. He may well have been the last man ever to feel sorry for Ricey on the field of play.

OFF.	DEF.	HEAD	BODY	LEGS
6½	7	7½	7½	6½

For the replay, Mickey had to plug a gaping hole in defence. He needed someone of physique and tenacity. Someone came to mind. He had only ever put Cormac at full-back once, for a Hastings Cup game in the misty past. But he was aware of him playing there occasionally for school and for Eglish, and saw in him a man who'd relish the challenge.

Before the Tuesday night training, Mickey called him aside to propose the switch back. No problem. Knowing Mickey had confidence in him to do it was good enough for him.

Project Switch hinged on secrecy, to catch Down on the hop. Cormac kept his side of the secret: he told no one at home about it, except me; and I told no one else. He was named at midfield as usual in the official line-up, and the team wasn't informed of the change till match-day. But from training manoeuvres some could see Mickey trying Cormac out at full-back. Word got out. The leak was later traced to the Moy, Friday evening.

When Daddy shuffled into his seat in the Gerry Arthurs Stand, supporters' tongues wagged his way. He was sitting among the other players' families, and they were well informed.

'Well, what about your lad at full-back the day?'

'Eh?'

He hadn't a clue what this was about. Then more asked. His face went beetroot as it dawned that Cormac hadn't divulged to him. He felt like Del Amitri when the bomb dropped.

Down hadn't heard either. They were shock-and-awed by a barrage of early Tyrone points and never recovered. Cormac had studied how to mark dangerous Dan Gordon – last week's hat-trick hero – but he had little to worry about, as the ball rarely came so far. Tyrone half-pincers stubbed out attacks at the launchpad. Down achieved only four shots from play in the entire match and lost by 15 points.

OFF.	DEF.	HEAD	BODY	LEGS
6	8½	9	8	7

'Cormac McAnallen is a dream player,' rejoiced Mickey to the press-pack. Project Switch had worked a dream. It would in time be lauded as a pivotal move of this campaign – indeed, of modern Gaelic football. There had been midfield/full-back converts before – Seán Walsh and Conor Deegan had won All-Irelands from both spots, and Colin Holmes jumped the lines for Tyrone routinely, almost unnoticed – but it was the instantaneous success that made Project Switch so celebrated. For Cormac, the credit he got was a swings-and-roundabouts thing: undervalued midfielder one week, Midas-touch new man on the square the next.

'There's just one thing,' I said to him, Columbo-like, at the kitchen-table next day. 'That's any chance of an All-Star gone now!'

He shrugged it off, unconcerned. Too early for such talk.

Reprogramming himself was a more immediate concern. The surprise factor was gone and beginner's luck wouldn't last. Now opponents could size him up. And in the expanses of Croke Park, big guns would find out a fake full-back.

Cormac signed up for his own one-man summer school. He channelled long holiday hours into mastering the subjects: how to run, mark and think like a full-back. He short-sprinted daily on our front lawn to sharpen his speed. He supped up advice from stalwarts of the square. He studied videos to see how Mick Lyons attacked the ball. He retrained his brain to be ever alert, to seek short kick-outs, to use faster hands, to cover and be covered, to be demonic in the hunt for every ball.

His assiduousness paid off in the All-Ireland quarter-final, against Fermanagh. While Tyrone dominated possession at the front end, Cormac kept a tidy kitchen. When required, he zoomed out afore and above Stephen Maguire, gathering and flicking to safety with impeccable timing. He stomped about with a vim and verve that seemed to inspire defensive colleagues, and he galloped out with the ball to instigate rapid counter-attacks. It was his first time draped in the county's No. 3 jersey. He looked like he'd been wearing it all his life.

Tyrone won by a whopping 19 points. Job done. Well, almost. 'We didn't meet the target!' he said to Paddy Tally afterwards, only half joking. Paddy had asked the players to set themselves targets for margins of victory. It wasn't an arrogance thing; it was their 'process-oriented goals' thinking. Having beaten Down by 15 points, they reckoned they could take Fermanagh by 20. Cormac always wanted to honour a deal.

OFF.	DEF.	HEAD	BODY	LEGS
7	8½	8½	8½	8

And as the hours ticked down to the semi-final, he wrote the following on a foolscap:

PERSONAL ASSESSMENT

5 THINGS I DID WELL IN THE LAST GAME
* Positioned myself well
* Played the ball quickly
* Didn't foul close to goals
* Made myself available for passes
* Held my man scoreless

3 THINGS I DID NOT DO WELL
* Didn't always take the ball at pace
* Didn't read the ball / fight the break ball well enough
* Wasn't exhausted coming off the field

5 THINGS I MUST DO TOMORROW
* Man the central area – Tackle anyone coming through
* Not foul within scoring range
* Be willing to take the ball & work it out of defence
* Play alongside my man – deny him possession
* Run, jump and tackle till exhaustion

*

The All-Ireland semi-final against Kerry was the biggest game of most of the squad's careers to date, he said beforehand. Munster teams at this stage had usually spooked northern teams – Tyrone especially. But Cormac and the boys stared this challenge in the eyeballs. They looked forward to beating Kerry.

Their fabulous form was one factor. The unprecedented competition for places was another. Everybody was available at last.

The stern of the ship was in line for changes. Gavin Devlin went straight in at centre half-back, with Ciaran Gourley transferring from there to corner-back in place of the unfortunate Dermot Carlin. When Devlin had received a three-month suspension in May, he feared he'd miss the entire championship. Cormac had kept consoling and coaxing him. 'Keep the head up, Horse. . . . You'll be back for the All-Ireland semi-final.' Right he was.

The original full-backs, Colin Holmes and Chris Lawn, had also both recovered from injury. Mickey kept faith in Cormac, though Declan O'Sullivan would be a different breed from the big stallions he'd marked so far. The Kerry lad was a coltish, quicksilver, two-footed, roaming, playmaking threat. Some pundits suspected Cormac wouldn't stick to him.

All that talk proved irrelevant. The two of them were left idle for most of the first half as Tyrone's middle and front sections hunted and gathered feverishly in packs. Peter had limped off before Cormac got his first touch from open play in the fourteenth minute. But with ball in hand, he played seemingly without fear, sallying forth, swapping passes and starting attacks. He even hand-passed with his left over a Kerry man's head for a colleague to run on to – something he'd hardly risk in a club game. This was Séamus Moynihan-esque dare-devil full-back play on a day when even the Kerry great couldn't exercise his own patent.

Cormac 'came through hell' in this game, he wrote later. It hotted up in the third quarter. Tyrone led by 0-9 to 0-2 when Kerry adopted more direct tactics, moving the more robust Johnny Crowley and then Dara Ó Cinnéide to the square. Yet, Cormac grew further in stature. He loped and leaped and intercepted with precision. Gumshield in hand, he was a vocal rear admiral. 'When he spoke in the backline, he gave a more calming reassurance than most,' Ciaran Gourley recalls. 'After a mistake, he'd try to encourage you rather than shout at you.'

At the end, Cormac faced the crowd bare-chested, hollered and raised his sinewy arms, with an inside-out Kerry jersey in his right hand. He linked shoulders with John Devine in uber-exuberance. These soon became iconic images of a famous win, a lifted yoke.

It was a major milestone. But Cormac couldn't say so to the semi-circle of dictaphones that converged on him in the corridor after Tyrone's lengthy post-match rituals. To admit it would have been to dim the focus on the ultimate goal. '[I]t's only a means to an end. If we don't do it in five weeks' time it will be quickly forgotten about.'

Within hours, that milestone became a millstone. 'Puke football' and other spiky words about the game – i.e. about Tyrone – peppered the airwaves and copy for Monday's southern papers.

Privately, Cormac said there was 'a bit of sour grapes' in the discourse. On TV, he stuck to a more diplomatic tone: the quality of the game was a matter of people's opinion, and no doubt neutrals who wanted lots of scores and free-flowing football were disappointed, but Tyrone's game-plan worked very well. And that game-plan was not to foul Kerry men; Mickey Harte had never sent them out to do that.

Whatever about his team, Cormac's own profile glowed brighter still. Having kept four men scoreless from play, he would be named 'star man' by the *Irish News*, and rated 8.5.

What did he think?

OFF.	DEF.	HEAD	BODY	LEGS
7	9	8½	8	8

★

The weekend after Tyrone beat Kerry, Eglish made the long return journey to Clann na nGael. The stakes were high. Both teams were stuck in a league-table log-jam; a win could send us into top-six territory, but defeat could knock us well down. There was needle, too. We sought to avenge our defeat in March, and a vocal local crowd made the venue intimidating. A plastic bottle was hurled over the fence. Despite Cormac's 3 points, we trailed narrowly in the last quarter. After several soft frees and a surfeit of stoppages, we scowled at the referee.

We raided forward for an equalizer. The chance fell to Cormac, over on the right. As he drew back on the trigger, a Clannsman charged at him from the left. He seemed to see the man out of the corner of his eye, for he corkscrewed wide. Then, BANG!

The hit was late. Later than Gay Byrne's stuffed owl in the back carriage of the final Enterprise train after signal failure and leaves on the track. Later than Jools Holland and James Last jamming on a mash-up of the *Sunday Game* theme-tune at a Coppers after-party.

Did I mention it was late?

It was lights out for Cormac and for Eglish. Concussion once again. We gathered up his stuff and Ashlene drove him to hospital – this time to Altnagelvin, Derry. But A&E was busy at 9.50; he'd be there till the early hours, if not overnight, and next-day plans would go out the window.

So he didn't wait. They left for Ashlene's family house, where she woke every two hours to check on him, as the hospital leaflet advised. By Sunday afternoon, they were with the Tyrone panel in Croke Park to watch the Armagh v. Donegal semi-final. To see him all the way home in the car, playing 'Name That Tune' with her and friends Dermot and Johanne McCloskey, and laughing non-stop, you'd think there was nothing wrong with him. And yet . . .

Tuesday, 2 September
Started back training tonight. I pulled out after warm-up due to ongoing headaches from Sat. night's concussion. Must have been 20 jerseys to sign. Hype building, teachers getting on nerves and pupil banter hasn't even started yet. I will be fine, just keep thinking positive, anything in the air is mine, on the ground I cut out the space. We must prepare to run down their throats, lose the ball, get up & go again. Gonna enjoy the hype & roll with it, no point in getting stressed, it's the same ball we always play with!

Thursday, 4 September
Headaches are worse, so didn't train tonight. Watched on though – team is flying. If we get a good start we could beat them well. I think we'll enjoy the next two weeks, the excitement is great. Even after that there's still plenty of time to get serious, so no over-hyping for the moment. Just embedding the belief of victory and the sight of Peter (& me) going up those steps & lifting Sam.

On Saturday the 6th, Cormac drove to Craigavon A&E for the tests he should've had a week earlier. The hospital records state:

Occipital headache radiating to front. Photophobia + neck stiffness yesterday. Lightheadedness. Unable to concentrate. Sleepiness. Nauseous today. No vomiting. Worse on straining. Better lying down.

An X-ray of his skull showed no swelling. He was put on painkillers and went home. But the pain remained.

Tuesday 9 September
Trained tonight. Brutally tough.
5 × 5 sets of 30 second sprints. After 2 sets I was knackered, my eyes weren't focusing too well – I went in: worried that this may hamper my fitness or mental toughness, but better being safe than a tragic hero.

Why on earth did Cormac contemplate the prospect of being a 'tragic hero', let alone write it down, nineteen days before the All-Ireland final? That's something we'll never fully fathom.

He was never one for morbid thoughts, or so we would have assumed. You could pass it off as diary fodder, a casual overstatement of emotion in a private setting. But he wasn't prone to wild statements of any form in any forum. He was a man of facts.

Clearly, he had been physically and mentally troubled often during 2003. The headaches must've been bad, to cause him to skip training. No one at home recalls him making a massive issue about them – though Mummy recently summoned up a memory of Cormac talking about feeling a sensation like his brain was rattling around in his head. Something like that, she thinks.

Reading his diary, we wonder.

Was something seriously wrong or was he overstating it in the diary?

If the former, did he try to tell us somehow and did we ignore him or miss signs?

Did he decide not to tell us, lest we disregard his complaints as exaggerated?

Was his eyesight blurred by lactate due to intense sprinting, or was something else causing dizziness?

Did he feel something in his heart back then?

It's not clear when the headaches abated, but Cormac returned to training.

★

September '03 was the craziest of months. A four-week run-up to the All-Ireland football final, Tyrone v. Armagh. The first time neighbours from one province would contest Sam.

Our home area hadn't seen such fervour since the O'Neill chieftains and their battles royale. Cormac, hopping across the county frontier to work, was stuck right in the middle of it.

There was the usual silliness of counties in finals: bunting, banal banners, spray-painted cars, dyed sheep, doggerel and ditties on FM playlists. 'We Didn't Start the Fire', Tyrone 2003 style, had the line, 'Cormac, number three / Wouldn't like to referee.' Purely a non sequitur, lyricist Hugh Sally assures me.

The hype hit new frequencies. There was lots of talk of age-old enmity, sure, but there were outbursts of ecumenism too. Flags and jerseys of the two counties were sold side by side, even in Daddy's shop. Armagh people wished Cormac good luck – just not too much of it.

There was goodwill all around him at home. 'Good Luck to Cormac' was writ large on overhead banners at the entrance to Eglish village, another passing Daly's yard, another at Barrett Concrete, and another at Jordan Engineering near home. There was a placard on Eglish GAA clubhouse, one from the camogie club down the road, and a big one at Derrylatinee P.S. His name even intruded on Holmesie's on the Benburb street banner.

The media hype was monumental. The Belfast dailies obsessed over the local derby lore, the holders-versus-hopefuls angle, and the underlying subtext that this pairing embodied an emboldened northern nationalism in the peacetime era. The Dublin ones focused on the six counties' debt to the munificence of Her Majesty's purse, and the inevitability – Nordies being Nordies – of brawls on the pitch and riots between fans.

Cormac must've been the most interviewed player before the final. After the team press-night, some younger guns who had answered all media calls to date suddenly – and wisely – muzzled up. Peter was flying quite low, due to his injury. But Cormac went out of his way as usual. He granted the Sundays and telly men several one-on-one meetings in Benburb. 'He'd hate to see you stuck for an interview,'

Malachy Clerkin observed in the *Sunday Tribune*. (And Daddy hated to see you refer to 'bric-a-brac' in his shop, Malachy.)

He maintained a cheery front. A fortnight out, at the *Irish News* Ulster GAA All-Stars dinner, he was clearly pleased as punch to receive his full-back award. On the front of the next day's paper, he and Seán Cavanagh were flashing toothy smiles among a beaming Tyrone bunch; but only Paul McGrane of the Armagh quartet could muster a half-grin.

Under the surface, Cormac found the weeks really dragging now. Constant match-chat made the days long. Pupils showed him their pictures with Armagh players and Sam, prophesying more of the same. *Whaddya think, Sir*? He stayed smiling, while privately wishing to swat it away. The Tír Eoghain bag over his shoulder and fluffy red pencil-case and red-and-white duster on his desk said enough.

'Hard to focus on school at the moment,' he wrote in his diary, wary of his mounting in-tray. Now he had charge of the A-Level Politics class. He was ambitious and eager to please, but maintaining focus on match preparation was the priority now; other things would have to wait. 'Starting to close out the crap as I get together with the team more.'

Ten days out, he had his assignment:

Thursday, 18 September
Found out tonight. Marking McDonnell. This is the big one. I break
it away, Ricey sweeps up. Every ball, every 30 seconds we must concentrate. We will win if we do this. Gear arrived this evening, all plus
insignia, absolutely brilliant, but not worth a damn if we don't win.
We will win – Armagh won't expect what we have.

Steven McDonnell was the big one. He had bagged 5-23 over the championship and surely Player of the Year awards already. His prowess high and low was the kernel of Armagh's long-ball tactics. This match-up was set in stone, Mickey said; but if McDonnell were to switch out, Cormac would stay to mark the new man and hold the square. Again, Mickey added, tell no one; you know the way these things could get back to Armagh.

Cormac wrote on a plain white page with a black permanent marker:

* IN HIS FACE
* 30 SECONDS
* MY BALL

He posted it up in his bedroom, so that it would be the first thing he'd see when he awoke in the morning. He needed something more, though.

He asked a favour of Fergus: could he Photoshop the Sam Maguire Cup in place of the NFL trophy in Peter's upstretched hands? Done. Up on the good wall.

That was doubly optimistic thinking. The team didn't know whether Peter would be fit to play. 'I didn't really ask too many questions,' he said later, 'and whenever I did, nobody was really too sure.' In theory, Cormac could've been leading the team out on to the Croke Park pitch. But that's not where his head was at. Without Peter, they'd probably have no cup to lift.

The mention of tickets was the one thing guaranteed to set Cormac off at home as the days ticked by. He begged to hear nothing of them, but still family members dragged him into their deliberations over allocations.

He escaped with the team for a weekend at the Dublin hotel, to acclimatize for the big-day preparations. At a team meeting, the players broke into groups and reached a consensus as to how to beat Armagh and beat them well. Cormac came home revitalized and jotted down more mental notes:

Sunday, 21 September
One week to go and blood is pumping. Don't want to be remembered for wrong reasons – we've got one chance – we write the script. Must go through hell to win this – no one said it would be easy. Next week – no papers, plenty of relaxation – no fools suffered at school. Remember – I came through hell against Kerry, I can do it again.

On Monday evening, he went up to Derry for adjustments by Marie McElhinney, the chiropractor. Ready for road.

On Tuesday evening, the team was named. Now he could tell his back-unit what he needed them to do.

On Wednesday afternoon, his last school class was interrupted by a 'security alert'. He ordered all out of his third-floor classroom, locked up, turned around and was greeted by 500 applauding pupils in a guard of honour with Tyrone colours all the way down the stairs, and a reception in the Crush Hall. 'I really didn't expect you had it in you,' he said at the bottom, genuinely touched by the gesture.

Wednesday, 24 September
Confident and calm. Have plan worked out and ready. Near side from wings, Ricey cover middle. From middle, jockey him one on each side. High balls are mine. In his face – 30 secs – My ball. Psycho for the ball.

Thursday afternoon, team rendezvous. Cormac was about to hand in his homework – a sheet of positive statements about each teammate – when he learned of his mistake. He had taken the brief to be a bit of fun.

Declan McCrossan: 'Will need an interpreter in London (as will Stevie).'
Cormac McGinley: 'Can use that engineering degree to design himself a few new knees & ankles.'
Brian McGuigan: 'Has recovered well from injury sustained when Greg McCartan threw the ball at him.'

Perturbed by his error, he sat down and wrote out a new set of comments, all complimentary. A game of golf, a team meeting, and a chance to wind down at last.

Friday, at home to rest and pack. The remainder of the run-in would be like clockwork, as ever with Mickey's teams.

Saturday noon, departure. Peter was declared fit to start. That left one more matter to be resolved: Ciaran Gourley's creaky shoulder. Paddy Tally called on Cormac and Conor Gormley during the evening session at the Cuala ground. They took it in turns to hammer Ciaran's humerus. He survived, and would play.

Retiring to his room after dinner, Cormac picked up an envelope from the ground, and opened it. Inside was a sheet of personal compliments from the other thirty players.

Eighteen of them used the words 'leader' or 'leadership'. The others were perhaps even nicer to read, for he was less used to hearing them: 'can play anywhere'; 'supremely focused'; 'most dedicated of trainers'; 'great temperament'; 'gives good simple advice'; 'steady influence on the players around him'; 'instils confidence'; 'tunnel vision for Tyrone football team'; 'never lets you down'; 'plays every minute of the game with the same intensity as the 1st minute'; and 'I have never seen a sign of weakness from him'.

Flattery wouldn't keep out the Armagh scores, however. His memos to self were the key. He picked up the Fitzpatrick Killiney Hotel notepad and pencilled them down again:

FIGHT OR FLIGHT?
DO IT – THINK ABOUT IT
IN HIS FACE – 30 SECS – MY BALL

Do all that, confine McDonnell to a humble score, and Tyrone would likely conquer. He was confident about all that as he tucked himself in. But the pressure of being the buck-stopper, with those internal memos pulsating around his brain, kept him awake.

Desperate, he got up, paced the corridor and headed for the lobby. There he met the peroxide blond mop of Mugsy. They would be at opposite ends of the pitch and in many ways they were polar opposites of each other. But here they were united in insomnia.

They talked through their duels, before Cormac concluded, 'All you can do is your best.'

On that simpler note, he returned to his room and nodded off, eventually.

★

In Croke Park, there was a flip-chart sheet taped to the dressing-room wall. This was Paddy Tally's precis of the Tyrone players' discussions seven days earlier, as to how exactly they would beat

Armagh. The team was going to have fifty-five per cent of midfield possession. They would lead by 0-8 to 0-5 at half-time, and win the game by 0-16 to 0-9.

Cormac shared this confidence, but there was no complacency; of all players, he couldn't afford it. The Armagh squad knew him inside-out. Ten of them had played alongside him at school or university, and two of the backroom team had worked with him. Ten times he had played inter-county against Armagh. Forget the Tyrone compliments sheet; they could have written a thesis about his strengths.

On this day, they saw him as a weak – even the weakest – link for Tyrone. Three times in a row, opposition teams had let him loll about the back lawn unchallenged for most of the game. He was still a novice, learning the ropes. When put to the test by the best, good, hard and early, might he not crumble? In truth, the same thought occurred to some of Cormac's biggest fans.

On this day, this Sunday of Sundays, Cormac would be tested; he would be made to feel pain. But he saw it coming and readied himself.

While the other 14 huddled as one after the parade, he was all fast-feet sprints back and forth and sideways, high knees to finish. When he burrowed in to join arms, the Circle was perfect.

Tyrone led 0-2 to 0-1 when the first real test came. For a full-back, the tests rarely exceed seven seconds.

Game time: 04:56–05:01. Diarmaid Marsden gave Gormley the slip, ransacked goal-ward and pulled the trigger at the square's edge. Sharp inhale. A tap-in now, surely. He swung back and . . . from behind, unseen, Cormac dived with one hand and tugged on his triceps. Marsden lost balance, sliced the kick, and the ball spun so wildly – whooh! – that it stayed in play and Tyrone gathered it. It was a humongous let-off. Gormley could mark down an IOU to No. 3.

It was also a foul, TBH. Not quite a stonewall penalty, but worth a free-kick anywhere else. Cormac got away with it as he had gone for the ball and had pulled so snappily that the ref couldn't be sure in real time. Credit to Armagh, who played on without complaint.

From that relief, Tyrone strung together three points to go 0-5 to 0-1 ahead.

17:18–17:27. Marsden catapulted the ball diagonally over the top to the right of the goal. 'Horse' Devlin, covering back, flailed at it. But McDonnell took it low on the ground, squirmed between Devlin and Cormac – who was trying to block the outlet to Ronan Clarke – and hooked it over with his left. 0-5 to 0-2.

27:22–27:25. McDonnell ran at a right angle towards the Cusack Stand to collect a fist-pass on the bounce, with Cormac in hot pursuit. Another man would turn, survey options, solo or pass. But McDonnell gathered, swung and kicked over his shoulder in one fluid motion, without a straight look at the target. No one in Ireland could've blocked it. 0-6 to 0-4.

The test was becoming tougher by the minute.

28:39–28:44. Cormac shouldered John McEntee 60 yards out, but the ball skipped across to McDonnell on the far flank, who panic-shot from 40 yards under pressure from Gourley. Wide.

30:30–30:33. Cormac strayed over halfway to join in an attack. The ball was lost, and he stiffened himself up to win it back with a side-to-side shudder. But he plunged in hastily and caught McGeeney on the midriff. It wasn't a very big hit, but there was a man down. Yellow card for Cormac – Tyrone's first. Harsh, he felt, compared to some stuff that was going unpunished. Like what would pass six minutes later.

34:52–34:57. A short Tyrone kick-out was intercepted and passed to McDonnell. McMenamin had his right side, so he dummied over to his left and shot while Cormac tried to block. Wide again.

36:28–36:34. Cormac bent down to pick up the ball from a ruck, and an Armagh man muscled him to the ground. On his knees, he was hit by one-two quick jabs to his face, and fell flat on his back. Punishment for the puncher: a free-kick and tick in the ref's notebook.

Half-time passed, noisily. Tyrone led by 0-8 to 0-4. With Peter staying inside for treatment, Cormac was nominal leader on the battlefield. But he let others lay down the law in the Circle. Game on again, he focused on his personal battle, calling repeatedly to his fellow backs:

1. Close down the space for long balls in behind them to full-forward; and

2. Two extra men under the breaks from any high ball.

This half went much better for Cormac. His pre-match

compliment for McMenamin – 'The sort of man you want to have beside you in the trenches' – was validated: Ricey ran repeatedly to his rescue. As the game got stuck in static warfare, and Tyrone stayed in front, McDonnell was living off scraps. The Armagh man foraged deep, but the lone point-shot that he got dropped short.

Cormac worked even more determinedly to deprive possession. Time and again, high and low, he got in with a fist to punch it away from McDonnell.

Coming down the stretch, 3 points ahead, still he worried. 'It wasn't the sort of game where your nerves went away and you relaxed,' he recalled later. 'Armagh could win the next ball, pump it into our square and anything could happen.'

Anything all but happened.

67:28–67:35.

Andrew McCann's high ball dropped on the Tyrone 21. Cormac went psycho for the ball, as promised, and called for it. 'MY BALL!' From the corner of his right eye he saw a nearby teammate whom he thought was staying down. No: he and Sean Cavanagh collided mid-air and the ball bounced off both of them towards Tony McEntee. On his knees, Cormac dived to put a hand in. But McEntee's fist-pass found McDonnell lying behind, six yards out.

Goal here! Cormac said to himself, as he lay prostrate on the grass. *McDonnell doesn't miss these.*

He didn't see Conor Gormley rushing in. He didn't even see The Block. He saw the aftermath, though. *A lifesaver!* IOU repaid with interest.

Back up on his toes, Cormac readied himself for another incoming missile. Later he would describe the feeling as 'living on the edge of your nerves hoping that something bad wouldn't happen'. It didn't. The ball ping-ponged about for a couple of minutes up at the other end. To the end.

Within seconds, a sea of bodies flooded the pitch. Thousands of faces whirling around him, one huge blur.

Through the Garda cordon, he gave a firm handshake to Armagh (and ex-Queen's) trainer, John McCloskey: 'Thanks for all the help you gave me in the past.'

He walked up the steps of the Hogan Stand and thought to himself, *It's like I imagined it, but I can't believe it.*

He stood halfway up the steps, looking into the crowd for people he knew, shaking his fist jubilantly. With a big animated face, he leaned forward to gesture to someone. 'Look!' he shouted repeatedly, pointing up to Peter. *This is perfect. Peter is the man we want to be lifting Sam.*

Cormac waited his turn to raise the cup. He had won the full set now – minor, under-21, senior.

When the commotion began to calm, he took down that flip-chart sheet from the wall, folded it and tucked it into his bag. It was now an artefact to be put in a bedroom drawer and taken out on some far-off day to illustrate the tale of Tyrone's first All-Ireland title.

*

When the final whistle went . . . I went running up the field and the first fella I actually met was my brother, Dónal. He just came straight up to my face and that was a bit of a shock too. And then once he had come on, we were being mobbed, and I was sort of carried over to the presentation area. [Interview for 'Northern Exposure' documentary, BBC NI, recorded 29 September 2003]

My ticket had me on the very front row of the Hogan Stand, about ground level in line with the '50'. For much of the second half, Cormac was in my direct eye-line. In the event of Tyrone winning, I was on a mission.

With that last parp of the whistle, I was off. My legs hurdled the hoarding and hit the turf running. My head felt dizzy with delight and the ethereality of invading like a frontiersman on virgin soil. My body hurtled towards its target. My arms girdled his waist from behind. My voice called to divert from his clinch with Collie Holmes, who had just beaten me to him. Then he twisted around and saw me. 'Dónal! Dónal!' he shouted, grabbed my arm and turned for the Hogan. But a tornado of fans swept him away and we lost contact.

Through the din, I dialled up Seán Bán Breathnach. After a

midweek *Raidió na Gaeltachta* interview, he insisted that I call for a favour if Tyrone won. True to his word, he answered. He wangled me past security and down the tunnel. Part of me felt guilty to have this privileged passage: I was never a bandwagoner, nor an accessor of VIP areas – let alone a team sanctuary – on any match-day. But this was one big chance to share Cormac's lifetime achievement with him, and I couldn't pass it up.

Our timing was perfect. The Circle had celebrated and sat down again. Reporters nudged against an open door. SBB led my way. I tiptoed in, fearing players might think, 'What's HE doing here?' I shook a few hands till I reached my man. 'Dónal!' Cue embraces, emotions and effusions. Seconds later, a photographer ushered us together. Snap! That image of us, shoulders locked with Sam in hands, would become our defining image as brothers.

None of that could happen nowadays. Croke Park celebrations have become so sanitized: hired goons in orange vests bar you from the pitch; men in dark suits say your name's not down; and dressing rooms stay more tightly shut. It's a pity. For Cormac probably sensed in those two encounters, more than any words I'd ever say, how proud he made me.

13. The Mornings After

He arose the next morning drowsy but tingling with that transcendental feeling: *Yeah, we've won it. And it's not a dream! No more football to be played now. We've won it; we've done what we said we'd do. This is the top of the world.*

That was his favourite moment, outside of glory day itself.

He saw life would never be quite the same again for that group of players. They were history-makers, mould-breakers, football earth-quakers. They'd always be the Edmund Hillarys and Roger Bannisters of Tyrone, regardless of who or what followed them. Even modest John Devine could see it. 'We're made men now,' he declared.

The *Irish News* had been running wraparound full-colour covers after the big games that summer. Today, that front page was dominated by Cormac, braying joy with his fist in the air, above the word 'CHAMPIONS'. That became the paper's top-selling issue of all time.

There was no chance of Cormac losing the run of himself. He saw this great triumph not as the natural end of the journey, but as another point on the path of glory.

OFF.	DEF.	HEAD	BODY	LEGS
6	7½	8	7	7½

The pattern of ink on his page suggests he didn't write this up till a fortnight later. Many another man would have jacked in the self-assessment by this stage, or awarded himself top marks out of pure glee.

Not Cormac. 6 out of 10 he evaluated himself for Offence. As winning full-back in an All-Ireland final, who had marked the most dangerous goal-scorer in the sport and who had crossed the halfway line a couple of times. He must've been thinking, *I must go forward more as full-back in future finals*.

He was equally level-headed in the many interviews he gave in the hours after the final. Live on the *Sunday Game* at the post-match banquet, he spoke highly of Armagh as outgoing champions and as people of goodwill. His line for the Six-One news was about having fulfilled his ambition – 'And now my ambition has to shift.' When journos fired questions about title number two, he said he'd make no bold predictions now, but in due course they intended to win more. Cue the heading, 'McAnallen Hungry For Even More All-Irelands'.

Back to that Monday morning. Something he said later, in an interview with Séamus Maloney for *The Sons of Sam*, I see now as the starting point, or perhaps the restart, of another emotion: 'You didn't have a minute to yourself because the moment you woke up you were trying to get breakfast, and there was a crowd in the lobby. Trying to get your bags on to the bus, little things like that were impossible; you were being mobbed. If you thought you could unwind the morning after, you had another think coming.'

On its own, that comment would be inconsequential. But such expressions would recur.

Aughnacloy was unrecognizable from his last homecoming, with the under-21s in 2000. Thousands jammed the streets today. He was determined to squeeze every last drop from these moments. He found the highest possible vantage point on the open-top bus. He reached his big open palms skyward for the aerial pictures. He got a camera and took a few pictures, looking down. He pointed and gestured towards friends and family, as he always did on these occasions, whatever the distance.

Omagh that evening was a sight never seen before. That long, sloped High Street – the site of death and bloodshed five years earlier – was now a vibrant, roaring amazon of white and red, and tens of thousands of heads. '*Tháinig ar lá*' proclaimed a shopfront banner at the top. A TG4 interviewer asked for a vox pop *as Gaeilge* from Cormac on stage.

'*Is é an oíche is fearr i mo shaol*,' he managed to utter amid the pandemonium.

The team diverted to stay the night in Donegal Town, oddly enough. Cormac was in big demand in the hotel the next morning. Folks from our grandparents' home areas flocked to see him. Obliging to the last, he said he'd return on a special trip. 'Cormac to Bring Sam to Letterbarrow', ran the story in the *Donegal Democrat*.

It was a long time since he had let his hair down with the Tyrone lads, so he made the most of these nights out while he could. He sang and shouted and jumped around, and had a few drinks too. But after the GOAL charity match at Omagh on Wednesday evening, he was back to the daily grind by Thursday.

He walked on air at school. Quiet congrats came his way, but no one caused a scene. 'I didn't say a lot either. I think I just had a big cheesy grin on my face. I didn't rub it in. They knew.'

But he did say something of note. He pinned a thank-you card on a school noticeboard:

> To all pupils who
> expressed best wishes before
> the final and / or congratulations
> afterwards, a big thank you
> – It was very much appreciated.
> Thanks especially to 8M for
> Their cards and 'survival kit'.
> C. McA.
> P.S. Commiserations to all
> Armaghians, you were there
> before and will be again!

Thursday evening, he was sitting in Havelock House, Belfast, being interviewed on UTV's *End to End*. That title could've applied to his part in the homecoming tour. Nearly every bush Sam beat about in east Tyrone, and even Stormont Castle, he was there. He was truly overwhelmed by the response everywhere.

On Saturday night, there was a slightly illicit, off-schedule detour to his native area. Neighbours packed out the Brantry BARD for the local champion.

Sam slept in our house and was spirited to Eglish under cover for our game with Dromore the next day. We lost by a point to the league leaders. We didn't want it as badly as they did – for they wanted it badly. When Cormac got on the ball, he heard a guttural voice taunting him. The words were immaterial, but who'd be barracking him at all, especially in this glory week?

It couldn't be.

It was.

His left-hand man from seven days earlier. Now in opposing trenches, he was on the receiving end of the grenades for the first time. Unhappily.

In the car-park, he handed over Sam for its trip to Dromore.

'What was that all about, Ricey?'

'*Rashin' fashin'RickRastardly,*' he mumbled, sheepishly. Or words to that effect.

Welcome back to club football, Cormac.

He went to visit Dermot Donaghy in the Royal Victoria Hospital. Dermot had been hit head-on by a wayward car on his return from Dublin to the Omagh homecoming. His aorta ruptured and only a clot saved him. The other driver died. The news put a bitter twist in Cormac's sweetest week, so he was glad to see his teammate in recovery. He was the only man who bothered to bring a useful gift – though Dermot had read Niall Quinn's book already.

Two days later, Sam made his formal visit to Eglish. The village had never known an evening like it. Cormac jumped on a pick-up truck platform outside Daly's yard and held the cup aloft past lines of cheering locals from 'chapel corner' to Connolly Park. At the club hall, hundreds crammed in. On stage, Mickey Harte praised the 'honest, hard people' of our club, and hinted at his plans for Cormac. 'My prediction is that one day he will bring this cup to Eglish as captain of the Tyrone seniors.'

Cormac spoke last. He praised the clubmen who had helped to put him there, especially Paddy McIntosh for those Sunday sessions long ago. And he threw down a challenge to the youngsters at the front, 'Who's gonna be the next player up on this stage. Is it you?' he asked, pointing. 'Or you?' Pointing again.

At Benburb, Cormac was back on speaking duty; it was really Holmesie's village, but he left it to Cormac to address the assemblage from the steps of the bus at 'Sean McGuigan's corner'. The cavalcade closed off the evening in the Moy, where Cormac had first kicked a leather ball.

Homecomings done, he longed for a return to relative normality. One way was to suspend the monastic diet. That sausage supper and battered fish was simply divine. And the slug in his lettuce at the wedding dinner that Friday must've been telling him to pig out a bit; why else land on *his* plate, after sliming through all the guests' salad in the kitchen?

Seriously though, he had so much to do, and so little time to do it. He worried that he had left his A-Level class badly behind, and he might struggle to make up ground, because another compromise rules trip to Australia loomed. A prospect that thrilled him before his debut in 2001 now troubled him. He was in two minds: torn between the honour of Ireland duty and all that he'd leave behind.

He discussed it with Ashlene. She told him straight: don't go. He made his mind up not to go. Then John O'Keeffe rang to tell him he was needed. He hmm-ed and hah-ed his way through the call up in his bedroom. He was even more conflicted now.

Downstairs, he and Ashlene sat on the sofa to watch *Meet the Parents*, again.

In walked Daddy. 'What's this rubbish yiz're watchin'?' he demanded, before sitting down to watch it with them.

The subject of Australia came up. Cormac intimated that he wasn't set.

'Sure why wouldn't you go? What's keeping you here?'

When Daddy put it like that, he found it hard to answer.

Eventually, Cormac decided to go. After all, the chance mightn't come again.

Mrs Martin accommodated his request for leave. In a mad rush, he diligently prepared plans for his classes during his three-week absence. But the worries didn't leave him.

★

Cormac kept a regular diary in Australia. The entries give a poignant insight into the mind of one who was struggling with life at the top.

Thursday, 16 October

Met up with team this evening at Citywest. It said I had to be there, *we* had to be there. Turned out that only about 8 of the players turned up this evening, the rest have obviously taken care of business before meeting up. Feeling under pressure to socialise with fellas who don't want to . . . Excellent gear though, loads of T-shirts, shorts, socks, tops, and nice suits.

O'Keefe [sic] even demanded that no one have any beer – even if we could have a drink then we could mix a little – as it is conversation is difficult with a lot of them.

Friday, 17 October

Trained this morning at Saggart. I know now that two weeks training is going to be a big trial for me. Back for lunch. Some eating in these team meals!

Was going to go playing golf this evening but had to jettison a bag – I had far too much stuff! After several phone calls [uncle] Seán eventually agreed to come out from the city, but it took him about 1 hr 30 mins to get out to the Citywest. By that time I felt terrible – his time is worth considerably more than the €40 it would have cost to transport the bags by taxi. Already I sense the Armagh players cold towards me – they're especially cliquish. I always feel, though, that someone else is having the craic, the funny conversations, and that I'm left out – so maybe there's not too much wrong after all.

Saturday, 18 October

Leaving for Australia, watched England v. S. Africa in world cup on TV in Heathrow . . . Feels like I've been away from home about a week. Me feeling a little detached from the core of the group has not been helped by being separated from everyone else on the long-haul flights. Still, it gives me time to do some reading without having to make conversation with someone who won't talk to me but will turn round and laugh away with the next fella.

Sunday, 19 October

Spent all day flying – mostly read Tony Adams' 'Addicted', got about ¼ way through it. In Singapore we went to a swimming pool / Jacuzzi facility outdoors. It was good, but again I felt left out – I don't know if there is any evidence to support this or if I am just being very insecure. If the latter, then this surely leads others to isolate me, whereas they would be drawn to the confident, strident figure who takes control. Still, slept for 6 hours from London to Singapore ('avec tablet'), good to pass journey much quicker.

Why such bad form and so lonely? 'A trip like this can be a bit of a drag if you've had a lot of football.' Trevor Giles' comments on TV were general in nature, but very true for Cormac. Insomnia was clearly another issue for him. He couldn't forget home either; he rang back to school to enquire about the Politics class. His fears about players ostracizing him were in part due to recent negative southern and Armagh reactions to all things Tyrone; indeed, the 'puke' stigma of '03 survives today.

Monday, 20 October
Arrived in Perth about 1 a.m., got to hotel room. We had talked plenty about how to avoid jetlag and getting good sleep once we got here. But I somehow knew that I wouldn't sleep. And so it transpired – I was roomed with Gary Cox, and he got to sleep after about 30 mins. I tossed and turned for hours – I thought I had all that over me – tried to watch TV to drop off, then read for a long time. I eventually got about 2 or 3 hours, but was very upset about the whole thing. This had better improve or it will undermine everything good about the whole trip.

Tuesday, 21 October
Played warm-up match today, vs 'The Black n White Mighty Fighting Swans' at Bassendean Oval. Started at full-back, but was caught out of position at the start – my man took a mark and scored the first over of the day – I don't think Jonno was too impressed. Word is that the Aussie full forward Barry Hall, 6' 4" & 16 st., is a big dirty brute. I will have my work cut out – playing full back ain't easy in this game. O'Keefe [sic] has also stipulated that no one is allowed down the street during the day, or

out to play golf or other attractions. What a joke – we'll be stuck all day in the 'team room' playing pool and table tennis. So far things are boring. Slept OK last night, with a tablet – it's not the answer!

Wednesday, 22 October
Had major bother sleeping last night. Didn't get a tablet off [Dr] Con, lay awake until 4 a.m. It's really getting inside my head now, not a physical problem at all. It's making me unhappy and – dare I say it – a little depressed. This evening was pure torture. Went to Governor's reception at 6 p.m., back at 7.30 p.m. Played pool for a while, some boys went away to casino or for dinner but I had to stay around to get traction treatment for my neck from Eamon [Ó Muircheartaigh] the physio. After that Paddy Christie was the only man about . . . [and] we got a sandwich back at the hotel. It was great, but I had to scoff it into me really quickly, I couldn't even enjoy it. I needed to talk to someone, so I rang Mummy. I broke down crying, just didn't feel happy at all. We talked it through and agreed that it was probably just me coming down off the high emotions and stress levels of the previous few weeks. Didn't want to bother Ashlene, but felt that it would be good to talk to her as well. She is my rock, and it did make me feel a whole lot better to talk to her. I love her and am missing her an awful lot, which no doubt is part of my unhappiness. After I was finished I went down to a meeting in the team room, where I got chatting to Con. I told him that I wasn't happy, and he picked up that I had been crying . . . He really helped me get my situation in perspective, and catch a grip.

Thursday, 23 October
Slept OK, with tablet – Getting my head round match tomorrow night, it's helping me get my mind off my emotions, but to be honest I'll be happy just to get it over with and a decent performance. Boredom of hanging round hotel is wrecking my head, and a lot of the others fellas also . . .

Friday, 24 October
First Test tonight, Subiaco Oval, 6.45. Super stadium, excellent

playing surface. Felt that I had got myself up for the match well enough, even though I still wasn't so sure of my total resolve if things started going badly. Match started OK, Hall physically imposing, but we were well on top for the first while. When he did get a couple of balls played in, he made excellent runs and took a couple of good marks. Forwards weren't working hard at all off the ball, and Aussies worked ball out too easy. Their main men had plenty of time to look for options up front, allowing Hall to make his run. 2nd quarter I denied his space a little better and he took no marks. 3rd quarter, a forward bore down 1 on 1 with Enda, shot it past him, and as I slid back to clear it I deflected it into our net. It was unlucky, and when Hall took a mark & scored an over a minute later I could easily have quit. Instead, I knuckled down and denied him possession well a couple of times. Their 3rd goal may also be pinned on me, as Pavlich (who I was marking at the time) won a mark after Brown had set a screen for me. I yelled at Brian White for ignoring the same offence twice in a row as I stood the mark, then the ball was popped over my head to the onrushing Harvey who crossed for Crawford to goal. There wasn't very much I could do, but ignorant people would no doubt point it out. 7 minutes from the end McGeeney & Chris Johnson got entangled, another Aussie came in and tried to walk over him, pushing him back. I thought 'to hell with this' and came in to match up with Johnson – nothing really, just holding jerseys. A minute later we both got yellow cards for 3rd man in – Hardly matters, we've lost at this stage anyway. I was totally proud of my actions. I felt that I did OK, especially considering where I had been earlier in the week. Afterwards . . . met up with team in Rosie O'Grady's. Stayed there till 1.30, then on to Paramount . . . plenty of craic – talked to many players for only the first time (this sort of night should have been on Monday or Tuesday) . . .

Sunday, 26 October
Had an awful night last night, one of those where you just wish for morning . . . I got chatting to Dessie Ryan in the Fenians pub across the road for about 2 hrs . . . Started [going out] at Northbridge, before going to Subiaco Hotel. Now if there'd been a good crowd,

and I had been in good form, it would have been excellent, but I was just not up to it and went on home. Phoned home (wished I was home with them), then tried to watch TV and read until I fell asleep, from around 11.30 to 3.00. Eventually went, woke up about 8. Slept on for another hour, and got breakfast and Mass. Mass was a great tonic, helped me clear my head and focus on my own needs and situation. Later on Sunday I wanted to watch the Rugby, but team officials dictated that we had to take a boat cruise along the Swan river in Perth. It was OK, nice bit of food and scenery was nice, but it dragged on a bit and WE WERE MISSING THE RUGBY . . . Back to hotel and early night for flight next morning (avec tablet – bien sûr – Je m'appelle Cormac!)

Made Ulster championship draw for next year – Tyrone v. Derry in prelim round – well done Cormac!

He faced his own trial by online media after the first Test. His performance became a cipher for Ireland's failings, not least in his struggles to contain Hall, the Aussies' 6′ 4″ target-man, with no real cover. He was spot-on with the 'big dirty brute' tagline, for Hall pinned those boxer's fists to his throat. The criticism from the media and online would be a mere historical trifle were Cormac not so upset, close to paranoia.

He was all chin-up in public. You could see him in the papers, laughing on a surfboard, apparently in his element. And there's no doubt he enjoyed some of the tour and fared better in the second Test. But he made his plans to fly home three days early.

Monday, 27 October
Up early for flight, feeling a little better. Interacting well with players and others like Brian Mullins & Marty Morrissey, but on my terms, not trying to get them to like me (which I had been doing). When we got to Melbourne we went straight into the hotel gym, which was amazing. We were told to do a good workout, but most of the fellas did 15 mins then went in . . . I got on with my work away from them and did twice as much. After dinner we went to casino. Set limit of $100, but could only find $25 table. Had it spent in 10

mins. I guess I'm just not a gambler. As days go on I feel lower, it is then that I wish I had the assurance of Ashlene to talk to, or at least my own environs at home. Well, only a week to go now anyway.

Tuesday, 28 October
Pretty uneventful day – trained in morning – myself & Odran slept in and got taxi to MCG. Later on, did laundry. Ate 'Moussaka' in Greek restaurant, then went to Internet café while clothes were drying. Looked at GAA Board, was disgusted what some people were saying about the 1st Match – That I was the reason Ireland lost, that I was humiliated, etc. I'll show them this week . . .

Wednesday, 29 October
Last Friday, after the match, I swore that watching the Aussies whoop it up after their victory was motivation enough for this week. Strangely though, my rage appears to have gone off the boil again for this week, and I am really going through the motions – as are most of the players on the team – despite our and the management's pronouncements that we're not . . . Mistakes are tolerated and an imperfect finish to exercises was accepted – the comparison with Harte again is striking. Anyway, doing my best to get myself wound up for the match – By Friday night I'll be fine.

Thursday, 30 October
When afternoon/evening comes and the groups start to make their arrangements for what they're going to do, they don't ever seem to ask me for my opinion, or let me in for a piece of the action. I have come to terms with that – I'm not about to start compromising who I am to fit in with their ideas – but you do wonder what the problem is. Are they jealous or do they see me as being on a different level, due to my high profile and success rate. Do they resent the respect with which I am held by journalists and management? It's hard to know. If it is, I can live with that very well – I know that I'd rather be the dependable one than the rough-edged rogue . . . However, if it's because of my personality and way of behaving (manner, voice, etc.) I would be more than offended, and disappointed at such immaturity . . .

Friday, 31 October

. . . After training all week and preparing to play full-back, O'Keefe [sic] starts to mention that I may be required to play out the field 'at times', with Canty going to full-back. Turns out he does this the whole day. Canty turns out the hero, they hardly play Hall at all all day. I play CHB – did OK – got plenty of ball, but use could have been better when I got it. We got major success in the first 3 quarters when we pushed up on their kick-outs, but in 4th we didn't, they worked it out, and went up the field to score easy 3s. I missed a couple of tackles that proved crucial, but on balance I pushed right up on my man for kick-outs and won a few of our own, so I was a positive factor. We won the match but lost the series. No big deal . . . Later on, PJ O'Brien's deadly craic . . .

Saturday, 1 November

Got up at 12, and no getting back to sleep . . . Went for Moussaka & milk, before hitting the Zoo . . . Lions, Lizards and Baboons being highlights, but probably no better than Belfast in the final analysis (no Hippos or Rhinos, not many bears) . . . Got back to hotel and left for Rugby. Excellent atmosphere before & during match . . . Telstra Dome itself is magnificent, really modern and well-designed . . . [S]ome boys (Hub, Coulter, Cass) didn't even make it to the match . . . More fool them, that's all I'll say – they missed a great match. Watching rugby on TV, you get no idea of the height that lineout jumpers reach or the height of Garryowen kicks. Horgan for Ireland was magnificent, as was Wood . . . Odie's friend was singing in a Reggae band in St Kilda later, so we went along. It was a Hotel ballroom, with an eclectic crowd . . . but it was a pretty good experience. Odie was dancing away – I had to dance also. I relaxed and enjoyed myself – it was cool. Later I got a chicken burrito (lovely) and headed back – My voice was gone!

Sunday, 2 November

Up early and enjoyed breakfast – you really enjoy the simple things at a time like this. Went to Mass – it was 1 hr 15 mins gone at Communion when I left – and met up with Dec Browne for shopping.

Went down with $1000 and all presents to buy, but 1st stop was to buy Aussie Rules ball . . . Ended up getting shoes for Dónal, books for Mum & Fergus, perfume for Philomena, shirts for Daddy & Aidan, and koala bear, rugby top for Ash. Also got chocolate covered macadamia nuts for Gandy, Molly, and ones at school. Bronté gave me a whole range of shirts yesterday, so I'll carve them up between Daddy, Dónal & myself . . . Went down with Decy, Odie, Cass & Paddy Christie for last meal, it was nice. Then back, get stuff together, and into taxi with Dec for the long journey home.

Monday, 3 November
After 34 hours of flying & waiting with Eamon O Muircheartaigh & Dec Browne, finally landed in Belfast City Airport at 8.00 p.m. Mummy was there to pick me up, we went home, it was very nice. Back to reality . . . I had maintained my dignity & sanity during the trip, and made the right decisions, considering my job, girlfriend, year I've had, and holiday to come, to come home early – Having reserve and doing your own thing – These are my lessons.

*

After-school netball was at full pelt when he rang Ashlene. Miss Moore was new to her job as a PE teacher in Claudy, north Derry. Cormac pretended he was still in Australia, about to head out for the night with the lads. But he was back in Tyrone already.

He drove up to her family home the next day while she was at school. Her parents were in on the secret, and let him park in the garage. When she arrived back and walked into the kitchen, there he was, drinking tea with her mother, Philomena. Shock, relief and delight.

The Moore house was an ideal getaway haven after his Australian trials. He always felt relaxed there, far from the pressures of work, family and football. He could just chill in the chair, his knee under peas from Philomena's freezer, and no one expecting him to do anything. She always stocked up on fish and veg ahead of his arrival.

The natives tried a little too hard to make him feel at home. Before the Bernie Burns Cup, the Faughanvale GAA Club's annual inter-townland tournament, Aidan, Ashlene's father, tried to recruit him for Gathgar, in a desperate effort to beat Greysteel, their deadly rivals. Gabriel, a neighbour, chipped in, 'Say you'uns are gettin' married and livin' here.' Cormac recoiled. A Burns Cup controversy would be an awful stain on his name. He confined his part to refereeing the football match and shouting encouragement to Ashlene from her father's support car as she ran to win the 5k race.

Time away in Australia had really given him a clear sense of his priorities in life. Surprising her with his early return was a way of telling Ashlene she was one of them. He had a bigger surprise in store for her. A few weeks later, he asked Mummy to go with him to help pick a ring. Then on a mid-December evening, her birthday, he popped the question.

The wedding planning got under way. They aimed to have the reception in Bundoran, and hoped for a date before the end of 2004. Whenever it would be, this wasn't meant to be a long engagement.

But Cormac's life had become so chaotic, it's a wonder he had time to get engaged at all. In the six weeks after his return from Australia, he was driving to special functions and gigs far and wide every other evening.

Monday, 10 November: interview for RTÉ All-Stars
    programme, Cookstown
Tuesday, 11 November: Derrytresk GAA hall function
Thursday, 13 November: Claudy school prizegiving [Derry]
Friday, 14 November: Ulster GAA Writers dinner, Bundoran
    [Donegal]
Monday, 17 November: Omagh District Council reception
Tuesday, 25 November: St Colm's HS, Ballinascreen
    prizegiving [Derry]
Friday, 28 November: All Stars, CityWest [Dublin]
Saturday, 29 November: Galbally club dinner, Cookstown
Sunday, 30 November: Tyrone Scór na nOg final, Cill Íseal
Monday, 1 December: youth presentation, Drumgoon [Cavan]
Friday, 5 December: Aldergrove GAA presentation, Crumlin
    [Antrim]

Saturday, 6 December: Ballintubber GAA presentation [Mayo]
Sunday, 7 December: Tyrone County Dinner, Kelly's Inn
Monday, 8 December: Fashion show, Cookstown
Wednesday, 10 December: BBC programme recording, The Moy
Friday, 12 December: Ardara presentation [Donegal]
Sunday, 14 December: youth presentation, Desertmartin [Derry]
Wednesday, 17 December: St Patrick's GS prizegiving [Armagh]
Thursday, 18 December: St Catherine's College prizegiving [Armagh]
Sunday, 21 December: Charity match, Tyrone v. SMA All-Stars, Omagh

Only one of those was purely out of personal interest. It was the night he confounded my mid-season forecast and won an All-Star. Four games old as a county full-back, he was *the* leading No. 3 in the land. And, oddly, he didn't face a stiff contest. His end-of-season flourish left him out in front of the pack. His legend was embellished with every retelling. He was in the top five of Pat Spillane's imaginary Gaelic football transfer market, valued at €13 million! Likewise, Colm O'Rourke was telling GAA functions that if he could 'buy' one player for his club, it'd be Cormac McAnallen. Yet, only for The Block on McDonnell, someone else would have been giving his interview on the live RTÉ All-Stars programme. On small things hinge big ones.

As for the circuit of club gigs, there was no agent involved; no fee quoted or expected. Cormac was simply doing as requested. He had something to celebrate and he was happy to share it with anyone who wanted part of it. He saw spreading the joy as his duty. And he enjoyed a lot of the gigs.

They still talk in Mayo about his trip to Ballintubber for a Bord na nÓg function. Tony O'Connor, one of the club youth officials, sets the scene:

The young lads were gobsmacked by what he said and how he spoke. He explained how he had been an average underage player, had listened to his trainers and was self-motivated. You could hear a pin drop in that room. The kids were in awe of him. Then, when a call came from Mid West Radio to do an interview, he said what he always said: 'No problem.' He would have chatted all night if they wanted him to. Even when he arrived that evening and we asked him how long he could stay, he said, 'Your time is my time.' . . . We brought him down to Geraghty's house that evening. They have five lads, are fanatical GAA followers, and there was mayhem when he arrived. Kids started arriving from everywhere. He had great banter with them all, there was a bit of slagging and he had time for all of them.

Up at the O'Connor house, he met Tony's sons, including eleven-year-old Cillian and eight-year-old Diarmuid. Two future Mayo stars, three Young Footballer of the Year awards between them. Then he and Ashlene were taken up to Corley's pub, where they auctioned off pairs of his shorts and socks and he told jokes and sang into the early hours.

The same story resounded from any club he visited: of his 'pin drop' speeches, endless autographs and photographs for young fans, talking to all comers till the end, never a hint of a hurry to leave, though he almost invariably had to rush on to another place.

Just one request he refused point-blank on principle. Suited up like a groom at the fashion-show in Cookstown, he was asked to pose with a model in bridal dress. *No thanks.* A week away from popping the question, he didn't want to appear in the papers with another B2B.

Meanwhile, he stuck to the teaching hours, school teams, Youth-Sport arrangements and everyday tasks. Thursday, 27 November 2003 was typical:

Ring Caroline McGrath ✓
Leave work for Friday ✓
Put in 'Order of Week' notice for next Mon/Fri ✓
Make Questions for Scór na nÓg final ✓
Change cover rota for Tomorrow (all day) ✓
Ask Mrs M for time off! ✓

Ring PJ O'Grady ✓
Leave in Suit for Drycleaning ✓
Buy new Shirt & Bow tie ✓
Post up F'Ball notice for 2moro ✓
Coaching Eglish, 7 PM ✓
Get copied: Senses sheet from 'Recording in History' (Yr 8) ✓
Blank wordsearch sheets ✓

He wasn't just doing things to appease people. He was still trying to improve himself and everything in which he was involved. He sat an interview for head of department. He rang around for jersey sponsors for school teams until Daddy stepped in to offer sponsorship from his furniture shop. 'Mention *Comórtas Peile na Gaeltachta* to Dónal,' he wrote on 18 November, and planted the seed of assembling a *Lár Uladh* team of Irish-speaking players from our area; he'd play as well.

Club duty called, too. Winning points for Eglish to stay up was paramount. After the All-Ireland, he had been the lynchpin in our draw at Carrickmore and brilliant win away at Clonoe. After his return from Australia, he put in another big shift to help Eglish to a narrow victory over Kildress. But a knock in the back while shooting caused his knee to hyperextend again.

*

His last Christmas with us was fleeting but purposeful. After Mass, he and I went to the Moy to put up a tree in Gandy's house and leave a present for his eighty-seventh birthday. We prayed at Granny's grave. We did full justice to Christmas dinner. We shared a tiny parcel of evening time. And as well-wishers inundated him on Stephen's night, I stood by his side, in awe of a lad on top of the world, yet as close to me as ever.

It was a very happy time for him, and for Ashlene. She arrived on Stephen's Day, packed and ready. They hit the Moy that night, 'for a quiet few'. It was anything but quiet. They got in the door of the 'Auction Rooms' but no further. Waves of people came to them, offering congratulations on football feats and their recent engagement. He had tried to keep the proposal secret at school – some chance!

Next morning, they flew off on the team holiday. Arabia would be a much merrier trip than Australia. And yet, amid all the jollity, there are more diary references to problems sleeping and relaxing, and a strange sense of detachment.

Saturday, 27 December
V. excited about setting off. Got to Belfast City Airport and checked in – First surprise! The woman who checked us in said she chose the name for her son while looking at the names of Tyrone players, and chose 'Cormac' . . . Anyway, got flying, marked a half-set of papers between Belfast & Heathrow, while being harassed by the 'kid from hell' in seat beside me, who jumped up & down, shouted & screamed, drove his elbows into me, and was pushing his dad, all while drinking 2 bottles of Fanta. His da merely molly-coddled him, asking him 'What's wrong' instead of giving him some manners.

Sunday, 28 December
Arrived in UAE (Abu Dhabi Airport) approx 8 a.m. . . . Everything on huge scale – 4-lane motorways, huge houses and mosques, ornate roundabouts, UAE flags & pictures of the ruler (Sheikh Zayed) absolutely everywhere. Into the Intercontinental Hotel – very luxurious . . . went on wee walk down by pool & beach. Looks really idyllic, white sands, beach soccer & volleyball areas . . . Later on, went down to hotel bar . . . I have an awful habit. If I find myself in a crowd I am always comparing myself to where everyone else is – are they having more craic than me? Does this mean I am not in the thick of things? It means that I don't enjoy many situations for what they are (relaxed, social gatherings) because I'm too busy looking around me to see what everyone else is doing. I'll try my best to snap out of this way of thinking. Went on to the bar at the Hilton – good craic had, especially on dancefloor with Ash – we are going to have a wonderful time here.

Monday, 29 December

Up reasonably early for the city tour ... Went back to hotel, had good day on beach. Started out looking round me at everyone else having *so much craic* – Playing volleyball, or drinking at the bar, or out swimming – when I should have been happy where I was – relaxing on a sunny beach in UAE. Soon changed though – got out in seas with a crowd & had game of keepy-uppy on platform – ended up a wrestling match to see who could stay on the longest. Great craic! ... Having bother sleeping these nights, even though I'm tired. Need to sort that out, it's wrecking my head.

Tuesday, 30 December

Good relaxing day today. Had breakfast, back to bed for a while, then up to Gym. Worked fairly hard, then up to pool for a swim. Played a fair bit of table-tennis against Ashlene, some wee American lad, Robbo, and Mattie Harte. Won them all comfortably enough ... Later on did some moonlight aqua jogging in the pool before dinner, a great time of day to do it.

Wednesday, 31 December

... Went for walk down to beach at 3:00. Tried throwing American football with J.D. – couldn't! ... Went for swim to take it all in on last day, swam out to bollards, then became very conscious of sea around, fearing sharks. Was glad to get back on to diving platform, then back to beach. We then went up for tennis ... I went aqua jogging again – feeling great.

The night began at 8.15, we gathered to walk over to island (well, not really, more a peninsula or causeway) where there was a barbecue in the sand already prepared ... After meal, Mickey took mic and made speech to mark end of year. Mickey Coleman sang 'Total Faith' ... Paddy Tally sang 'Angels'. Finally, I knew it would happen, Mickey asked me up to sing 'The Music Man'. Not the time or the place, but I couldn't refuse. Went through with it – Cringe! Never mind. On to disco. Mad. Everyone in group on grass. Top DJs – Great music. 12 o'clock – hugs & kisses all round – very nice. Auld Lang Syne, then into Fatman Scoop 'If you got a $50 bill' etc., 50 Cent 'In da Club', Punjabi MC. Dancing for Ireland . . . Some great photos – best 1 a team photo . . . Later on, stealing plastic mobile phone inflatable, and chatting to Tally & Dooher about next year . . .

Thursday, 1 January
Got up again for Breakfast (doing very well at this) . . . A full 2 hour trip to Dubai . . . Passed the huge gleaming towers rising up in the middle of the city, truly remarkable in their make up of gold, glass and marble. They are so built to keep them cool, even in summer . . . Oh yeah, me & Ash agreed the other night that we would love to come out here for a year or two to teach. Flights paid, accommodation paid, no taxes to pay! . . . I found sleeping difficult enough . . . Got to sleep about 1:30. Thank God.

Days of water-park rides and quad-biking over sand-dunes made for an enjoyable end to the trip. When everyone else had gone to bed, he stayed up to 2.30 a.m. playing darts with Mark Harte. 'Last leg lasted 20 mins trying to hit a double – Yeeeeesss!'

*

On his designated day with the cup, 13 January 2004, he was determined to bring cheer to a lot of old friends.

Start of Tullysaran Basketball, 2.30 (LG)
Start of St Catherine's Badminton, 3.45 (LG)
Sam Maguire for a day?
Launch of YS St Catherine's, 3:30
Mrs M
Council officials
Promo shots at Priory House
Cup to Deccie McKeever
Bring to Moy – Gandy / Teresa / Anna
Derrylatinee, 10–12
Leo McGeary?
Tony Byrne

To Derrylatinee, where he spoke less of his own glory, and more of the value to pupils in having pastimes outside of school and keeping them up in future.

To St Catherine's, where staff-members and school teams – both Tyrone and Armagh folks – jumped in for pictures with the cup.

To Leo McGeary in Collegeland, who'd told him among strawberry beds half a lifetime earlier that he'd need to be fit to solo through a hedge to play in an All-Ireland final.

To aunt Mary McAnallen's house in Dungannon, to which aunt Hannah had come from Dundalk and aunt Margaret from Mayo, with Charlemont St neighbours in for the party too.

To the Moy, where four generations of his O'Neill relations crowded around, Gandy playing the fiddle as ever while his great-grandson Max sat in the cup. Then to a few doors down Jockey Lane, and his great-aunt Joan McAnallen.

But there was high drama before he left the Moy. While putting Sam in the back of his silver VW Golf, in the Co-op car park, he made the mistake of leaving the key in the front.

The car's electrics were going haywire: it was locking and opening sporadically without warning. Now, the car was firmly locked. He could wait for hours in the cold evening, and it mightn't open. But if he left the scene, it could open at any time, with this seven-kilogram slab of silver sitting there, begging to be taken and smuggled away up the main Dungannon–Armagh road. Imagining 'Sam Maguire Stolen' headlines, he started to panic. Eventually Fergus came to the rescue with a spare key.

*

Cormac wasn't waiting to be captain, but he was the captain-in-waiting. He knew Peter was in the twilight of his career and due to rest after his ankle op. There were older, more experienced players than him about, but having always been a captain or vice-captain on Mickey's teams he was now next in line.

When Mickey put it to him this time, he said few words in response, but his glinting eyes told of quiet pride. He didn't intend things to change a lot: he would try to communicate with teammates

237

much as he had before, and he expected them to say their bit too. Nonetheless, he wanted to do justice to the role. To set the right tone from the start, he pencilled down some notes for his maiden speech to the team as captain, on 24 January:

Proud to lead team
Represent fairly – Openness
New boys welcome – Integrate – Deed – Word
Last year's meeting – Mickey & Peter
We know we can now
Belief – Dangers of listening to media
Duty to win – Young ones (Role Models)
Supporters – £1500 a table
to Ourselves (Man in Mirror)
Most young – had success
Couldn't stand end of career – won all by 23
Best chance we'll ever have

One point in that speech resonated then and still resonates in players' memories: that in ten years' time he wouldn't want to look back on a career with only one All-Ireland senior medal. 'I don't want anyone in this room looking back and saying the same.'

The news went public, with Kieran Shannon's report in the *Sunday Tribune* hours later. Mickey was quoted paying more compliments to Cormac. 'He's not the most vocal but the best way he leads is by example . . . He's as focused for a training session in Omagh as he would be for an All-Ireland final.' And one more thing: 'I have no doubt that if Cormac McAnallen is injury-free, he will always start on my teams.'

The caveat was significant. Cormac was far from injury-free. The knee was still niggling away at him, especially when kicking with his right. His November scan had shown a heavily sprained LCL ligament and meniscal cartilage damage, but no tear, and he had stuck to the advice to take a ten-week break from competitive games. He had aqua-jogged. He had taken supplements to speed up recovery: glucosamine, ginseng, cod-liver oil, calcium and Pharmaton; anti-inflammatories too. Yet it hadn't improved as much as expected over the winter. He watched the January McKenna Cup group games, with woolly hat and hoodie on head, worried. Would he, like Peter sitting beside him, have to miss a big slice of the season?

Fortunately, Louis O'Connor, the new Tyrone team physio, was an expert in knee and groin injuries. With a renewed urgency, Cormac went to his practice at Magherafelt twice in the third week of January. Staring at shelves full of books from the treatment table, Cormac thought, *He can't have read all of them.* Out came random questions about various volumes. The new physio passed the test.

Cormac was given an extreme wobble-board, a real balance-tester. Within a week, he had the knack of it. Louis became the latest admirer of his determination to overcome any challenge. But there was still pain, and it had spread to the inside of the knee. Could this be a medial ligament or cartilage strain, and might it yet require an operation?

At midweek training, he felt he wasn't quite right yet. For Tyrone's National League opener, away to Dublin on 1 February, Mickey kept

COMPONENT	TEST	SCORE & % OF TARGET	SCORE & % OF TARGET
		15 January 2003	4 February 2004
Body Fat (of 100%)	Sum of 7 skinfolds	49.6 mm (100%)	42.1 (100%)
Upper Body Strength	3-rep. max. benchpress	82 kg (64%)	85 kg (70%)
Bodyweight	Bodymass per 3-rep. max.	0.91 (71%)	0.96 (88%)
Abdominal Strength	7-stage core test	5 (71%)	6 (86%)
Flexibility	Sit & Reach	31 cm (80%)	32 cm (85%)
Leg Power	Vertical Jump	63 cm (72%)	55 cm
Speed & Agility	40-m. split-sprint (best of 6)	9.06 seconds (47%)	9.04 seconds
Fatigue Index	Recovery Time (average of 6)	2.04 seconds (75%)	1.67 seconds
Aerobic Fitness	(Bleep test)	121 runs (58.5%)	127 runs (67%)

him in reserve. But not for long. A half-time sub, in at full-back, he faced into the elements: a howling wind, icy rain and a fired-up home team at Parnell Park. Just fifteen seconds in, the Dublin full-forward, Ray Cosgrove, boomed the ball over the bar. Welcome back, Cormac. Gradually, play subsided to a series of petty fouls, bloody bodies, silly stoppages, big brawls and quarrelling camps. Dublin held on to win by a point and shatter Tyrone's long unbeaten record.

Cormac and the lads could look on the defeat as a timely wake-up call, to end the backslapping jamboree since the All-Ireland victory. He could also excuse his own rustiness after being so long out of action, and the 0-8 to 0-9 final score reflected no shame on his defence.

The team's mid-week fitness test at Galbally would give him further cause for confidence. Despite several setbacks and layoffs, he was fitter, faster, stronger and leaner than a year earlier – than ever.

Paddy Tally had tailored the targets for the physique required for top-level inter-county Gaelic football. It really was a matter of inches at that level, for one centimetre further could raise a score by several percentage points. Cormac's year-on-year improvement was remarkable. His 49.6 millimetres had already hit the 100% ideal for body fat in January 2003, but he lost another 7.5 millimetres of fat in the intervening year. The one drop he recorded, for the vertical jump, was entirely down to that knee. It wasn't called 'jumper's knee' for nothing.

As he became used to the captain's mantle on his shoulders, it dawned on Cormac that he might have to make one or two changes. He was now one of the last – if not the last – members of the squad who had not joined the GPA. In the off-chance that this could somehow put him at odds with the rest of the team, he decided to submit a membership form.

The next Sunday, 8 February, he led the senior team out of the tunnel for the first time. His leg was heavily wrapped from thigh down, more than ever. His interception started the move for the first goal and helped Tyrone build up an 8-point lead. Unlike the massacre of six months earlier, however, Fermanagh fought back and Stephen Maguire put it up to him. After ceding a wad of possession and two close-in frees, he swapped places with Conor Gormley at the break.

He fared little better at centre half-back; his poor clearances led to 2 Fermanagh points and his general play was below par. Tyrone won, but some people at Healy Park that day began to wonder again about his best position for the long term.

The next game would tell a tale. Away to Longford, joint top of the table and surprise packets so far. His personal assignment was Niall Sheridan, the shaven-headed, bicycle-shorted, burliest, fiercest forward in inter-county football. Within a quarter of an hour, the pair of them were booked. But Tyrone got well on top; Cormac was kicking without pain, and Sheridan felt weak – by his own admission – after recent weight-loss due to the Atkins diet. When Tyrone had the points in the bag, the captain came off for a rest late on. No point in wearing out the leg today.

The very next day, 16 February, Cormac was at the Belfast Knee Clinic for another scan. Mr Nicholas, the orthopaedic consultant, diagnosed a slight improvement, advised no surgery required and to keep at the strengthening exercises.

Now he could look forward to the coming Sunday's McKenna Cup final and the chance to lift a first trophy as Tyrone senior captain.

★

One February evening in the house, Cormac spoke of feeling chest pains. Mummy thinks she told him to get it checked out; that was her default response to any ailment, if she couldn't work it out herself. Daddy imagined a muscle strain from lifting weights. Cormac may have said it a second time, but memories are hazy. One thing is for sure, though: if they had the merest notion that a chest pain could be as serious for a young athlete as for the aged, both parents would've sent him to a GP or A&E.

We assumed Cormac could read his own body. He knew his resting heart-rate and understood his low BPM – thirty-five, he had told Mummy a while before – to be typical of a fit athlete. He had worn a heart-rate monitor at gym sessions in '03. If he had sharp chest pains, surely he'd impress that on us, as he did with regard to his knee, cheekbone and concussion injuries.

He had a couple of other issues that we overlooked or didn't fully appreciate then. There was some insomnia, as his diary in Australia records. And he had been sleepwalking: several times in the previous year he had rambled aimlessly from his bed, like when Joe Kernan encountered him on a corridor after the All-Stars dinner in November.

Then there was the tiredness factor. In passing he had mentioned feeling tired. We knew he burned the candle at both ends. The drawers of his mahogany desk trundled late into nights as he prepared lessons. Past midnight on Thursdays he taped *This Week*, the new BBC 2 politics show, for his A-Level class; one night Mummy found him asleep on the job. Getting up for school was a real struggle some mornings. And Ashlene, who had heeded his fatigue more than the rest of us, saw him nod off once or twice when she was driving.

Again, though, it's a big leap from tiredness to mortal danger – one we'd never have made then. Maybe it's a non-issue altogether. Don't so many of us seem to run on fumes, but manage to keep running anyway?

Despite those few complaints, he maintained a steady and largely positive countenance. Whatever was asked of him in the last eight weeks, he did if he could. Writing an article of MacRory Cup memories for the final programme. Giving an interview for cousin Anne Kelly's business studies thesis, and the usual media. Obliging and engaging at more club functions: Bellaghy, Eglish, Lisnaskea, Club Tyrone and Rostrevor in January – the last two on one evening. Receiving the *Belfast Telegraph* Sports Personality of the Year award for Peter in Belfast on the 26th. Smiling at Rockcorry club presentations on 10 February; regaling at the Aghaloo dinner dance on the 21st. Being his same pleasant and industrious self at school. At the gym, he wasn't flagging.

*

Des Cahill: *Tá mise le fear a bhuaigh Craobh na hÉireann i mbliana, Cormac McAnallen of Tyrone.* And Cormac, your brother Dónal is playing today. He wouldn't be used to this kind of occasion; you'd be used to it.

Cormac: No, I suppose. He would've played in club championship finals and things like that, but this would be just maybe
a step higher than that. And it's live television, so, yeah, it's a
big game, I'm sure. He's lookin' forward to it now; a bit nervous, but he's gonna give it everything, I'm sure.

[*The Underdogs*, TG4, 14 December 2003]

During Cormac's *annus mirabilis*, a much smaller footballing drama
was playing itself out for me. Adare Productions were recruiting for
a TV series, *The Underdogs*, in which a team of footballers who had
never played for a county team trained to take on the Dubs.

Plenty would say that I made the cut as Cormac's brother and an
Irish-speaker, ticking the TG4 boxes for a story. And they'd be right,
largely. More fleshy than flashy at the May trials, I was lucky to get a
call-back. But there's a twist: once on the panel, I shed two stone, got
fitter than ever, and earned a first-team place, ahead of some useful
players. And Cormac had a big part in all that, too.

He had launched my recovery months earlier, in the winter. I
had been stagnating through injuries and ill-fortune and indolence,
without really noticing. He saw it though, so he dragged me out
training with him on 7.30 a.m. road runs. He was by my side in the
gym, setting targets: could I pull 2,000 metres in under seven minutes on the rowing-machine? He wheedled me into a Stephen's
Day game of football tennis on the Eglish pitch. Then his knee buckled and my progress stalled. But when I went to the 'dogs', he was
my whisperer. He taught me new tricks and threw bones of wisdom
my way. From him I learned the fat content of every food on the
shelf, and how to eat ascetically. When we climbed Croagh Patrick
in July, after a cousin's wedding, he acted as my hare, racing ahead
of me.

It's funny now to see the TV caption for his interview. 'Cormac
McAnallen: *Deartháir Dhónail*'.

The *Underdogs* experiment culminated with that live challenge
match against Dublin in December. In the run-up, the TV people
cornered me with a question: *Do you feel you're now coming out from
your brother's shadow?* They only showed the answer, of course.

A watcher might think that sibling rivalry was my motive. But I was just happy to be bettering myself, to be achieving something as a footballer.

The night before the match, he rang me to give me this advice: 'Remember – the script isn't written yet. You write your own script.'

The next morning, he and Ashlene drove from Donegal to Parnell Park. They had to be back to Derry for a youth presentation at 7 p.m. But he wouldn't think of missing that match.

We led the Dubs for fifty-five minutes and lost by a point. Yes, they were out of season, but they were mostly first-teamers, and getting stuck in rightly; they even had a man sent off. After doing my jobs like a dutiful St Bernard, I had been – whisper it – moderately effective, and my master was proud.

★

Another subplot of the All-Ireland summer was my sense of protectiveness towards Cormac, in the wake of his head injuries. The Eglish v. Errigal championship match that June was Cormac's first in four weeks. Shortly before throw-in, I was passing the referee, Mickey Hughes, when I was overcome with an urge to say something.

'Mickey, watch out for Cormac's cheekbone. He's taken a few hits lately.'

He gave me a stern look and a brusque reply as if to say, *Don't be trying to influence me! I'll referee the match as I see it, no favours.*

It was never my style to chat up a referee before a match. I'd never have said the like of that for my own sake. And Cormac had no idea I'd said it. I don't even know exactly what I intended to achieve. My words were impulsive, born out of concern for a brother whose last two games had ended with a cracked face and concussion. I feared another stray elbow, foot or limb coming at him.

When the next one came at Clann na nGael two months later, I was virtually foaming at the mouth. I'm not now. Any bad blood about Cormac's various knocks that year is long gone. Time heals. But in any analysis of my brother's last year, I have to consider what

I – and what we all – did and didn't do to support him, directly or indirectly.

At times we failed to offer enough. When he rang home from Australia in bits, my initial response was to chastise him. 'Catch yourself on, Cormac! You're the man who has everything!' I didn't really consider the possibility that life could be tough at the top. When I listened longer, I felt sorry for him and guilty for my haste.

At times we added to a burden that was already a mile high. I dragged him to Belfast Newspaper Library for two days' research in July. I begged lifts to and from Aldergrove airport in mid-February '04. I nagged him to agree to buy the site up the road for house-building – not really my business – when Daddy put pressure on, despite his tender age and obvious need to think things over. Countless others asked much of him too. He was public property in constant transit. He hadn't time to get half the signatures on Tyrone jerseys that people gave him, so I sometimes helped him, forging 'autographs' in thick black ink.

The last card I ever wrote to him read:

> *Breithlá shona duit*
> Happy 24th birthday Cormster, but
> just remember – I'd still beat you
> in a scrap.
> Dónal

I didn't actually believe that. It was more sibling code for *You've achieved so much more than me and I respect all you've done. But don't underestimate me yet, yeboya!*

We were at that mid-twenties stage of maturity, of clarity, of appreciating what really matters beyond rivalries, wins and defeats. We were gaining a clearer vision of our individual and family futures. We were coming to realize that we'd factor in each other's long-term plans. And we presumed there would be a very long term.

Alas, in our final embrace, when Cormac needed me most, I wasn't able to protect him.

14.   Last Rites

Sunday, 22 February 2004
Bringing cup down to Eglish Yoof, 12:00 ✖
McKenna Cup final, Tyrone v. Donegal
Balleybofey [sic], 2:30 ✓
Scór Sinsear Semi-Final, Omagh, 8 p.m. ✓

The Eglish 'Yoof' were in for a big surprise that afternoon. The Sam Maguire Cup turned up at their under-10 practice, courtesy of Cormac. He couldn't be there that day, but he had come to talk to them before. 'Who do you want to be like?' demanded their coach, Seán Byrne. There could only be one answer.

Four weeks after being appointed to the role, he captained the Tyrone senior football team in the McKenna Cup final. This was only his third start of 2004 since the knee injury had blighted his January.

That right knee was still worrying Cormac in the dressing room at Ballybofey. To Brian Dooher he confided his fear that he mightn't be fit to jump high enough. As county full-back for only the seventh time, he had a daunting assignment. Brendan Devenney was in prolific form, a hat-trick hero the week before against Monaghan. Thankfully, with Tyrone fielding thirteen of the All-Ireland winning side, everything worked to perfection. Tyrone movements flowed up the pitch with ease, each pass put on a plate and the players interconnected in virtual telepathy. Tyrone's 18-point victory, by 1-22 to 0-7, was the county's biggest-ever margin away to Donegal.

At the final whistle, Cormac had to decline his opponent's request to swap jerseys, as he had to look the part in his county *geansaí* for the trophy presentation. Devenney would later present his Donegal 14 jersey to our family.

This was Cormac's ninth trophy lift as a Tyrone captain, at the outset of his eighth season playing for various county teams. Today's triumph meant that the county held the full set of Ulster and All-Ireland senior football titles at once. 'This was the Eglish man's first trophy as senior captain,' stated the *Dungannon Observer* report, 'and no doubt it will not be his last.' A man who had turned twenty-four only eleven days earlier would surely have several years to prove the truth of that.

All of the after-match duties took half an hour or more, on a bitterly cold day, and at a time when he needed to put ice on that knee. He made little of the delays at the time, though in private he conceded later that he had been freezing.

While others went into full celebration mode, he was doing everything by the book. In the showers, he took out his toothbrush. 'Why?' others asked. To counteract the sugar of energy drinks, he replied. He was on his own in that ritual.

On the bus home, Cormac took out some politics books to prepare for the next day's A-Level class.

He disembarked at Omagh and continued school prep for a couple of hours while waiting for Cathal Murtagh and me. We went on to St Patrick's High School for a Tyrone Scór semi-final. We were the county quiz champions, gunning for our fourth title. I had told him not to bother as we could likely qualify without him. But Cormac wouldn't miss a quiz and he insisted on taking part. We qualified for the county final the following Sunday.

> Monday, 23 February 2004
> Start of 2nd Badminton Course ✓
> (Organise, Barat or Crush Hall?) – Collect £5
> -> Give out 1st Certificate to participants
> YS Kickboxing – Collect Money ✓
> Put up notice for Yr 8 Football Course ✓
> Phone McSorley's re Glucosamine & Other supplement
> Gym, LA Fitness, 5 PM ✓
> Line up handout for Wednesday's Lesson (Politics) ✓

Mondays were Mr McAnallen's most hectic days at St Catherine's College, Armagh. He had 8A, 8R and 10H for single History lessons; doubles for Year 12 IT and Year 8 PE; and a Year 13 A-level Politics lesson.

Teaching done, he went on to the gym at Armagh City Hotel, where he had been training as much as in his native county since January. It was still quite new, very high-tech and the 'in' gym for people from our end of Tyrone as well as Armagh. Cormac's training partners were Collie Holmes, and Paul Feeney of Eglish, both of whom were living in Armagh.

They were doing some tough weightlifting these days: drop-down sets, starting with heavy kilos and going until failure, then lightening the load. On evenings like this, Armagh players like McGeeney and McGrane also used the gym. Cormac cringed to think they'd see him struggling on an empty bar to finish, looking like a weakling.

To all appearances, though, he was in the shape of his life.

Tuesday, 24 February 2004
Buy Wedding Present for Gavin Devlin ✓
Start of new Tullysaran Basketball course
Visit for photoshoot
Ring Roan re Volleyball course
Phone Paul Duggan St Paul's Eglish ✓
Phone Great Northern

Another busy day at school. Form-class 8M up first, and finishing with 9A for History – navigating the Ulster Plantation today. Sandwiched between all the other classes was a triple-period for his extra role as school co-ordinator for YouthSport.

The wedding on Friday would be good fun. Most of the Tyrone team would be there for their No. 6's big day. This would be their first collective get-together with their ladies since the Dubai trip at the New Year, and coming as it did at the end of a crazy winter of celebration functions it would also mark a line in the sand for a serious campaign ahead.

He was the next Tyrone player due to be married. Since his engagement to Ashlene two months earlier, he had intended to move on his own wedding-reception plans. They had talked of a December date, but time was against them. And today again, he didn't get around to ringing the Great Northern Hotel in Bundoran. There was just so much on.

Wednesday, 25 February 2004
All Day PSHE course, Craigavon T.C., 9.15 ✓ (Behind Brownlow
Integrated)
Room re Volleyball
First Trust Dungannon re Mortgage ✓
Room for wedding ✓
Gym, LA, 5 PM ✓

Ash Wednesday marked the start of Lent. In previous years, he had gone off chips for Lent, as well as the few sweet things he ate. This time, Cormac resolved to stop biting his nails.

No teaching today, due to the citizenship course at Craigavon. A day off lessons is often welcome relief for teachers, but with so much going on at school at this time – not least an internal inspection – he'd rather have been getting on with work.

After school, he took the girls' football teams for their weekly combined practice session at Sherry's Field, opposite school.

He tied down at last the mortgage meeting with the bank. It was for his site in the townland of Gortmerron, half a mile or so from our home place in the Brantry. The plot was on a hill, and adjacent to the BARD cultural centre, so familiar to us. On a good day, you could see as far as the Mourne mountains. Daddy had done most of the negotiations over the previous year, and only in recent weeks had Cormac come to consider and agree to the purchase. Now he just had to sign the legal contract.

Here he would build a future for his new family.

Thursday, 26 February 2004
Give Helen 2 ICT lessons for observation
↑ If successful Put Armada Quiz on Shared Resources ✓
Give membership money to Roisín Jordan ✓
Meeting, First Trust, 4 PM ✓
~~Meeting with Paul Duggan, Council Offices, 3.30~~
Tyrone Training – Richard Nicholas' bill – P.J. re Players' Fund
Yr 13 – Prepare test exercises ⎫
9A & 9R – Statistics displays ⎬ Sort, & laminate 10G ICT work ⎫
8M B'AS Displays ⎭ ⎬

Thursday was usually one of the lighter teaching loads. The triple-period A-Level class was the exception. Having striven so hard all year to get to grips with the subject, and having missed another double with them yesterday, he put in a solid 110 minutes today, studying past papers.

He also had to prepare classes for his absence the next day. As well as the Armada quiz, he set the Year 9 classes a task concerning causes of the English Civil War and a list of ten Protestant Reformation terms to learn for a spelling test.

Heavy overnight snow had left some roads in a treacherous state. Whether that evening's planned Tyrone session went ahead at Omagh is somewhat lost in hazy memories, but that unticked box suggests that it was called off. At any rate, Cormac drove up to Ashlene's house at Greysteel, north Derry. They walked around a circuit of the area in the dark evening, then ate toasted sandwiches while watching *Meet the Parents* for the umpteenth time and reciting the dialogue line by line.

Friday, 27 February 2004
Gavin Devlin's wedding, Tullyglass House Hotel ✓
Mass Pomeroy @ 12.00

Cormac and Ashlene took it easy on Friday morning and didn't go to the church ceremony. After lunchtime, they departed for the reception at Ballymena. The journey was shortened by a ritual singalong to the Burt Bacharach CD ('Raindrops Keep Fallin' on My Head') and a comical rendition of 'Save Your Love' by Renee and Renato.

At the reception, memories of Dubai formed much of the conversation. So too did first sights of the engagement ring and their own impending nuptials.

Saturday, 28 February 2004
Lámh Dhearg Centenary dinner ✓
Europa Hotel (Jim Herron)
Staying over

Early on Saturday afternoon, they left for Belfast. First stop was Corrigan Park on the west side, for the Sigerson Cup final. It was Queen's University's first final since Cormac and Co. won in 2000. Cormac and Ashlene took their places high up the bank. In front of them stood Mark Harte, then myself and Gerald O'Donoghue of Wexford. To our left stood Ruairí and Conall Ó Máirtín of Eglish and Charlie Pat McCartan of Down. The banter exceeded the match itself in quality. The industrious Queen's side's defence-first style – described as 'Gaelic league' by one reporter – eventually lost out to a star-studded IT Sligo team.

After a brief post-match shopping expedition in the city centre, Cormac and Ashlene arrived at the Europa Hotel to attend the centenary dinner of Lámh Dhearg GAA Club, Hannahstown. This was his fourteenth club function as a special guest, covering nine counties, in the space of three months. This would be his last on the schedule. He failed to notice that it was a black-tie affair and arrived wearing his ordinary suit. Someone gave him a dickie bow, which looked rather incongruous atop his blue shirt, but he didn't mind.

I attended a separate dinner in the Europa Hotel that night but, strangely, our paths did not cross. In fact, I didn't even know he was going to be there, till some of my own company informed me of his presence. By the time I called in to see him, he had gone to bed early.

Sunday, 29 February 2004
~~Tyrone training~~
Eglish match v. Culloville ✓

At 9.00 a.m., Leap Sunday, he rang home from Belfast. I answered from my bed. He wanted to play in Eglish's challenge match away to Culloville, around noon, and he asked me to meet him with his kit-bag. I couldn't play as I was recovering from a finger operation, and had to go elsewhere that day. To his annoyance then and to my regret now, I declined his request. Our teammate Brendan Donnelly called to collect the bag instead.

Before leaving Belfast, Cormac called at the Catholic chaplaincy at Queen's to say a few prayers. He realized that on this busy weekend, unusually for him, he would probably not get to Mass. The door was locked, however.

Culloville is in deepest south Armagh, sixty miles from Belfast and over an hour away. No one expected Cormac to play. Inter-county players of his stature and schedule rarely put themselves out for club challenge games, and he had no diktat from our new manager, Mattie McGleenan. Yet, he thought about the three-month gap since his previous club game, and the start of the all-county league campaign in a few short weeks, and decided he should be there.

He arrived as the game was about to start, so he stayed on the sideline for the duration of the first half. It mattered little. Our team was suitably experimental for a friendly, with a couple of young players making their senior debuts. But once he heard he'd be going in as a sub, he launched into an intense warm-up. 'It was as if he was preparing for an All-Ireland final,' recalls Dermot Donaghy.

In retrospect, his participation in that humble club match appears as one of several neat coincidences that occurred in his last week. It was as though he was saying an unconscious goodbye to the club and colleagues with whom he had grown up; he ought to take his bow in the black jersey of *An Eaglais*.

Cormac and Ashlene took the wrong road out of Culloville and had to double back towards the ground, where Conor Daly, the last man out, sent them on the right path. At Castleblayney they stopped for a round of pitch and putt. They could never get enough sport, and of course they had to compete. He led at the end of the nine holes; however, she invoked the special dispensation of a winner-takes-all tenth, which she duly won.

Following dinner, he drove home. They called first at their new site. He walked into the field and surveyed the scene for a few minutes. Though the grass was coarse and overgrown with wet rushes amid descending dusk, he could begin to picture the prospect of their new home. He spoke of having large windows and labouring on the job during the summer holidays. As they left, they waved at Mary Hughes, standing opposite, outside her house; she had looked after us some days when we were young.

A quick visit to our parents' house for a cup of tea generated discussions of wedding plans. Daddy mooted Armagh as a place to live during the house-building phase. Cormac gave Mummy a CD of Dromore Diocesan Youth Choir. She urged him to put on a woolly hat to protect him from the cold.

Back on the road, they stopped outside Eglish so he could pay his club membership fee. The end of February was the deadline, he had been reminded by Róisín Jordan. She was the new club secretary, learning the ropes; a decade later, she'd be the first female county chairman in the GAA. She wasn't in this evening, but Cormac left his £30 annual dues.

Onwards to Greysteel. He felt a little tired after several long stints at the wheel that weekend, so Ashlene drove. Along the way they played 'Mallet's Mallet', *sans maillet*, but the word-association threads kept leading to morbid terms, so they stopped.

Destination reached, he spent a while preparing acetate sheets to project in the next day's Politics class. Then he took a welcome call, which had been prefaced by a text:

> Big lad met donal last night outside the bot – got your number. How are things – has sporting super stardom changed you?

Long time, no hear. It was Gavin Andrews, his old Queen's Computer-Based Learning classmate. Stardom was coming Gavin's way too. He would become a BBC NI sports reporter, and graduate in due course to presenter and housewives' favourite.

The evening rounded off with a treat. Cormac sat down with Ashlene to watch the DVD of the All-Ireland final victory of five months earlier. It was the first time he had watched the game in full. And it was purely for enjoyment. Still, looking at the decisive sequences, he was reminded of the fine line between glory and grief.

Monday, 1 March 2004
Start of Roan Volleyball
Start of Internal Audit (to Fri 5th)
Charting pupil progress by accompanying individuals
Quality of relationships – Praise/Chance to communicate
Ring St Malachy's – Leona can't come ✓
Drop round form to S & S [Saints & Scholars P.S.]
Sort out Freddie K's form(s)
Get Leona to sign Tullysaran form
Gym, P Feeney, 5 PM ✓

Before 7 a.m., Cormac left Derry for Armagh. Ashlene waved at him through an open window and he beeped back. At 8.40 she rang him to check he had arrived safely.

It was an especially busy day. He had to prepare for the internal inspection, which he learned had been confirmed to start the following day; to carry out routine YouthSport tasks; and to teach the ordinary classes.

In second period, each pupil in 8A was given the name of a candidate for King of England in 1066 and had to make a pitch on his behalf, even if they doubted his credentials. Ann-Marie Donaghy didn't believe in her claimant, but Sir persuaded her to make the case before the class anyway. At the dinner-table that evening, she was proud to tell her parents of her top marks.

A teacher can have scores of conversations in one day. Many people recall meeting Mr McAnallen at St Catherine's that day. At break-time, he cracked a joke with some teachers. During lunchtime, he enquired of a close friend about his new motor: 'Why did you need to buy a new jeep?'

'I'll take you for a spin in it tomorrow,' vowed Kieran Gallagher, seeing nothing awry about him.

By that stage, however, it seems that he had given a few indications that he wasn't feeling a hundred per cent. He may have said something to his A-Level class in period 4. In the canteen for lunch, he asked a dinner-lady for a strawberry yoghurt and mentioned a sore throat. On the corridors, pupils saw him drinking from a blue Powerade bottle, as usual.

He pressed on. Teachers become inured to enduring tough school-days, fighting through till last bell, and he wasn't one for pulling a sickie.

There were five periods to go that afternoon. For the first two, he drove down to the Barat building in the far corner of the premises, to ensure he would be there on time. After tutoring the Year 12 class in the computer suite, time for something completely different. In periods 8 and 9, he was instructing the Irish-medium boys of 8I and 9I in the basic skills of rugby.

Driving back up the hill to his last lesson, he met Ciara McKeever, captain of the under-16 and under-19 teams, and her mother, on a corner. Ciara was off school with an ankle injury, but called in for some books. She'd be at the Wednesday practice session, she said, though it'd mean her mother driving from Portadown again just so that she could watch on crutches. He was pleased to have a captain leading by example, showing dedication like his own. 'She definitely has the heart for it,' he remarked to Mrs McKeever.

Mr McAnallen's last lesson took him back to 1066, with 8R. This class was still preparing their speeches; they would begin tomorrow.

The final bell rang. Mary Corr, a cleaning-lady, talked to him at about 3.30, coming out of the reprographics room.

'How are you?'

As usual, he took that as not just a greeting, but a question to be answered, honestly. He mentioned feeling stuffed up, perhaps for a few days now.

'You'll be glad to get home.'

'I'll be going to the gym. But I'll not be staying long.'

All teachers stayed on till 4.30 to attend to paperwork, as they had to do each Monday. Up the stairs to his room, D31, to prepare for his formal observation the next day. Might as well get ahead of himself in his files. He took a plastic pocket and wrote on top with a brown acetate marker: NOTES ON LIB DEMS – DICTATED 24/2/04 & 02/03/04.

He nearly got locked in: the caretaker had turned keys on most of D block before realizing that Cormac was still there. He had much more to do, but he'd have to pack up now.

Along the corridor, coming up to 4.45, he met Therese Donnelly, a business studies teacher. They didn't often cross paths, but right then she needed a hand. He helped her lift a plasma screen into the Crush Hall.

'Are you training tonight?'

'Naw, not trainin' the night. Goin' to the gym. I'll take it easy. Not feelin' the best. Just gonna go into the pool.' They touched on the next day's audit. He said he wasn't as far on with work as he'd hoped, since having the wedding on Friday and so on.

On leaving, at around 5, Bernadette the cleaning-lady advised him to take care in descending the newly washed stairs. He replied with a joke and a 'See you tomorrow'.

At the filling-station adjoining the Killylea Road he picked up a decidedly green-looking banana and joined the queue behind Marie McManus, a home economics teacher. The pending inspection came up, inevitably.

At the gym, he met up with Paul and Collie. Brendan Donnelly, a recent Tyrone call-up, joined them. Cormac put on a Tyrone training-top, having nothing else with him. 'That's the last thing you should wear in Armagh,' Collie teased. There were other Eglish players as well: Declan McKeever and Felix Daly had come together, Kieran Jordan by himself. Six of our clubmen working out under their own steam in an Armagh gym was odd but good to see.

Despite his prior vows to go easy, once he had stretched on the mats, Cormac couldn't resist the urge to take part. They grabbed the chin-up bar – his gym Achilles heel – for thirty pull-ups each, and ditto on the dips. They pumped a good few weights, but tiredness from the previous day's game and talk about Friday's wedding tempered their intensity. Lifting done, they took a dip in the pool. Cormac thrashed the water as much as he swam, and Paul urged him to improve his breathing technique. Then they finished off in the jacuzzi and steam room for a short stint.

Cormac and Brendan left for home first. On his way out, Cormac bought two apples, handed one to Brendan and started to eat his own. He said he would give Brendan a lift to Tyrone training at Omagh the next evening, as it was his turn. Cormac drove in front for the next nine miles till their paths diverged, close to home.

That same evening, as dusk descended, I was driving home from Cavan. If you had told me right then that someone in my family would die that night, I would have presumed my own doom and prayed for forgiveness for the next life. Through spectacular mismanagement, I was at the wheel of a car with both dipped headlights blown. So it was full headlights most of the way, and none at all in places. It was an anxious drive and I was grateful to reach home before 7 p.m.

Cormac would not have allowed that to happen.

*

At about 7.30 p.m. he arrived home.

He sat down to dinner: a chicken and pasta dish, made with customary care by Mummy. He knew the value of prompt reloading after a workout; the more proteins the better. He asked for and ate second helpings.

Our paths intersected in the kitchen; it had been two days since we'd seen each other. Good tidings gave way to a silly, brotherly row. The Sigerson Cup final highlights were on TG4's *Ard San Aer*. He wanted to watch without distraction, but I wanted to record it on VHS, which entailed changing channels and checking the tape briefly. Tempers rose. He was right, of course: the piece was too short to warrant the bother and have I ever looked at it since? At least we spoke no more cross words to one another.

8.30 p.m. on Mondays meant only one thing in our house. Normally Cormac threw down the gauntlet, but this evening he seemed slow off the mark.

'Do you not want to play *University Challenge*, Cormac?' Mummy enjoined. He switched over to BBC 2. Jeremy Paxman introduced the first quarter-final of the season: Magdalen College, Oxford, versus Northern College of Music, Manchester. Mother and son locked horns, frantically calling out guesses before the teams on screen buzzed. He sat nearest the telly, writing down the scores on a notepad, and ran a tight ship: no second answers were allowed, no interrupting the other's bonus questions, and no copying answers from the teams on screen. There were occasional quarrels about who got in first. His arbitrations weren't always accepted.

Cormac won, as usual. Magdalen won the other battle, with a captain from Norn Iron, a rare thing and a point of interest in our house. We joked that Magdalen would be investigated for fielding illegal players – a recurrent feature of varsity Gaelic football. Might a redbrick university register a team of quiz sharks as mature students for a shot at glory, we wondered.

Jeremy said his 'Goodbye' and Cormac went to prepare school-work on the computer. On his way we relayed two fresh requests for him, received by home phone that day. One: to speak to a youth group after a Mass in Clogher diocese. Two: to write a letter to a far-away elderly man who was ailing.

That's when he said, with a sigh, 'This is gonna have to stop soon. It's all becoming a bit much.'

I sympathized with him that there weren't more young people of his ilk, so that he wouldn't be in such demand. I'd never called him a role model, but that's what I was getting at.

After 9 p.m., Cormac put together a few Powerpoint slides, entitled '3 Claimants', on 1066 and all that, for 8M, first lesson. Depic-tions of William of Normandy and Harold Godwin were not too hard to find, but for Harald Hardraada he had to rely on clip-art of a cartoon Viking. He packed it in at 11.10, to judge by the 'last modi-fied' time. Finished or not, he gave way to Fergus, who had been agitating to use the computer for a while.

Upstairs, he prepared for the next day. It was probably then that he updated his diary. Beside the tasks for 1 March, as most days before, were ticked boxes. He entered the following mundane tasks on the page for Tuesday 2 March:

Sort arrangements for U-14 match v. Lismore
Bus / Notice about training
Sort out homework for 8R inspection

At some stage I called upstairs to impart a couple of trivial anecdotes from the press. One of them was so trifling that I am almost afraid to write it: I mentioned that three Ulster players had been picked on the camogie team of the century, and straight away he said he thought there was only one.

At about 11.30, later than normal, he rang Ashlene. He mentioned that he felt exhausted and under pressure, but there was no talk of sickness. Booking the wedding reception came up again. He prom-ised to visit her later in the week at the Lough Erne-side outdoor centre where she'd be staying with a school group. The call ended close to midnight.

He fell asleep at some stage in the next hour. During that time, I was briefly upstairs and called to him from the landing, something about a recent book-launch. He may have replied, *or did he*? Downstairs again, nearer 12.30 a.m., I called up to tell him I saw he was right about the camogie trivia, but I heard no response and assumed he was asleep. About then also, Mummy slipped into his room to take an item of clothing off the heater; she too thought he was dozing.

A night-owl by nature, I stayed up doing postgraduate study. It was far from intense tonight – simply filing away research notes from Cavan County Library that day. I sat on a long chair in the living room, lever-arch on my lap and telly on low volume. Usually I'd work till 1.00–1.30, but these notes were copious and I wanted all done. The clock passed 2.30 a.m.

The defining moment of our lives came at 3.00 a.m. – give or take a minute or two.

First I heard a loud noise upstairs through the door behind me, which was slightly ajar. It sounded like a snore initially. It was coming from one of the boys' bedrooms. Cormac's room was directly above where I sat, but Fergus in the room opposite was more prone to snore.

The noise quickly became a constant drone, escalating in volume. Now I thought it might be a strange prank of some sort. I went out to the hallway and called, 'What's going on up there?' No one answered but the drone continued. I ran up to investigate.

On the landing I realized that the noise was coming from Cormac's bedroom. I walked around the corner, entered and flicked on the light. There he lay on his back, tilted slightly to one side, with his duvet half lifted as though he had tried to get up. His eyes were open, staring into space and there was some sort of mucus on his lip.

I knew something was seriously wrong – but surely not the absolute worst. Cormac was simply too young and healthy for that. Instinct told me he might have had an epileptic fit, from an undetected problem; I recalled the strange case of a cousin who had a seizure due to the flashing lights of Sonic the Hedgehog years earlier. If not that, could Cormac be choking on his own vomit?

Now I realize that the noise was the 'death rattle', which I had heard once before, when our grandmother died in a nursing home. At this moment, however, I made no such association. The noise had reduced to an exhaling wheeze by the time I got to Cormac. These were truly the last gasps. I shook him and shouted his name in an attempt to rouse him. I didn't know what else to do. I knew nothing of CPR. I ran and called to the most medically minded among us. 'Mummy! Come quickly! I think Cormac's had some sort of fit!'

Mummy came in, called his name and looked for a pulse, to no avail. Then she turned him sideways to the recovery position, to see was he choking on something. She hoped she was doing it right, but wasn't sure. Daddy was awoken by the commotion, and I woke Fergus.

3.15 a.m.: I thundered downstairs to ring 999 from the main landline. Describing what was wrong with Cormac and our exact location wasn't easy. An ambulance was assigned at 3.17.

3.17 a.m.: Simultaneously, Mummy rang Dr Anjun Ghosh for guidance on artificial respiration. A retired local GP and family friend, he answered from his bed. Immediately he presumed she must be phoning about Daddy. Teresa, Anjun's wife, awoke. A former general nurse and a trained first-aider, she came on to the line to say she'd come over. 'I'll go with you,' said Anjun, who couldn't drive since a recent knee operation. After two minutes and thirteen seconds, they hung up and got dressed to go.

3.20–3.30 a.m. approx. We tried what we could with our limited knowledge. A few attempted compressions, half-baked breaths of life. But it was futile. He wouldn't stir. Absolute disbelief consumed us. How could this be happening to Cormac, of all people? Daddy felt cold feet; minutes later, they seemed colder yet. 'I think the poor child's dead,' he declared in a high pitch that I had never heard him reach before. Then he drove out to meet the ambulance, as the 999 operator had requested. Finding a remote house like ours at that dark hour was no small task in the pre-Satnav era. Daddy wanted out of the house anyway, for he could do nothing there to bring his second son back.

3.30 a.m. approx. The Ghoshes arrived. Frosted, slippery roads made their normal 8–10-minute journey that much harder, but they didn't waste a second. And in the absence of an ambulance, there was no one who could have been of more help to us in our hour of need. Anjun tried cardiac massage but Cormac remained static. While he persevered, we fell back on our faith. Teresa, a very firm believer, led us in prayer. She launched into the Chaplet of Divine Mercy. An Our Father, a Hail Mary, an Apostle's Creed, and five decades of the Rosary. One line stands out in my memory. 'For the sake of His sorrowful passion, have mercy on us and on the whole world.'

3.34 a.m. The ambulance crew arrived at the house. That's the official record. To Mummy, and Teresa Ghosh, it seemed to take agonizingly longer. Ditto Daddy, who had sat alone at the end of our boreen, half a mile from home, with his lights on full beam, waiting for them, terrified as to what was happening in the house.

This was our last forlorn hope. A pair of paramedics set to work, feeding in oxygen and rigging up a defibrillator to try to shock the inanimate body back to life. The family huddled outside the doorway, at a safe distance from the defib's first bolts, hoping against hope.

Fr Breslan landed very shortly after. Daddy had had the presence of mind to call him and, despite the unearthly hour, he too answered first time. Our parish priest of fourteen years was known for his diligence in administering the last rites. Usually he'd ask everyone to leave the room for a few minutes while he carried out his duties. This time, however, he had to work around the rescue efforts, standing clear for a defib shock before anointing Cormac's forehead as absolution.

Shock after shock was administered, with no change of condition to report. Ten minutes turned to twenty, twenty to thirty . . . We tried to shut down panic and despair, but tears were pouring forth.

I drew one last sliver of hope from the apparent logic of history. No sportsman I could think of had ever died like this. You'd have to go back half a century to find a GAA player of this standing dying from natural causes in his prime. The deaths of John Joe O'Reilly and P. J. Duke of Cavan in the 1950s sprang to mind, but both of them were known to be ill prior to passing. I could recall that some athletes had died in car crashes or other accidents, and others due to substance abuse. But Cormac never smoked or took drugs, rarely drank alcohol, had no recent accident to report, and showed no serious health symptoms that we knew of. How could he have died in bed in this way? Was it not a sort of deep coma?

But some time after 4.00 a.m. the attempted resuscitation drew to a close and Dr Ghosh confirmed the worst: Cormac was dead.

With that grim realization, we were wrapped in a cocoon of numbness and resignation. For the first time ever, we threw ourselves into a group hug. Now we were just four, and we would have to stick together through whatever troubles and trials lay ahead.

We had to start telling people. Daddy rang his cousin, Eamonn McAnallen, who lived nearby, and it was not long after 4 a.m. when he and his brother Kieran arrived. In retrospect, it's amazing how many people lifted their landlines at crazy hours that morning. A phone ringing in the darkness was so alarming that it demanded to be answered.

At 4.14 a.m. I made the hardest call. Some people suggested to wait a while before ringing Ashlene, as the news would be too devastating for her to take at that hour. But she had to be one of the first to hear, I reckoned; to find out from others or even the radio would be worse. So I rang her family house, the only number I could find for her. Her mother, Philomena, answered. I didn't even know her name; we had never spoken before. As soon as I introduced myself, she sensed something was seriously wrong.

I had barely begun to relate the awful news when she started to cry, and I heard hysterical shrieking in the background. Ashlene had been awoken by the ring and suspected bad news about a grandparent. I had no adequate answers for their questions. A few moments later, Ashlene rang back in a frenzy, entreating me to put Cormac on the phone now. 'I can't,' I repeated helplessly.

The mystery of Cormac's death was arguably greater for Ashlene than for us. When she last spoke to him, less than five hours earlier, there was no inkling of a problem. Now she had to hear this news from us, over an hour and a half away, with no physical evidence to begin to make sense of it all. Neighbours drove her and her parents to our house at breakneck speed along the dark road.

Between 4.30 and 5.00 a.m., the police landed, having been notified by the ambulance service. Detective Constable Logan and a colleague had to carry out their own enquiries and report. As a matter of procedure they cordoned off Cormac's bedroom and surveyed the scene for a short while.

There were no marks on his body, but they had to ask the standard questions. As the person who found him, I was required to give an account of the circumstances. Recounting the story was hard, given my exhausted and emotional state; before uniformed constables it was acutely so. The questions were cold and searching, and compassion was necessarily withheld. At the back of my mind was a slight concern that they might treat me as a suspect in this sudden, strange and unexplained death. But in fairness, they never tried to insinuate anything untoward, and they didn't interview me again.

They requested to see items belonging to Cormac. A search of his schoolbag found only books; a hunt through his kitbag, nothing but football gear. They took a half-empty water-bottle from his room and another from his car for forensics.

Fergus found his mobile phone. On it he read two bizarre, creepy text messages received the previous evening. These would play on our mind a lot over the next couple of days as we tried to make sense of what had just happened.

At 5.10 a.m., another doctor arrived at the scene, having been called by the police. Cormac was officially pronounced dead at this point.

Informing close relatives was the next painful task.

'It's Cormac.' Daddy's voice trembled down the line to his brother Seán in Louth.

'*What do you mean "It's Cormac"?*'

'He's dead.'

'*He can't be! What're you saying, Brendan?*'

And so on. Seán was thus handed the baton to ring the rest of the McAnallens.

A pre-dawn call wasn't in itself strange to Paudge Quinn. An undertaker is always alert. He was also renowned as the poacher of Tyrone's only All-Ireland senior final goal, and owner of a roadside hostelry where GAA fans dined – and where Cormac's captaincy had been announced five weeks earlier. But the news of this death shocked Paudge as much as anyone. From him the message would spread rapidly to Mickey Harte and the GAA network and the media.

At about 6 a.m. Daddy rang Mrs Martin. Cormac would not be coming to school today.

Ashlene arrived around then, rushing to Cormac's room. She walked straight through the police cordon at the doorway, sat down beside him and tried to talk to him.

It was 6.25 a.m. when Mummy steeled herself to ring her sisters. Only Anna Kelly in Carland answered first time.

Sunrise came at 7.10 that morning, but for us there was no light. Relatives were already arriving at the house, where they were bound to be. Neighbours had begun to report for duty: to sympathize; to mourn; to understand; to help out. Everyone wanted to know how this had happened, though some were afraid to ask, and we were at a loss to explain.

All we knew was that with Cormac's death our lives had changed, utterly.

15.   The Wake

Better being safe than a tragic hero. The thing that Cormac had written he didn't want to be, he became. He was now the most tragic hero in Irish sport for a long time.

The morning of 02/03/04 is bookmarked in many minds for one of the most staggering pieces of news they ever heard.

Some of the earliest calls around the parish were very tentative.

At 6.30–6.45: *Did you hear any news this morning?*

This would be too wild a rumour to spread without substance.

Each call and text met utter disbelief at first.

What?! Cormac? That can't be right. Who told you?

It had to be a silly rumour.

Maybe they mean Brendan, his father, thought more than a few.

Some tried to go back to sleep, others rang around in the hope of disproving it. When the same story echoed back from different sources, they worried.

Hundreds of people learned of it that way before it was officially announced.

The first public broadcasts were at local churches. Parishioners in nearby Donaghmore heard Fr McAleer announce it at 7.30 a.m. Mass.

Early risers in Benburb could see the shutters down on our shop, with the notice: 'Closed due to death in the family'.

At Terry McCann's, the shop and main meeting-house in Eglish village, about a dozen people were present when the news came on air.

Thousands heard the story break on radio at 8.00 a.m. while on their way to work. That's how many of Cormac's teaching colleagues heard, if they hadn't been phoned already. Some had to pull in to the side of the road to take in what they were hearing.

Others still at home read the headline on Aertel, or saw Sarah Travers read 'news just in' at 8.28 on BBC NI.

More still heard Mickey Harte's radio interview on RTÉ at 8.35.

Hordes of teary-eyed pupils shared the story on school buses about Tyrone and Armagh. Niamh Marley of 8A had just started rehearsing her 1066 speech for Mr McAnallen's lesson when the news came on the car radio. Her father Noel, of Armagh's 1977 All-Ireland final team, stopped and doubled back to the house to check that he heard right. Mrs M confirmed it.

Our house had become a hive of people. Relatives and neighbours getting down to work, Uncle Seán as bronze commander, Kellys and Downeys and Donnellys on the frontline. Club officials and county board men offering help to manage the swarms of humanity heading our way.

The crunch of advancing feet still reverberates in my mind. The early ones crunched softly through the frosty muck and the thin fringe of snow in the fields around about, where they parked. This sound passed. But the harsher noise of mourners plodding through the stones of our yard, like the chewing of crackerbread, lasted all week.

By 9 a.m., a statement of sympathy from the Taoiseach was carried on the news. It had become truly a national event. Such was the 'what?' factor, people didn't wait for the water cooler – they phoned a friend. The ripple effect was best encapsulated by the writer Eamonn Sweeney, down in Cork. He got the news in a 9.30 call from someone who wasn't a GAA fan. 'And then there was another phone call, and another.'

Just about everyone who knew Cormac had heard by now. Most turned up for work. But a lot of close companions had similar experiences in their various workplaces: in their stunned daze, they couldn't concentrate, concluded that they ought to be somewhere else, and went or were sent home again.

St Catherine's was shell-shocked. A fraught stillness suffused every corridor. At first bell, form classes had the news confirmed to them. They teetered over to the main hall for assemblies. Announcements, prayers, and elegiac airs on strings. All punctuated with tears and pin-drop silence. A few pupils, who were genuinely overcome, were allowed to go home. Timetabled lessons were suspended for the day.

But the school had to deliver important lessons in life, there and then, with no time to plan. Many of the pupils had never known someone so close to them die, or at least not one so young. Mrs Martin, as principal, was very conscious of their responsibility to make sense of this tragedy for pupils in a language they would understand. 'We had to discuss it in a way that wouldn't frighten, but make them united in common grief. We were conscious of every word, every gesture in light of the fragile state of our young people.'

Gloom descended also on St Patrick's, our old school. Between here and St Catherine's, enrolment from Eglish had grown exponentially, from one or two to a full busload, since Cormac had left in '97. There may have been an element of *If it's good enough for Cormac, it's good enough for us*. A goodly gaggle of the boys were deeply affected, and a couple of the male teachers who tried to counsel them ended up bawling in front of them.

Back at home, full bookcase after full bookcase was lifted out of the house to make space for people.

The press started to land, access all areas. In the corner of the yard important people hovered about, phone to ear, trying to get a signal.

Our house was filling up with people, but it had never felt so empty. We had never felt emptier.

By 9.30 a.m., the patriarchs of the Tyrone football team were standing in our sitting room.

Around 10.00 a.m., Big Eamonn McAnallen and Leo McKeever, the Brantry's tallest and burliest men respectively, carried Cormac's corpse down the stairs, with Paudge in tow. He was taken away for a post-mortem in Belfast City Mortuary.

'It's not fair,' Fergus muttered to visitors. It was the simplest expression of what everyone was thinking.

Ashlene could hardly speak. She was flanked by friends, and greeted with consoling hugs, but her disposition was almost catatonic. Her life had hit a hairpin bend and could never turn back to its former direction. 'We'll do whatever we can to support you,' Daddy said. Nothing could change this fact, however: she had lost Cormac; she would have to find a different path.

I tuned in the radio in the conservatory after 11 a.m. I seemed to need confirmation that it had actually happened, and to gauge what people were saying. Michelle Nic Grianna was talking about it on Raidió na Gaeltachta, while the local Q101 was playing tribute-tracks in lieu of its schedule.

Around midday, I went up to my own room and switched on BBC Radio Ulster. Instead of the usual political crisis, Cormac was the subject of *Talkback*. Our old friend Paddy Gallen was speaking about the young boy who had accompanied him to countless matches in years past, long before the world knew him. But there wasn't much time for us to nostalgize.

Outside Cormac's bedroom was a policeman standing guard, armed with a sub-machine gun. It was just me and him upstairs. How surreal this had become.

Away from the house, police were interviewing his gym posse from the previous night. Had they noticed anything out of the ordinary?

In Eglish too, the GAA club pulled heads together for an emergency meeting. How to deal with the press? Who would steward where and when? How to fit so many cars into the Brantry boreens for the wake? How to handle the crowd at the funeral?

Someone flew a kite for Armagh cathedral, but Eglish was the only place for it. Yet nobody knew exactly how many people our little St Patrick's could hold. Daddy, for one, feared that an over-packed gallery could collapse the supporting pillars. Out came the measuring-tape, and a capacity of about 600 was set.

Tyrone's home league game against Cork, scheduled for Omagh the following Sunday, and the county Scór Sinsear final at Bally-gawley that same Sunday evening, were postponed. Cormac would have been competing in both.

People tried to comfort us with statements like, 'Well, at least he was at home with his family. Wouldn't it have been a lot worse if he had been away and something happened to him?'

That meant nothing to me. How he had died didn't really matter. What's dead is lost and gone forever, and we had lost him surely. I was also slightly gnawed with guilt, for not fully appreciating what we had till it was gone, and the hunch that we – I – might've been able to save him.

I remained in a state of incomprehension. I reminded people that he had always seemed durable, a man without weakness. On a certain level I regarded it as God's will – whatever that entails – but I couldn't accept it as pure fate.

As with the rest of the family, I needed to know what had killed Cormac.

The state pathologist, Professor Jack Crane, had completed the autopsy before lunchtime on Tuesday, but could not categorically pinpoint a single cause of death. Most of Cormac's organs were reported 'Normal' or typical of a dead body. Cormac's brain, the report said, 'seemed swollen, with flattening of the convolutions and grooving of the unci [tenorium cerebellum]. It was normal on section.'

The heart was described as '490 gm. Of quite good size but not unequivocally enlarged.' My translation: 'It might be a bit bigger than an ordinary heart, but not unusually so for a sportsman and not enough so to identify it as the source of the problem.'

The decision was taken to keep his body overnight for more tests. Stomach contents and fluid samples were handed over to police forensics. Pathology also retained tissue samples, fluids and the heart. There would be further tests in the morning. These medical updates were relayed back to us – Mummy in the main – through a police liaison.

From all this uncertainty, a 'rare viral infection of the heart' was floated as a possible cause of death. We can't recall exactly who suggested it first, but the media seemed to pick it up. They had to have a line of speculation to satisfy their audiences' curiosity. Not much harm in that, perhaps; if they hadn't signposted natural causes, some people might have suspected something unnatural. We had to accept it as a plausible explanation. Very occasionally, the sort of viruses that cause normal respiratory infections can spread to the heart of an otherwise healthy person, causing unstable electrical heart rhythms and even cardiac arrest.

Many other thoughts were racing through our heads at the same time.

269

Was it because of plain fatigue? We recalled his sounding tired the previous night. Had he trained too hard at the gym, or in general?

Some folk cited his busy schedule and reckoned his body gave in to exhaustion.

Mary Thomas, a cleaning lady at St Catherine's, had told him months earlier to lose no more weight. 'Don't start!' he replied. 'My mother's at me already.'

Pointing to pictures of him lifting the McKenna Cup a week before, a couple of our aunts claimed they had thought then that he seemed very gaunt. *He didn't look well at all*, they said.

Hmmm. We wondered. Maybe there was something in that. Burn-out had recently become a buzzword in the GAA, in view of the busy work and training schedules of top-level players; academic studies into it were already under way. But much tireder and thinner people weren't just dropping like that. This seemed too extreme a consequence of fatigue.

I couldn't help but think of all the blows to the head that Cormac had sustained in recent months. That was the one obvious affliction he had suffered. I said this to people whom I trusted. Still, it was only a notion.

One more thing was nagging away at me. It was an outlandish, freaky thought. I could really talk about it to two people, and we had hardly time to speak.

It went back to the last two text-messages Cormac received:

> +4477xxx-xxxxxx
> 01/03/04 16:23
> Ur GOING DOWN
> Cormac: [. . .]

> +4477xxx-xxxxxx
> 01/03/04 19:34
> Get ready to die
> on court

Our family has never disclosed these two last texts publicly before. But they were foremost in my thoughts for two days after

Cormac's death. I will never forget the chilling feeling that they sent through me.

Someone had warned he was going to die, twice. Then he died, seven or eight hours later.

We couldn't work them out, especially the 'on court' bit, but they looked like threats. We couldn't identify the sender either. The number wasn't saved, didn't appear anywhere else among his messages, and wasn't to be seen in his diary when we checked it. Did Cormac even know who had sent them?

Our minds went into overdrive, sparking off into wild possibilities.

Did some shadowy figure actually want Cormac dead? Had they tried to kill him? Was he poisoned? Who could possibly have it in for him, of all people? Could 'on court' refer to something legal?

And how did Cormac react when he got those messages? Did he feel threatened, or at least taken aback by the language? Did it cause him to think – momentarily – of his own death? It was upsetting to think that 'Get ready to die' was one of the last things he read.

Fergus and I told Daddy, and the police. We said nothing to Mummy yet. With so many people about, and private moments hard to come by, we didn't want to add to her or anyone else's distress unnecessarily. We also had to keep quiet in case it became the stuff of tabloid headlines. Let police investigations take their course first.

We went to bed on Tuesday night, knackered, withered, bewildered and more than a little spooked.

Wednesday, 3 March

Cormac's story was wrapped around all the morning papers. It had already been on the *Belfast Telegraph* cover by Tuesday lunchtime. The *Irish News* reproduced the full-cover portrait of Cormac from after the All-Ireland final, replacing 'CHAMPIONS' with 'DEATH OF A CHAMPION'. Terms like 'future GAA president' were bandied about, even though Cormac had never indicated any such ambitions.

It went global too. *The Times* and the *Independent* took it to Great Britain. The Irish correspondent for Associated Press sat down in our living room, fine-tuning his story to string out syndicated news for any American papers taking interest. Sky News carried it long enough for aunt Maggie's pupils in Qatar to see it.

Yet it remained a truly Irish story. And as the Irish public learned more detail of Cormac's life and last deeds, the story became more poignant still. The young captain plotting another All-Ireland for his county. The committed clubman playing that Sunday. The quiz fanatic watching *University Challenge* on his last evening with his mother, and due on the Scór stage on Sunday evening. The fiancé making wedding plans. The clean-living boy who didn't deserve to die. It was a tale of pure dedication and old-fashioned chivalry that made people well up. It caused many people to wonder openly whether they were putting enough back in, according to one columnist.

The talk was tending to mythologize Cormac, if not canonize him. The comparisons ranged from Cú Chulainn to King Cormac to Michael Collins. That's why I tempered the superlatives when we gave our first TV interviews that day. We hadn't gone looking for the cameras, but when requested we acquiesced – just as Cormac was wont to do. After speaking of what a great brother he was, I added: 'Some people are talking about him as if he was a saint. He wasn't a saint; he was just a good solid lad.' I was merely trying to point out his private, human side. For a long time afterwards, I regretted saying that, as though I had deflected from the greatness that everyone else was heralding. On reflection now, I'm glad I said it; he wouldn't have wanted any fabrication of his memory.

Mid-afternoon, Cormac came home. We met the hearse at the Tamnamore roundabout, exit 14 off the M1, returning from Belfast. As the cortège crawled left at the new Eglish junction roundabout, workmen downed tools and stood to pay their respects.

Eglish was a *village noir*. Black flags hung from telegraph poles. Black-draped parishioners formed a long guard of honour, blessing themselves as we passed through.

We lifted Cormac around the house, and laid him in the conservatory. Here he would lie in state. Open coffin, we got to see him again. He was dressed in a suit, looking smart but a ghostly spectre of his former self.

The Wake was officially on now. Ulster Catholics must be the wake specialists of Western civilization. We have the full Irish wake at home for two nights, no discount. 'House private' is rare here; evening removal to the church, simply unheard of. It never occurred to us to close the doors to the public. All comers would be welcomed.

We were in for a crazy time.

We stood as a family beside Cormac, with an endless line of people shuffling towards us. The evening grew darker, but the queue kept getting longer. Around the house and halfway up the lane it swirled.

There were so many familiar faces, from the recent or distant past: locals, club colleagues, members of other clubs and traditions, old schoolmates, university friends, family colleagues, and streams of schoolgirls and staff from St Catherine's. Lots of the faces were as well known to me as they would have been to Cormac. At times it felt like I was standing at my own wake, only the crowd was too big. There were so many more we didn't know, but their proudly worn club gear identified them. I tried to address everyone by name, through calculation or guesswork or simply asking who they were, and I thanked them for coming. I meant it, for we were grateful to know that Cormac meant so much to them.

Looking through the in-house books of condolence many years later, I see signatures from thirty of the thirty-two counties that week.

They came in droves from certain pockets around the country. There was a big squad from Ballintubber, paying respects for Cormac's visit to Mayo. From Faughanvale, Co. Derry, they flocked in solidarity with Ashlene.

Then there were the public representatives, players and managers from every corner of the land. You could tell the story of modern Gaelic football through some of the visiting sympathizers. Nearly every All-Ireland winning team of half a century was represented.

There was Jack Mahon of Galway '56. And Kevin Beahan of Louth '57.

Kevin Heffernan, captain of Dublin '58, and chief of staff of Heffo's Army.

And Sean O'Neill of Down '60–61 and '68, our former mentor at Queen's.

And Mick O'Dwyer of Kerry 1959–70, leading a herd of Laois lads. And Power and O'Keeffe of the 1975–86 golden boys.

From Dublin, 1974–83, came Brian Mullins.

Seeing Matt Connor of Offaly '82 wheel himself towards us was truly touching.

From Meath 1987–8 came O'Rourke, Coyle and Flynn. And Tony Davis from Cork 1989–90.

And O'Rourke and Kane and McCartan of Down 1991/94.

And Molloy, Boyle and McHugh of Donegal '92. And Jimmy McGuinness, confiding that something similar had happened to his brother.

Take your pick from Derry '93.

From Meath '96/'99 came Geraghty, plus Seán Boylan.

And Kerry '97/2000 sent O'Keeffe, Moynihan, Ó Cinnéide and Darragh Ó Sé, reaching out a hand to erstwhile adversaries.

Kevin Walsh, Padhraic Joyce, Declan Meehan and Joe Bergin of Galway '98/'01.

Armagh '02 were there to a man.

And the Tyrone squad sat in dugout formation around our kitchen, pale shadows of their usual selves.

Just the hundred All-Ireland medals between them, knocking about our homeplace. Many other current star players came also, from all over Ulster to the Dubs and midlands and the depths of Munster. Like Ireland teammates Declan Browne, Graham Canty and Colin Corkery, the one big-name Gaelic footballer who was known to play with a heart condition.

Others had never broken bread with Cormac, but they went as they thought it the right thing to do. The presence of Brian Cody and D. J. Carey was a totem of support from the hurling community. Likewise Joe McDonagh and Nickey Brennan. And seemingly every reporter or TV personality who had ever interviewed Cormac turned up too.

To see one of the above coming near Eglish would normally be a big deal. Yet now here they were, shuffling through our hallway, standing sheepishly in our front room. And we had but a twinkling to spend with each one, for the pressure of numbers forced people to pass on through.

Only now were we coming to realize the level of respect Cormac had among the GAA and the wider public. Man, woman, boy and girl identified him as a role model – their own role model. We were undoubtedly cheered by what they had to say. We just wished we could have found out another way.

Tomás 'Mousey' Dougan handed me his MacRory Cup runners-up medal from 1997; we had Cormac's already, but to refuse his genuine gesture of sorrow would seem rude. Brian McEniff gave us a Railway Cup medal for the '03 tournament – which Cormac had missed due to injury, and for which we presumed he would receive no reward. Now, posthumously, he had completed the set of national medals from inter-county upwards. Strangest of all, a man from Laois handed me a piece of rubble from the old Cusack Stand.

Meanwhile, in the corner behind Cormac, at the head of the coffin, sat the ultimate prize in Gaelic football. Tyrone people had longed to touch the Sam Maguire Cup for almost a century. Now they barely even looked at it.

Equally muted, amid this maelstrom, sat the McGirrs in the sitting room. Since Paul's very public passing, they had borne their sorrows privately for seven years. Looking on as Tyrone scaled the pinnacle at last, the family must have wondered what might have been. Now two of the '97 minor team were gone, and we were just beginning to taste what the McGirrs had gone through.

★

The riddle of the morbid text-messages was resolved by Wednesday.

The police had tracked down the message-sender, interviewed him, and sent him on his way. It turned out that he had met Cormac recently, and was challenging him to a game of squash. Writing 'Ur Going Down' and 'Get ready to die on court' was his form of pre-match banter. There's a moral in that story for anyone writing a text, even in jest.

At least that news ruled out murder, manslaughter and telekinetic homicide.

What had killed Cormac then?

In a Belfast laboratory, his heart was examined by microscopy. The report came back during Wednesday. As before, the cardiac structure was found to be sound. Note was taken of some white blood cells in the muscular wall of the left ventricle, but, again, these did not equate to a fatal defect.

The viral-infection theory was somewhat debunked by these results. A virus would be expected to produce inflammation of the heart muscle (myocarditis), but none was in evidence. Several genetic conditions could be discounted too.

In the absence of obvious defects or symptoms, the search for the reason for Cormac's death turned elsewhere. It could still be a hereditary cardiac condition, but that would not be determined this week. We were told that his heart would be sent to London or America for additional tests by expert cardiac pathologists.

By this stage, the virus theory was being accepted and reported as fact by the media. We had not yet sufficient detail or time or nerve to challenge it.

What had killed Cormac? We would be putting him in his grave without knowing for sure.

Thursday, 4 March

Never had Eglish seen such a week, nor its people played such a blinder.

Few places could do mourning like Eglish. Quiet solemnitude is the village's default mode. Perhaps the only parish in Ireland without a pub, there was no drowning of sorrows to be seen. McCann's shop window, opposite the church, was decorated with the back-page of a newspaper. 'A Born Leader and a Perfect Ambassador', it read.

Mixed in with their sadness, the locals exuded an intense pride that they had helped to sculpt his flesh and bone. Redolent of Mat the Thrasher and *Knocknagow* in 1879, Cormac had sported and won 'for the credit of the little village'. He had put this little-known place on the map.

Quite a few people took off work on Tuesday and didn't return for the rest of the week. They were marshalling crowds and making plans and serving tea and sandwiches. Some businesses were on virtual standstill for four days. Local construction firms gave up their yards for parking. It was a community effort the like of which I'd never seen before.

The GAA club initiated a park-and-ride scheme that ferried crowds to and from the wake. In among the fleet was the *Blackboard Jungle* minibus that Cormac's team had won for the school seven years earlier. He never got his trip in it. Now it was bringing hundreds of people to him.

On the eve of the funeral, locals were working frantically to get ready: putting up loudspeakers, setting up a big screen in the club hall, finalizing plans to close the village the following morning, and scheduling shuttle-runs in and out. Fr Breslan, a retiring sort stuck in the middle of an imbroglio, consented to one TV camera in the church – in a fixed position, on the gallery.

It was for media duties that we escaped the house that afternoon to visit the club. We were there to record interviews for a special BBC programme on Cormac, to be shown on Sunday. The 'Good Luck to Cormac from all in *An Eaglais*' placard was still affixed to the exterior of the clubhouse. A display of his awards and medals and jerseys, curated weeks earlier by Liz Daly, adorned a glass cabinet in the foyer.

Camera rolling, Jerome Quinn asked me what I'd say to Cormac if I had the chance. '*Tar ar ais*,' I said, spontaneously. *Come back.*

★

Every passing day, we grew in amazement at the impact of Cormac's life and death.

Countless thousands signed books of condolence, in person and online – the first time I had heard of this. Tyrone folk and Armagh schoolgirls and GAA fans around the world were logging in to write tributes. In Dublin, some Tyrone people wore county jerseys on their midweek commutes to work, as an act of solidarity. In Belfast, Tyrone students wore them en masse – within a day, the shelves of the O'Neills store were cleared of all Red-Hand-embroidered attire. In Sydney, Tyrone natives organized a special Mass.

Clannish Ulstermen like to show their sympathy in print, too. The *Irish News* carried thirteen columns of death-notices for Cormac that week.

We were overwhelmed by the extent of sympathy expressed by sportspeople right across the community that week. This tragedy seemed to transcend sporting boundaries like few things before.

Cormac's death was a 'shock to everyone in sport in Ireland', said Brian O'Driscoll on the TV news, as the Irish rugby team trained to play in Twickenham that weekend. A minute's silence was observed at Ravenhill, before the Celtic League rugby match between Ulster and Munster. Ditto at Leinster v. Cardiff, in Donnybrook. And at the inter-city boxing tournament, Belfast v. Dublin. And at Dennis Taylor's testimonial. And at a cross-hurling/shinty match between Catholic and Protestant schools from Belfast, played on Phoenix Park.

Joe and Rodney McAree of Dungannon Swifts FC called at the house. The IFA President, Jim Boyce, would attend the funeral.

The affection from Armagh GAA fans was noteworthy. They weren't far off Tyrone in the scale of their outpouring. Some Armachians flew flags from their houses in tribute. Even diehards who had come to detest the red hand both for a hundred reasons and for none at all downed cudgels and said aloud, 'He was one Tyrone player I had time for. He felt almost like one of our own.'

The goodwill stretched far beyond sporting realms. Local authorities were passing motions of sympathy, from Coleraine Borough to Passage West Town Council. Omagh District Council suspended its meeting that week as a mark of respect.

Sympathy and Mass cards were stacking up in the house. No need for the letterbox, they were just passed along in a chain from whoever was standing at the open front door. By the end of that month, we had about 3,000 cards and letters.

Thirteen years on, I opened up boxes of them. It was fascinating to read through them again, for they capture the emotional impact of Cormac's death in some ways better than memory.

They came from old pals, former classmates, staff colleagues and pupils of Cormac, relatives and friends of the family. 'This is the most difficult letter I have ever had to write.' So many of them opened like that.

They came from random admirers, high and low, from Leaving-Certers to Zimmer-framers. They told anecdotes of meeting Cormac, or simply admiring him from a distance through the years.

They came from families who had lost a child suddenly, some in similar circumstances. Many devout people wrote of 'the mystery of God's plan', enclosed prayer-cards and religious medals, and promised to pray for us.

They came from primary-school pupils, in letters of gratitude to Cormac, artwork, and acronyms of his name. 'Courageous, Outstanding, Robust, Modest, Achieved a lot, Courteous' wrote Yvonne O'Neill of Glencull.

They came from GAA clubs in nearly every county – from big boys like Nemo Rangers and Castlebar to tiny clubs like Glack, The Neale and Tara Rocks. From Chicago and Huddersfield and Sydney.

They came from prelates and priests and nuns far and wide. From Bishop Daly, who waved the white hankie on Bloody Sunday '72, to a Protestant clergyman in Derry. From Fr Peter McCarville in Onigbongbo, Nigeria, and Fr Oliver Stansfield in Ngong Hills, Kenya.

They came from all walks of education. School principals. The CCMS, ASTI and NASUWT and an alphabet soup of others. Lecturers from QUB and UCD, university sportspeople, authorities, and a vice-chancellor too.

One came from Seamus Heaney, to Mrs Martin: 'Keep the spirit level high as ever.'

They came from pensive GAA veterans. From medics Gerry McEntee in Meath and Dr Felix McKnight in Perth, WA. From Val Andrews, who disclosed that his sons frequently re-enacted Cormac's palmed goal that cost his Cavan team the 2001 Ulster final. From too many more to mention.

They came from public bodies. Foras na Gaeilge, the RTÉ Authority and two sports councils – ISC and SCNI.

They came from the private sectors of insurance, crystal and soft drinks.

They came from other sports. The IRFU President, the Ulster

Branch, and Ballymena RFC too. Conor O'Shea, M.D. of London Irish.

Ronnie McFall, manager of Portadown FC.

Hockey's Ulster Branch president, and the Dungannon and Cookstown clubs.

The Australian Football League.

They came from polar ends of the political spectrum. A letter from Paul Murphy MP, Secretary of State for NI. A telegram from Ruairí Ó Brádaigh. Letters from TDs, nationalist and unionist councillors. An epistle from Garda Commissioner Noel Conroy. A card signed by republican prisoners in Portlaoise.

Had this lot ever found common cause before?

The most astounding of all was a letter from the Imperial Grand Black Chapter of the British Commonwealth. That's the full name of the Royal Black Preceptory, the elite society of Orangemen. Catholics in general have a negative perception of the preceptory, and no one would have expected it to send us a letter. Yet it did, and with real meaning:

> This land would be a much happier and contented place if only other young people could aspire to and emulate the high standards which Cormac had set. I pray that his exceptional example may be followed.
>
> I would respectfully ask you to accept the condolences of the membership of the Royal Black Institution and in particular the sincere sympathy of those members who live in County Tyrone. They, together with everyone else in the wider community, are deeply saddened by the sudden bereavement you have suffered.
>
> . . . Yours most sincerely,
>
> W.J. Logan
>
> Sovereign Grand Master.

Wow! That really took us aback. It was truly symbolic of changing attitudes in Ulster. It was backed up by countless handshakes from besuited, homespun Protestant neighbours, letters and cards from unionist citizens we didn't even know, and a kindly soundbite from the Presbyterian Moderator – Rev. Ken Newell – on TV news. From those days to this, I never looked at the orange–green divide quite the same again.

My favourite of all, though, was the card that was signed simply, 'All the people on Tory Island'.

That evening, the pilgrimage of mourners lengthened again. It didn't really taper off till well past midnight. We were frazzled and half-frozen from the chill coming through the conservatory door. And I felt all stodged up after three days of the Wake Diet. Tea and sandwiches and biscuits, pinched off passing trays, and eaten one-handed between handshakes, while standing up. To make matters worse, someone had used a humungous tub of Flora to make the sandwiches. I couldn't but think, *Cormac did not authorize this muck!*

You need black humour to get through. Meeting an Eglish colleague who had spat bullets at us in a team meeting, I couldn't help myself. 'Who's gonna pass me the ball now?!' I asked with a half-grin. I promptly forgot I had ever asked. But over a dozen years later, he still recalled it.

Early morning, I retired to my own bed. On previous nights I had stayed with a local couple, Dermot and Betty Casey, for some respite. Since Monday's all-nighter, alas, I wasn't fit to sit up with Cormac past dawn. But with neighbours and relatives doing night-shifts, at least he wasn't alone.

Friday, 5 March

All week we had hoped that this day wouldn't come, but it came.

I was so worn out, I hadn't prepared a stitch to wear. With my suit and the black tie provided by Uncle Seán, I ended up putting on Cormac's pale-blue shirt – the same one he had worn to dinner at the Europa the previous Saturday.

Ten o'clock was the appointed start of the funeral procession. But with visitors still arriving anew in the house to offer condolences, it was hard to make headway.

Eventually, people exited in stages, and wider family peeled away to leave just the four of us with Cormac. It was our first time alone together since his passing on Tuesday morning. Given only a few seconds, we took a couple of minutes.

Seeing Cormac lie serenely at rest, with all the crowds and cups and ceremony stripped away, immediately I thought back to the two of us as wee boys. Those endless days, even before he said he seemed to be five forever, when the world cared not a jot about him.

I made a spontaneous request of Mummy.

'Sing those songs you used to sing to Cormac as lullabies. The ones that always made him cry.'

'Which ones?'

'Y'know, "It won't be long till our wedding day", and the one with the "ice-cream castles in the air".'

For all that she was grieving deeply, Mummy granted my request. She quivered through a few lines of 'She Moved Through the Fair' and 'Both Sides Now'. Since Tuesday morning we had been pent up, putting on brave faces, but now the tears flowed. If there was a right time to release emotion, this was it.

We said our final goodbyes and closed the casket.

For the first mile out, we walked and lifted him along the narrow laneways of the Brantry, flanked by Eglish players to our left and Tyrone men to the right. I harked back to so many days we had taken this same route home from school, only in reverse. Proceeding down the slope towards Tullygiven Point, we passed through the plantation where overhanging trees draw a dark veil over the road. Morning sun rays pierced the canopies and an audition of springtime birdsong filled the air above us. A roadside streamlet gushed and tinkled. It was Elysian and eerie at once.

The scheduled 11.00 a.m. start had long passed by the time we reached Eglish. Paused on the slope outside the church, we were encircled by a small nation of people standing motionless.

We entered to a fiddle solo, played by Gandy, eighty-seven years young. *An Chúilfhionn. The Coolin. The Fair-Haired One.*

The altar was more decorated than any I've ever seen, before or since. There were silver trophies, several jerseys, and large portraits of Cormac. Jerseys also draped his coffin. The Catholic hierarchy had recently issued an edict against such secular trappings at funerals. Cormac would've blushed to see the rules set aside for him, I thought to myself.

In the compact intimacy of our church, no one is more than twenty yards away. In the pew next to us were emissaries of state, north and south. Among the colony of dark suits, along the left side – what's still called the women's side – sat the Tyrone team as one. Directly above them on the gallery sat the entire Armagh team.

The four concelebrating clergymen had all known Cormac. Cardinal Seán Brady described him as a 'noble hero' and 'an icon in the proper sense of that term'. Fr Breslan spoke of him as a parishioner who 'did not berate his faith': 'his love for his faith could not have been better'. They shared the altar with Frs Donaghy and McAleer, who had taught and coached him at school. Bishop Lagan, who had confirmed him in this church fourteen years before, was also present.

Fergus and I delivered the biblical readings, but there was no eulogy or speech on behalf of the family. A couple of others recited poems from the lectern, independently. But we, the McAnallens, sought no special pedestals for Cormac. Besides, what could we say that had not already been said? His life had spoken for itself.

Receive his soul and present him to God the Most High.

It was time to take our brother to his eternal repose.

Daddy and Uncle Seán took the front; Fergus and Aidan Moore, the middle; me and Uncle Peter, the back.

'God is by my side,' the choir sang us out. I hoped so.

He was heavy, my brother. He dug deep into our shoulders as we walked out into silence. Between the peals of the church bell, I could hear only the snap and whirr of photographers' cameras. Realizing that this was our very last journey, I keened again.

Past chapel corner, we halted to let the next lot lift. The 500-metre stretch from there to cemetery was lined thick with guards of honour – of St Catherine's pupils, university teammates, teams from other counties, two players from each club in Tyrone, and so on.

Seeing a garish big floral wreath, inscribed 'MACCA', in the hearse, it dawned on me: the university housemates had been left out of the lifting rota. That was quickly sorted.

We turned left into the cemetery.

The grave that they dug him was the first in a new row. Beside and behind was only green grass.

We prayed, pulleyed him down slowly, and pitched in our flowers.

We uttered one last decade, halfway through which the *Sé do Bheatha Mhuires* fell to the family to lead.

Sin a bhfuil, we thought.

Then out of nowhere came the *pièce de résistance*. The voice of Micheál Ó Muircheartaigh crackled in the wind, accompanied by a lamenting flute. I had no notion this was coming.

Only while writing this book did I learn that Micheál had been approached by Pat Treanor, the Brantry's hirsute musician, during the Mass, with a poem scribbled on a page: *Perhaps it would be worth reciting at graveside.* Micheál replied, *Would the family want that?* Pat got word to Daddy, and a nod back. Micheál could hardly read the words, but he had heard them before, so he spent much of the requiem copying them out more clearly.

I had no idea about any of this at the time. But if I had to choose a bardic gatecrasher for a funeral, it would be Micheál, *Saoi na nGael*.

> *Less than a minute remains on the clock,*
> *As I tighten my lace and turn down my sock.*

It sounded vaguely familiar.

> *. . . Is that the crowd I hear, or is it the ghosts*
> *Of men before me who have faced the same test,*
> *And never once failed to give it their best.*

Now I realized I didn't know it, but it seemed perfectly apt for Cormac.

> *My father he gave me the love for it all,*
> *When he guided my arms to strike that first ball.*

The tears were welling up inside me.

> *. . . From boys in a field to a big crowd roar,*
> *There's never been anything to excite me more.*
> *. . . It's a dream that's consumed me since I was a boy.*

Yep, that was us.

> *My feet pound the ground, my foot sends the ball,*
> *It sails through the air over men who are tall.*

When Micheál lilted these words, you could see it clearly.

> *Then dipping and curling, it finds the goal,*
> *And just for a moment I'm in touch with my soul.*

That opened my sluicegates. The moment was hauntingly evocative. The poem, by Brendan Kane, was entitled 'The Beautiful Game'. It was the perfect coda to the occasion, if there could be such a thing.

*

Right to the end of the funeral, we tried to conform to others' plans and accede to each request. Though burning low on adrenalin, we kept on greeting, thanking and praising sympathizers – for we were so grateful.

Beneath the talk and behind the smiles, we were struggling with the vastness of our grief. That scarcely needs to be said. But a couple more misgivings were taking seed, in my mind anyhow. One was the sense that people were taking decisions about Cormac's legacy without consulting us, fully or at all. The second was the growing realization that not every sympathizer had entirely noble intentions.

I had spied only shards of evidence for these concerns during the week, but anecdotally we began to learn of people positioning themselves strategically for attention, and cameras. Posturing as dear friends. Pushing for places and brazenly name-dropping. Politicos parading through while pals and neighbours stood back. Pressmen imagining. Parkers noseying. (Many years before I discovered that some wake-goers just want a gawk and a gossip.)

None of these matters perturbed me at that time, nor should they have. They were clues, however, as to a future issue for us: did we have first say over Cormac's memory, or was it simply public property?

Now, as custodians of his memory, we had to consider always: *What would Cormac really want?*

16.   Aftermath

Now that Cormac was gone, nothing could ever be the same again.

There was a huge, irreplaceable void in our family.

Beyond that, who we were and how we lived changed overnight. Our roles as Cormac's Father, Cormac's Mother, and Cormac's Brothers were perpetuated, magnified and vested with new meaning. Life, and death, had thrust new responsibilities on us. As if to ram home the fact, the UTV programme broadcast on the Sunday week after his death was called 'Cormac McAnallen: The Legacy'.

As we saw it, our responsibility was about much more than keeping his memory alive. For our family, it was also about trying to live up to the high ideals associated with his memory; to continue his pursuit of perfection.

The exaltation of his name, and the veneration of his life, continued for a long time. His grave became a shrine. For weeks afterwards, a Persian rug of flowers spread from it across the row. Any day you drove past, you could see a steady trickle of figures up the pathway, and a lucky dip of licence-plates parked roadside.

From home we saw a thickening of traffic on the boreen opposite, with cars edging along and slowing to a halt at the farmer's gate that allowed a view of our house; we could only surmise that they were strangers, curious to see where Cormac McAnallen had grown up.

We became much more recognizable. When people met us for the first time, many could guess who we were from our surname alone. Some surmised privately.

Others asked, 'Are you anything to the lad that died?'

We got so used to that question that we could virtually see the cogs moving in their brains before they uttered it.

Many identified us from the media coverage. Never could I have imagined that I'd hear, 'I recognized you from the cover of the *Irish Sun*.'

Quite a few saw a physical resemblance and calculated the rest. Often people lapsed into addressing me as 'Cormac'. Moments later, they'd realize their error and apologize profusely. They didn't need to: they weren't dragging up a painful memory, for that memory had never left me in the first place.

At the same time, Cormac's constant shadow could be a bit over-bearing. I felt that nothing I could ever do would be as good as the one who went before. Chris Lawn spoke of a similar feeling when he resumed Tyrone full-back duties.

We remained on high alert for months. Nothing, least of all life itself, seemed certain any more. On the odd night, before going to sleep, I'd wonder, *Will I wake up in the morning?* A few times, without our knowing, Mummy sat up to watch us. Others talked of similar anxieties. The problem with being hyperconscious of your heartbeat is that you can misread or imagine an irregular rhythm. One evening in early May, I thought I felt a heaviness in my heart, and I related as much to Daddy. Off we went to the hospital. The doctors didn't want to take any chances, and kept me in for a week.

Anyone named McAnallen was being watched out for. Shauna McAnallen in Dundalk was pulled aside before her Junior Cert Irish exam to inform her there was a comprehension question on her cousin Cormac.

Often in the early months, when I heard a weird fact or funny story, I'd instinctively think, *Wait till I tell Cormac.* Microseconds later, the penny would drop.

But for many months to come, he remained a very real, living fig-ure in my dreams. There was a match about to start on telly, when the presenter's voice changed pitch to declare that he had a very special guest with him in studio.

'Cormac, first of all, it's great to see you. I have to ask the question everyone's asking: where have you been for the last while?! You've kinda been missed!'

'Well, Jerome, I suppose this has all been a shock to the supporters out there. Em, what can I say? Sorry I scared you! Everything had just got so much after the All-Ireland. I felt I really needed a break, and I sort of thought it better to slip off quietly. I had done something like this once before when I was a student in Belfast and, eh, that worked then. Obviously, it backfired this time, as there's been such a fuss. Again, I'm sorry about that. It's all over now anyway.'

'I think I can say, on behalf of everyone watching today, "Welcome back, Cormac". We'll hear more from you later. But before all that, we have to announce the winner of last week's competition . . .'

Then the signal went, and I awoke.

★

Each day brought poignant new tasks.

Giving back bags of footballs to school.

Handing back fluorescent bibs to county-board men.

Dealing with union reps to iron out his pension.

Sorting out the paperwork for his site.

Standing in for Cormac at functions that he had been set to do.

But as we sifted through his stuff, we found so many little things that filled us with wonderment.

The Trócaire box on his window ledge brimmed over with coinage; was it £70 or £80? We left it in on Good Friday.

There was his wallet, €555.50 and £40 in expenses cheques from broadcast interviews and clubs he'd visited around the country, going back four months. Was he going to lodge them at all, or was he holding on to them to donate to the players' fund?

There was his subscription to Queen's University GAA Academy from October 2003.

And there too was a letter from Queen's library, dated 20 February 2004, thanking him for his donation to its book fund appeal. His nameplate would be inserted in two of the library's books, it said: *Defining John Bull: political caricature and national identity in late Georgian England*, by Tamara L. Hunt; *Social Psychology of the Self-concept*, by Morris Rosenberg and Howard B. Kaplan.

That one blew me away. How many guys his age would feel the civic duty to donate to such a fund, let alone devote the time to sending it away?

Everything he owned, every item he scribbled on, now assumed something of a sacred quality. None of it would bring him back, but giving it away would be like losing a little, authentic memory of him.

The vast majority of the sympathy cards and letters were not answered. I reckoned that if we got five of us around a table for a solid weekend, we could have penned most of the replies. I besought others to join me for a Friday-to-Sunday session, flat out. But no one was biting. The prospect was too frightening. And I couldn't face doing it all by myself. So they remained unwritten. Which saddened me, for those people had been so kind to us in their messages, and many of them had recounted their own tragic tales. I hoped they'd understand that there was only so much we could do.

People respond to death in vastly different ways. Some people try to get back to daily business as soon as possible, to escape from the darkness and keep their minds occupied with anything but. Daddy and Fergus got out and about and back to work in Benburb within a couple of weeks. I was in a bit of a bind, though: I had been studying from home, and I didn't really think I could leave it to Mummy to deal with everything that kept coming our way. So I stayed about the house most days. Somebody had to.

Morning to midnight, visiting friends kept us company, shared stories, offered advice and left mementoes. Strangers called too, to express sympathy or spend some time with us, and became new friends.

Then there was the admin. Hour on hour, the phone-calls kept coming.

Not a week passed without new media requests. For comment on an article or documentary on sudden deaths. For a reaction to the latest such death. For a quote about Tyrone's progress. For a feature on how our lives were progressing.

★

The Irish, and the GAA especially, are obsessed with naming things after the dead. No other nation, or sporting organization, comes close.

And so the Cormac Boom began. Babies as far away as Cork were given his name, their parents wrote to tell us. The number of newborn Cormacs in Ireland rose by forty-four per cent in 2004, and a further eighteen per cent in 2005. The 260 born in '05 remains the highest since records began.

In May, the Mullaghmore and Castleview Community Association – MACCA, by chance – in Omagh planted fifteen trees with a central stone inscription in tribute to Cormac.

Queen's University awarded its Graduate of the Year Award posthumously to Cormac in July. Senator George Mitchell, the Chancellor, presented the trophy.

Shortly before the first International Rules Test in October 2004, the Cormac McAnallen Cup came to be. Some people, especially in Tyrone where opponents to the series were many, would prefer his name on a national GAA cup instead. But we weren't up for that debate. If Cormac was honoured to play for Ireland, we should be honoured to have this prestigious prize named after him. It's a fine piece of silver too – Croke Park personnel reckon it's one of the best they know. Yours truly translated the text to Irish, and took it to a jeweller's for engraving.

The Australian dimension took another twist in 2005, when Cormac McAnallen's GAA Club was formed in Sydney. This was the initiative of a few Tyrone natives, strangers to us, but young and full of enthusiasm. A GAA club in a foreign city can have an ephemeral existence; with no permanent home to call their own, it can take only a couple of key personnel to move on for such a club to fold. This outfit had grand ambitions, however. They went big on recruitment and PR. The publicity blindsided us a bit. It was while browsing online one day that I first heard tell of the club.

'No matter how many years pass, we will never picture Cormac any older than twenty-four years of age.' So read our family message to the club's launch function. We thought of how a club of twenty-somethings on their travels is forever young in its own way. Training on Bondi, playing beach football tournaments, fancy-dressing and revelling as their own community. They couldn't have been further removed from where we were, psychologically as well as geographically.

The 'Macs' grew stronger. Recruiting exiles from all over Ireland, they fielded in men's and women's football, plus camogie, from the early days. Hurling started a few years later.

Having a club at the opposite end of the world named after your younger brother takes a while to get used to. Seeing a fixture for McAnallen's v. Michael Cusack's, or playing in Pádraig Pearse's tournament, it seemed Cormac had entered the pantheon of Irish nationalist heroes.

★

There was no grand design behind Campa Chormaic.

Daddy had suggested holding a cultural summer camp for children in our native area, dedicated to Cormac.

The right people were around to make it happen. In spring or early summer 2005, Daddy and I sat down with Conall Ó Máirtín, our long-serving teammate, and his father Micheál. We brainstormed.

It'd be a five-day camp. Mornings of Irish classes and cultural activities in the BARD, Gaelic games at the Eglish pitch, and then home. Foras na Gaeilge would help to fund it. Conall pushed it on. We'd try it once anyhow. If forty children attended, we'd call it a success.

About seventy came, the vast majority from the parish. The place was a-buzz. We had a crew of local teachers and volunteers and special guest coaches. We had a special green camp *geansaí*. We had awoken the sleepy Brantry countryside with the romping of sturdy children. We had stirred a pride of place within them. '*Dúil sa Dúchas*' became our catchcry.

We threw the ball in again in 2006. This time it was a fortnight-long festival, and some 200 boys and girls came: from all over east Tyrone, in the main, but also pupils from St Catherine's, and a few from Belfast and Antrim. We had definitely tapped into something now. It was like a fun-size Gaeltacht up the road, which suited home-bird pupils and parents.

★

The Tyrone football team regrouped. There was group counselling and sharing of tragic experiences. They reminded themselves of

Cormac's opening speech as captain. They retired the No. 3 *geansaí* for the year and vowed to win another title for him.

They returned to action the Sunday week after his death, playing at Castlebar. For one day, Mayo became a site of football pilgrimage for Tyrone people. There was prayerful silence, during which the squad stood in the shape of the number 3. And there were miraculous visions too, for everything the Tyrone players did seemed to work, gusts of wind puffing the ball over the bar as if to order.

Mission complete, Tyrone gradually settled down to football reality. Cormac was badly missed as captain, as a steadying influence on the team, and as a hero to fans. And he left a hole to be filled in the defence. Yet, the bittersweet truth was that the Tyrone team was strong enough to replace Cormac, and to win games without him. All through 2004, before every training session and game, they formed a circle and reflected for thirty seconds on their old teammate and his attitude.

League, Ulster and All-Ireland titles were lost. In the flat aftermath, players talked as though they had let down the man himself. In retrospect, observers said it was never meant to be: Cormac's shadow hung over them too heavily. Perhaps. But retaining the All-Ireland would have been tough anyhow.

When your son or brother is playing at the top level, you see the pains and trials at first hand, and you get talking to the other players, and you're privy to inner workings, and you hear team news first, and you have people asking all the time, 'Is your boy ready for Sunday?' and you share in his nervous excitement, and your eyes constantly scan back to him, irrespective of where the ball is, and you feel the joys and agonies so sharply, and you celebrate or commiserate with him, and you help in your own little way to prepare for the next game.

And then that's all gone. And watching football is a much hollower experience. And victory is a duller thrill. And you wish for things as they were. And you know they can't be. And you question whether you really need to be there.

We had all gone to the first game in Castlebar, cherishing each divine moment, then falling back into our prolonged regret. We sent a 'good luck' card to the dressing room before the match. 'The Courage of Cormac's Parents' ran the *Evening Herald* cover the next day – a slow news day. Our parents were brave enough to go to most of the big games that year. They even visited the dressing room after the quarter-final defeat to Mayo.

I stayed at home after Castlebar. But had Tyrone made it to the semis, I would probably have gone. And I felt a profound sadness when they were knocked out. I had let myself sip of the belief that Cormac's team would win Sam, and bring about a fairytale ending.

2005 was a new year and a new phase. Cormac was rarely talked about in Tyrone dressing rooms now. A special symbol on their jerseys – a circle with thirty-one spikes – signified the thirty squad members and the one absent. He stayed in the back of their minds, but Mickey and the players had to look forward. As they progressed, I jumped on the bandwagon again.

The All-Ireland was the day of destiny for Cormac's team. They broke the *omertà* at last. Leaving the hotel for Croke Park, the players spoke of his vow to win a second title. At half-time, Mickey asked them to think of the thirty-first spike. 'What would he do now?'

It was a cliffhanger, and right to the end I didn't really expect them to win. So when they did, the emotional release was unlike anything I'd known before. This time, I didn't care to invade the pitch, but I felt – we felt – an indescribably intense pride.

It peaked when Brian Dooher raised the cup and started his speech. Straight away, he tipped his hat to 'the most important man' to be thanked.

'This man should be here instead of me, receiving this cup today. His name is Cormac McAnallen. Two months before Cormac was taken away from us, he told this bunch of players that he didn't want to be part of a Tyrone team that only won one All-Ireland. Well, Cormac, you now have two.'

The crowd paid probably the simplest and yet the most beautiful tribute ever paid to our boy. People don't mention it now, but I found it deeply moving.

'Cor-mac! Cor-mac! Cor-mac! Cor-mac!'

I could have listened to the crowd chant his name all day. It was spontaneous, and genuine, and touching. They had been thinking of him as one.

'We Did It For Cormac' was the resounding headline of the next day's papers. And Brian and Mickey and Sam slipped off undercover to the grave before the official homecoming. Acts of completion.

*

For Eglish, Cormac was irreplaceable.

He had been our one-off all-terrain model. Now, in one go, the engine was ripped out, the steering ruined and the suspension wrecked, and any spare parts we could source were never going to work as well. We weren't ready for the road ahead.

We tried to convince ourselves that we could defy adversity – *for Cormac*. For a few weeks, and after two intensely satisfying wins from our first four games, it seemed possible.

Then the wheels came off the wagon. Every defeat exposed our sorry state more starkly. We were rudderless and amorphous – a situation accentuated by the retirement of several veterans around that time. Nobody dared say it aloud, but our minds lapsed into balming the pain of each loss with the consolation that football didn't really matter so much any more; at least we had our lives, and look what became of the man who gave everything. This germ in turn caused a downward spiral: players would have an extra drink out, debate whether we were good enough for this level now, and slacken off in their efforts accordingly.

The club had put up a long portrait of Cormac on a foam board in both the home dressing rooms, mounted on the wall facing us on our way out to the pitch. It's a picture of him stationary with ball in hand, about to take a free-kick. There's a look on his face as if to say, '*Is anyone going to make a run for me here, or what?*'

Naturally, that image became a regular reference-point in team talks. What was meant to inspire could also have the converse effect, however. That picture was becoming a constant reminder of our failure to live up to expectations.

My glass case of emotion could crack over the smallest thing, but I had to internalize it. Like when someone called out during a game, 'We've gone dead, lads!' or 'C'mon, we're dyin' here!' I could only think, *We're not dead. Please don't use words like that.* (Ditto when run-down mobile batteries were spoken of.) And for our armbands, I thought black on black jerseys looked like nothing, but the white one I made kept sliding down my sleeve and putting me off my game.

Gamesmanship bugged me too. In my idealistic naivety, I had pre-sumed that all the clubs' tributes to Cormac the hero and role model would translate to chivalry when they next met Eglish. Fat chance. Some clubs saw us as roadkill, to be driven over again and put out of our misery. Never before had I seen an opposing squad kick six or seven balls at our '21' in unison, so as to delay a kick-out and prevent a late equalizer.

Heading home, with or without others, I couldn't dissect games like I used to with Cormac. It was a lonelier, emptier experience all round. It ended quite abruptly for me. After a hammering by Cooks-town one July evening, I hobbled off the pitch with a dead leg. (There was that word again.) Next thing I knew, my pelvis was badly tilted, my back buckled. I couldn't even run. That's how I stayed, in agony, for three years.

Eglish were relegated at the season's end. A second relegation fol-lowed in 2005, and by autumn 2006 the club was in the lower rungs of the third division. It was one last-day play-off from being the first team in Tyrone to drop from top to bottom, senior to junior, in con-secutive seasons. You could micro-analyse those three years to find many different faults, but ultimately the hangover from Cormac's death was the common denominator, the alpha and omega of our problems. Winning that play-off bought us some time, thankfully.

It was 2007 when the tide turned. A new wave of young spirits were winning as minors and claiming places on the senior team. They were the first upcoming generation in Eglish to glean some positive legacy from Cormac's death. A homegrown management team was snapping the whip. Old hands were renewing pledges to the cause. The Cormac factor changed too. He was still standing on sentry as we togged out, and he figured on our training-tops' insig-nia, but direct mentions became fewer in the inner sanctum. As we climbed the table and the mood lifted, the need to invoke his name receded.

Happily, I returned that summer. At last I could run again. I squeezed into a pair of boots from Cormac's room – they could've been his All-Ireland boots for all I knew; there was no way of knowing – and ran back onto Fr Connolly Park. Starting afresh from base-level, I was fit only to be a bit-part player. But that was OK for now. Eglish football let me live and breathe and see the sun again. My job spec now read: answer the spice-boys' deep philosophic posers; sing 'This Charming Man' into a beer-bottle; and if we win the league, host a party. Well, we did, and I did.

We were a charmed team again. League restructuring lifted us back up two flights where we belonged. Inside twelve months, we had gone from candidates for the fourth division to being promoted back to the first.

Eglish had regained equilibrium at last.

*

'Fair play to you, Sir.' That's what Mrs Kilpatrick and caretaker Eugene Weir found written on his board when they opened up Cormac's classroom, D31, one week after he died. They were looking for a football kit, but dreaded to go in. The message could only have been written by a pupil during his last day, without his noticing. Now it served as a fitting epitaph.

No teacher would relish taking over in such circumstances, but manfully they did it. The bulk of the burden fell to Mr Rafferty – or Pat John, as he was well known to our family. He was retired and was acting as a supply history teacher when called upon. He felt honoured to step into the *bearna baoil*. Bringing the A-Level Politics class back on track would be his toughest task. They were the pupils who had hung most on Sir's every word and handout. Now Mr Rafferty had the daunting workload of learning the curricular content afresh on the job until the end of the school year. A new young teacher, Ryan White, was appointed for 2004/5. Upon receipt of Mr McAnallen's files, he felt a sense of mission, and put the Politics class through extra after-school lessons from September; come June, they were rewarded in their results.

Starting in 2005, the 'Cormac McAnallen Leadership Lecture' became the headline event of the school calendar, with a packed audience of pupils and invited guests. We were there each year.

The girls' footballers were heartbroken to lose Sir. There were practical problems too. By her own admission, the assistant coach, Miss Creighan, was 'thrown into the lion's den'. But the team responded with real maturity. They organized charity games in his name. Some senior girls started to lead parts of training sessions.

The younger girls kept following his instructions, practising with their weak feet. In 2004/5, the under-14 team formed a huddle before every game. Hands in. 'On three, "McAnallen".' Two years later, as the under-16 team, they won the All-Ireland Schools Junior C final at Breifne Park. It was a first-ever national football title for St Catherine's. Mr McAnallen had left them with a rich legacy.

*

I suppose the whole idea of having services for heart diseases in Ireland began to take shape after the death of Cormac McAnallen in 2004. Sudden cardiac death in the young had been occurring before that, but it hadn't really come to the public's attention. People didn't report it. It was only when some very high-profile sporty people, who should have been the fittest in the land, died of heart rhythm disorders that people began to take note. [Dr Deirdre Ward, consultant cardiologist at the Tallaght Hospital screening centre, interviewed in the *Irish Times*, 17 November 2015]

So public and so mysterious had Cormac's tragedy been, and so many people would be potentially affected by similar issues, that we had to act.

We had to learn quickly about Sudden Adult Death Syndrome (SADS). One of the first things we discovered was that lots of young people had died suddenly before, but with much less publicity afforded to their cases.

Within days of Cormac's departure, we were contacted by many parents who had suddenly lost a son or daughter to heart conditions, mostly undiagnosed. These families had endured instant and devastating loss, and feelings of sorrow and guilt. A lack of public information and infrastructure to address their issues had exacerbated their bewilderment. They found that authorities in Ireland barely knew of the problem, let alone how to tackle it. Due to widespread ignorance concerning these conditions, some families had had to deal with misconceptions or rumours that their loved ones' deaths at home or on the road at night had been caused by substance abuse or suicide. These parents shared a common goal to prevent further deaths of this type. But they were disparate, seldom-heard voices.

The more we as a family talked to these bereaved, and heard what the experts had to say, the more we sensed our duty to raise awareness of these conditions. We didn't have to try to drum up interest; the media were already on the case. Simply by telling Cormac's story, and opening up the conversation to discuss heart conditions in general, we could raise awareness of the problem.

In Britain, the Cardiac Risk in the Young (CRY) charity was beginning to make some headway at that time. A private member's bill for increased provision of heart-screening was being tabled by Dari Taylor MP (Labour), on behalf of CRY, at Westminster on 10 March 2004; in addressing the Commons, she referred to victims like the 'young Irish footballer Cormac McAnallen', who had died the previous week.

The charitable sector in Ireland was much weaker. CRY had small separate operations north and south of the border which relied on a couple of families, but there was no national structure or island-wide co-ordination.

News of the sudden death of John McCall on 27 March shook the nation again. Just ten days after captaining Armagh Royal School to the Ulster Schools' Cup, he collapsed and died while playing for the Ireland under-19 rugby team in South Africa. There were extraordinary parallels with Cormac: two recent winning captains, based at schools in Armagh, dying without warning in the prime of their youth.

We became spokespeople and ambassadors for the cause before the month was out. Coverage continued to be fair, sympathetic and supportive for the most part, though certain Dublin media tried the angle that high-intensity training regimes mixed with illicit substances might be responsible for such deaths. The insinuation was either that – in its worst interpretation – these young amateur footballers had gone over to the dark side, like bodybuilders and pro cyclists who had met their demise due to steroids and EPO blood-doping; or that legitimate supplements such as protein shakes or creatine could have lethal consequences. About three weeks after Cormac's death, a pushy *Prime Time* researcher pressed Mummy to travel to Dublin for a live interview on a feature about SADS among sportspeople and *y'know, what they might be taking.*

Maybe these were understandable suspicions, for so little was known about SADS back then. Let's be honest. Inasmuch as people in Ireland had learned of Marc-Viven Foé, the twenty-eight-year-old Manchester City and Cameroon midfielder, dropping dead during the Confederations Cup semi-final at Lyon in June 2003, many had probably drawn the conclusion that he had ingested or injected something he shouldn't have, or that he had contracted a tropical illness. We knew nothing then of hypertrophic cardiomyopathy (HCM), the inflammation of the heart caused by exercise, and the cause of death determined by Foé's autopsy.

Thankfully, so many people could attest to the wholesome lifestyles of Cormac and John McCall, local heroes beyond reproach. (Indeed, it soon transpired that John had also died from HCM.) And few took the creatine hypothesis seriously. It had no medical basis. If it were toxic, sports stars worldwide would have been dropping like flies. Nowadays, if you were to push such a line, you'd be laughed out of court. But we were wary of it then, for we realized that a pointed comment or innuendo by a scandal-mongering journalist could tarnish Cormac's name.

On the night of the month's memory Mass – taxi to Dublin – Mummy and Ashlene went on the *Late Late Show*. We persuaded Mummy to take up the offer as it could be a platform to divulge the nature of SADS before the country. It proved fruitful. Interviews with survivors of similar conditions, including Antrim footballer Kevin Madden, widened the discussion to include the benefits of screening. And a presentation by Professor Bill McKenna, a Canadian cardiologist who had examined a sample of Cormac's heart in London, educated the nation about some of the different heart defects.

Prof. McKenna helped to identify Long QT Syndrome as the most likely cause of Cormac's death. This was explained to us as a range of conditions in which the electrical current to a person's heart can be disrupted. In particular, bearers of the LQT3 gene mutation could suffer abnormal heart rhythms during sleep.

Daddy was given a research project. Could he go back to his McAnallen family tree and identify other members of the family who had died young? He drilled down and found that a couple of cousins and a few other relatives on his mother's (McGee) side of the family had died suddenly at a young age. When we went to the London Heart Hospital for screening tests that summer, Daddy's ECG appeared to be typical of Long QT, and this, along with his accounts of fainting a couple of times as a boy, and the family history, was accepted by Prof. McKenna as a strong indicator of LQT3. Daddy was deemed to be a carrier of the condition. The rest of us were given the all-clear.

*

Cormac's death had really opened eyes. Month after month, cases of young people dying on pitches and in their beds were being given headline stories, each one tied back to Cormac.

In September, the Irish Heart Foundation convened the first national conference on Sudden Cardiac Death prevention, attended by 800 physicians. (The event was organized by Dr Joseph Galvin of the Mater Hospital, Dublin, who became a regular support for us thereafter.) Two weeks later, the Department of Health in Dublin appointed a national Taskforce on Sudden Cardiac Death to produce a report.

All the while, our phone hopped. It had become an unofficial charity hotline. For concerned parents whose children had shown symptoms of a weak heart and wanted advice on where to go next. For similarly bereaved mothers who saw that we had a media platform that they had never had, and encouraged us to promote the cause. For friends who offered to help us to raise awareness and funds to fight SADS. The Tyrone squad set the ball rolling by organizing a fund-raising concert at Quinn's Corner.

It was becoming clear that a charity in Cormac's memory was necessary. Club Tyrone, the PR and fund-raising auxiliary of the county board, threw its mighty shoulders into laying the groundwork and erecting the scaffolding. In December '04 it arranged press launches in Belfast and Croke Park for the announcement of a gala banquet. Brian O'Driscoll and Brian Kerr were invited to speak alongside Peter Canavan, to demonstrate that this charity would be for all people, not just GAA members. Daddy met BOD with a punch to the body, just to see if he was tight enough. Happily, his father, Dr Gary, was there on standby.

The branding of the new charity was also intended to appeal across the sporting spectrum. Niall Laird, the creative hand of Club Tyrone, designed a logo depicting a silhouette figure with ball in hand, against a backdrop of green fields, shrubbery and hills. The silhouette signified how SADS could remove a seemingly fit and healthy person from this world, whatever their background.

We decided to call it The Cormac Trust. Cormac would be recognizable on first-name terms, without our unwieldy surname that many struggle to spell. Plus, it was to be bigger than one family or code; it was for society as a whole. And the word 'Trust' seemed fitting of the man.

Tables for the 'Heart of Gold' banquet sold out inside a week. On an emotional night in February 2005, it raised £121,000. Quite a war-chest for a charity that had yet to take shape.

The Trust was formally established the following month, with the following aims:

to raise awareness of SADS among young people, and its causes;
to promote cardiac screening for young people;
to inform and lobby authorities for more screening facilities;
to provide defibrillators in the local region, with training in their use and CPR.

Back in February 2004, did I even know what a defibrillator was? I'd seen people (and ET) being shocked on hospital beds in films, but no more. By the end of 2006, the Cormac Trust had provided eighty of the devices free of charge to Gaelic, rugby, soccer and golf clubs, fire brigades, leisure centres and other community facilities in Tyrone, with training thrown in. For a while Tyrone had probably more defibs than any other county. The Trust extended its provision of defibs to some clubs and communities in surrounding counties. Liam Nelis, Paul Doris and Dr Gareth Loughrey did ferocious work in driving this programme on behalf of the Trust.

The Trust's work was being done on an entirely voluntary basis. The vast majority of its funding outlay went on the purchase of defibrillators – over £1,000 a pop – and training. You'd struggle to find many charities producing such a bang per buck.

It wasn't without hiccups. Months after receiving defibs, some clubs had locked them in a cupboard, away from view. This was no more than human error; volunteer officials were already over-stretched with duties. Nevertheless, the lesson in this was that clubs and communities should be encouraged to raise funds for their own defibs, in order to increase their sense of ownership and public aware-ness of the devices.

In 2007, we as a family helped the GAA to set up its first national defibrillator programme, whereby clubs could avail themselves of the devices at a reduced price. Still, some Luddite attitudes persisted in the public sphere. I had a meeting with a university health and safety official in the south to urge for the provision of defibs to cater for the thousands of students on campus. The response: there's one in the nearby hospital, and nobody's trained, and if we used one but weren't insured, yadda yadda . . . But four months later, the first defib on campus was unveiled.

Achieving some of the Trust's other aims proved still more arduous.

Raising awareness and lobbying meant more than achieving reams of publicity for Cormac and other SADS victims. It meant convey-ing several complex, even slightly conflicting, messages at one time.

An amount of publicity was targeted at sportspeople, because vig-orous activity could trigger conditions for some of them. To this end, a Trust poster ('Are You Fit For It?') was circulated to sports clubs nationwide.

On the other hand, there was a need to tackle the public

misconception that SADS affected only athletes, pushing themselves too hard. This impression caused frustration among other bereaved parents whose children did little sport.

We strove to counter such false impressions. In a feature for the Trust website, I wrote profiles of young men and women from all over Ireland who had died of these conditions. It was to show that people had different types of condition, that they died in different ways, and that our cause was not just about Cormac.

Pushing for more screening proved to be the hardest task for the Trust. Our family placed a lot of importance on screening, because it's the intervention most likely to save someone in Cormac's position: if you don't know you have an irregular heartbeat, and your heart stops while you're asleep, there's only a slim chance that someone will be able to recognize what's happening and revive you with a defib.

Screening encompasses some or all of the following, escalating in terms of complexity:

1. completion of a questionnaire regarding symptoms;
2. electrocardiogram tests (ECGs), which measure heart rhythm and electrical activity;
3. echocardiograms (or echos), which are ultrasound examinations of the structure of the heart and surrounding blood-vessels; and
4. genetic testing.

ECGs tend to be the most effective method of detecting Long QT syndrome in most cases. Had Cormac been screened in this way, the presence of Long QT – if indeed that's what he had – would probably have been determined while he was alive. But the condition can't be clinically identified after death.

Before Cormac's death, cardiac screening had been a rarity in Ireland; tests were carried out mainly on those who presented symptoms of an obvious irregularity. In the world of sport, screening was essentially within the confine of professional teams outside of Ireland. After Cormac's death, there was a rapid upsurge in demand for ECGs and echos in Ireland. Top-level sports teams, and families who suspected a heart defect, led the charge. Having learned of these potentially life-threatening conditions, they wanted to be sure. Senior teams from Tyrone, Armagh and Kilkenny were among the first screened; when their tests threw up a few heart anomalies, others began to request their own.

Many doctors, fearing they'd be inundated, urged caution in their public utterances on the subject. Ireland did not have an abundance of equipment to conduct heart screening nor of experts to read the results. They argued that merely a tiny minority of people had significant, detectable defects. They contended that mass screening would involve a significant number of 'false positives' – results that could be read as showing heart arrhythmia, where in fact none existed – and lead to undue worries, retirements from sport, and problems in obtaining life-insurance cover. Furthermore, they stressed the occurrence of 'false negatives', where certain heart conditions might not show up in screening and a person could be given the all-clear, with potentially fatal consequences. These were all valid points.

Our family heeded them, but still saw the need to make screening more accessible: however imperfect, it would save lives. We referred to the recently published findings of a long-term study in Italy, where participants in competitive sport are required to receive heart screening. Following the introduction of screening, SADS deaths among athletes in the Veneto region dropped from 3.6/100,000 person-years in 1979–80 to 0.4/100,000 in 2003–4, whereas the incidence of sudden death among the unscreened non-athletic population hardly changed. We argued that official policy closer to home ought to be as proactive in diagnosis for unsuspecting youths as for older adults in respect of illnesses. We advocated widened access to questionnaire and ECG screening across the 11–35 age-cohort – broadly considered the most at risk of SADS – and primarily for those playing sport. We argued that increased provision could be facilitated by public health services and private initiatives, so that anyone who wished to take the precaution could be screened with ease. We recognized that this would require great investment from government and sporting organizations, but we held that it was still the right thing to do.

We felt certain that Cormac would have wanted to know if he had a potentially lethal condition. His probable reaction to such a diagnosis would be harder to predict. Had he found out in summer '03 that he had a potentially fatal heart condition, would he have wanted to play on until the All-Ireland final? Alternatively, had he found out after that summer, with an All-Ireland medal in the bag, might he have been willing to take a break from the game or even retire, his highest sporting ambition having been fulfilled?

Change was coming, anyhow. The Dublin government's Task-force on Sudden Cardiac Death report, by sheer coincidence, was published on the second anniversary of Cormac's death, 2 March 2006. This report, 'Reducing the Risk', recommended ECG stress tests for all top-level athletes, and for families who had a history of relevant symptoms.

By 2006, CRY NI was hosting quarterly screening sessions at the University of Ulster for anyone who wanted it. In Dublin, the Mater Hospital set up a family screening clinic in 2007, and the Tallaght screening centre – funded by CRY Ireland – opened in 2008.

The GAA proved to be a harder nut to crack than you might think. For several years, we advocated that the association set up a mobile screening unit, which could travel the country to screen teams and individuals for a small fee. Commercial sponsorship and Trust contributions would have covered much of the cost. I drew up a detailed proposal for this, incorporating input from cardiologists and advice from CRY in Britain as to how their mobile unit worked. I submitted it to Croke Park officials. Response: zip, nada, no *focal* at all.

In 2007, the GAA's national medical committee proposed a trial screening programme of 500 players – chosen at random – and this was carried out over two years. Meanwhile, various county and club squads went for screening off their own bat.

*

The letter finally arrived in September 2006. We don't know why it took so long to come; presumably, the to and fro between medical experts had elongated the process.

The question: did we want a public inquest into Cormac's death?

After discussions with the coroner Mummy relayed our decision in January 2007. *No, thanks.*

Why not? Having accepted the Long QT theory of experts who had examined Cormac's case, we didn't have the appetite to go through this lengthy process in public. Also, we believed that an inquest was likely to tell us little new. The autopsy had discovered no visible heart defects, and we knew that the official inquest record for many sudden cardiac deaths where physical proof of the cause was not visible stated 'cause of death: unascertained'. Long QT could not be proven retrospectively. And a verdict of 'unascertained', reportedly baldly in the media, might be misinterpreted as meaning that Cormac's death was not heart-related, and this might in turn undermine the positive effects of the work of the Trust.

In the subsequent decade, even as we availed ourselves of new forms of genetic testing on Cormac's heart, we didn't look back on that decision. But while working on this book, and re-running Cormac's last laps, I have felt some fresh doubts about his cause of death. In particular, I have found myself dwelling on the head traumas he suffered towards the end of his life.

Before I started working on this book, I recalled that Cormac sustained three such traumas in his last year or so. Now, his medical records tell me that the three I recall were preceded by another, in November 2002. In a league play-off against Cookstown, he received a blow to the jaw. Five weeks later, on re-examination of the X-rays, a consultant noticed 'two small lucent lines' on the mandible – a possible undisplaced fracture.

So Cormac had four different significant head injuries in his last sixteen months. He was treated in three different hospitals, saw different doctors, and didn't check in with our GP. On autopsy, his brain 'seemed swollen'. Had there been tighter protocols about the reporting of concussion and treatment, could any bigger problem – if it existed – have been detected?

There is, of course, no obvious connection between head injuries and the heart. But recently, I've heard a theory from a person who treated Cormac during that period and recalls his headaches. It concerns the vagus nerve, which starts in the brainstem and networks with most internal organs. The left vagus nerve supplies the AV node, which is part of the electrical conduction system of the heart. In effect, the nerve controls your heart-rate. Stimulation of the nerve can therefore impede electrical impulses as they attempt to travel from the atrial chambers to the ventricular chambers – this is a recognized condition known as 'heart block'. So, could cranial trauma have impinged upon or inflamed the vagus nerve, in turn disrupting the regular signal to his heart, and thereby triggering cardiac arrest?

This theory is very much at odds with medical orthodoxy, and for this and other reasons it can be only speculative at present. My informant is not a medical doctor; nor am I. A vagal origin of sudden death has been hypothesized by some scientists, though not clearly demonstrated – so I read online, in articles by Dr Paolo Alboni, an Italian cardiologist. Unlike other unorthodox theories I have heard about Cormac's death that I won't mention here, I am willing to keep an open mind on the vagus theory. It strikes a chord with me on one level: the vagus also forms an essential part of the parasympathetic system, which calms down organs after 'fight-or-flight' adrenaline responses to danger, and Cormac was unusually overanxious in those last few months.

Still, I have to keep such ideas in proportion. Of all the boxers, rugby players and American footballers who have suffered concussion, few if any are known to have died soon afterwards with SADS-like symptoms. If nothing else, I think that Cormac's catalogue of head injuries, and the symptoms he suffered afterwards, underlines again the need for more post-concussive care in Gaelic games.

Cormac's death certificate was signed by Mummy on 28 August 2007. For Cause of Death, it states: 'Unascertained (Sudden Arrythmogenic Death Syndrome)'. It's unlikely we'll ever be able to say anything more definite with utter certainty. Some day, advances in the development of genetic cardiac screening may enable us to clarify whether or not hereditary disease was a factor, or *the* factor. Until such time, we'll stick with the Long QT explanation.

17. Remembering Cormac

> I am the Music Man,
> I come from down your way
> And I can play.
> What do I play?
> I play the piano.
> *Pia–pia–pia–no* . . .

Today, there are hundreds of things that trigger memories of Cormac. So many of them are musical.

To many of Tyrone's golden generation, Cormac will always be the Music Man. That song was his party-piece, and the times he performed it stand out in Tyrone players' memories.

Peter Canavan recalls Cormac singing it on a senior team weekend at Limerick in 2001, their first proper bonding session in two years; he was pleased to see how much at ease the lad was among his elders.

Further renditions followed the '03 All-Ireland. And then Mickey called on him for one in Dubai on New Year's Eve, when everyone else had eyes on the beach party across the way.

When Cormac was gone, that childish song could sound like a tear-jerker. One night on the All-Stars tour of Hong Kong in January '05, someone from another county started singing 'The Music Man'. While the other lads loved it, the Tyrone players present were weeping for the man who should've been there and picco-picco-picco-lo-ing for them.

'Gold' by Spandau Ballet was the other song they linked to Cormac. That's what he chose for the Tyrone team CD in 2003. He got a bit of stick over that one; shouts of 'Next!' on the bus, they say. The purpose of the exercise, he thought, was to pick music that was distinctive and inspiring, not necessarily your favourite song.

Lads picking U2 numbers were simply playing it safe. 'Gold' was the theme tune for many 1980s BBC sporting montages he had watched as a youngster, such as 'Sports Personality of the Year'; in his mind, it recalled past heroes and reminded them of the present prize at stake.

That song took on new meaning after Cormac died. It was a regular request on Omagh's Q101 station on 2 March and that week. Years of 'Friday Night 80s' shows later, it'd still hit me.

Relatives recall him going up to sing a duet of 'The Fields of Athenry' with Mummy at the worldwide McAnallen family gathering in summer 2000, and thinking *Isn't that great of him, not being afraid to go up and do that.*

Colleagues at St Benildus' remember him singing 'The Boys from the County Armagh' at their Christmas social in '01, and thinking, *Wow! That's very ecumenical.*

After his death, people made music in his memory. Fiona Kelly, whom he coached in football at St Catherine's, composed a flute instrumental, *'Tar ar ais'*. Malachy Duffin, a trad musician from Antrim, wrote a song of the same title. Damien Molloy, a trad singer from Dungannon, wrote a song in Cormac's name. The most famous piece was 'The Brantry Boy' by Mickey Coleman, a Tyrone teammate and singer-songwriter. Mickey released it as a single, and still performs it on stages around Ireland and America. I stay at a distance, if I can, when these songs are sung. I don't find laments about Cormac easy listening.

I prefer to remember him in a higher tempo. His high-pitched 'World in Union'. His 'Lethal!' mix-tape of late-'90s trance. And tunes that remind me of happy times together – moshing to 'In Bloom', or the laughing bout in the car to 'Because We Got High' on his road home from Australia, or the fresh riffs of 'Take Me Out' in our last trip to the gym together.

And one more tune.

It's him warbling the chorus of 'We Have All the Time in the World', with a deep, gravelly voice and Satchmo smile.

With all the cares of the world far behind us.

★

We've done our best to be true to Cormac's memory. To stay proud. To move forward, without forgetting.

There are few harder burdens to bear than the loss of a child. But our parents did not crumble or crumple. They accepted the yoke placed on their shoulders and they pulled like dogs. Distributing defibs brings a feelgood factor, but long debates about sudden death and its complex, often nebulous causes don't make for pleasant pastimes. It took a lot out of them, but it also gave them a strong sense of purpose. It took them around the four provinces to clubs, schools and community halls. It took them to Stormont, Westminster, Italy and New York. They collaborated with cardiologists and parlayed with Professors Casey, McKeown and Mossey – trustees and patrons of the Trust. So often I listened in awe of Mummy as she took tough questions from Joe Duffy or Stephen Nolan in her stride.

Our parents kept up other interests to maintain their sanity. Daddy bought the pub next to the family Spar shop in Benburb. We had a name at the ready. The name that Cormac had jokingly suggested for it, long before Daddy conceived of buying it: 'The Bottle of Benburb'. It stuck, and The Bottle has boomed. Since expanded to include function rooms, it's where we eat as a family on anniversaries and special occasions.

Their historical projects didn't end, either. They helped to form a committee that produced *The Book of Eglish*, a 512-page volume published in 2011. Daddy's still a driving force for local heritage schemes, and the go-to man about Benburb for American tourists.

Fergus has managed the finances of the two businesses, maintained the Trust's Facebook page and taken snaps at events. He wrote a sporting biography too – about another Ulster champion who died tragically. *King Fisher* tells the story of rally-driver Bertie Fisher, who perished along with a son and daughter in a helicopter crash in 2001.

Ashlene's married now, living and teaching in north Derry. She and Pádhraic have four children: a girl and three boys. Pádhraic is known as 'The Bee', but he's all buzz and no sting. We're very happy for them, and we see them a couple of times each year. Ashlene has been through a lot and has come out the other end.

★

Being Cormac's Brother can be like a goodwill magnet. This is especially so with long-toothed folk at GAA events and wakes. Like this:

Phonsie: D'you know who this is, Sadie?
Sadie: Who is it?
Phonsie: This is Cormac McAnallen's Brother.
Me: I'm sorry about your father.
Sadie: Och, is it? You look wile similar. Sure it's awful good of you to come. You've had your own troubles to deal with.
Me: We all have our cross to bear. Everyone's lost somebody close to them. Ours is just better known than most.
Sadie: D'you know this man, Wishie? . . .

I still get called his name. Frequently. If they realize their error, I say, 'Don't worry. I'm honoured.' It's said by people outside the GAA gene pool as much as by those within. In recent years, several strangers who would never have seen him play have done it in public. A Trinity College professor called me Cormac as I addressed a seminar group. A BBC NI presenter directed a question to Cormac where I stood on stage before a schools' audience at Enniskillen. A producer for RTÉ gave instructions to Cormac where I sat awaiting questions for a historical documentary.

The Cormac connection is the main reason I've stayed off social media. I don't want to say or do anything that would taint Cormac's image, or detract from the work of the Trust. It's his shadow again. If it didn't knock my confidence, it certainly made me more risk-averse.

Writing this book has helped me to unshackle myself from all that.

*

'To an Athlete Dying Young', a poem written by A. E. Housman in 1896, was referenced here and there in that fateful week of March 2004. Although many poems were penned about Cormac himself, and 'The Beautiful Game' marked the celebrated climax of the funeral, Housman's is the piece of verse that has moved me most ever since. Any time I see Robert Redford recite it in *Out of Africa*, or read it on a page, it stirs something inside me.

> The time you won your town the race
> We chaired you through the market-place;
> Man and boy stood cheering by,
> And home we brought you shoulder-high.

That was the homecomings of 1998 and 2003, Cormac being carted into Eglish on a trailer, crowds applauding on every side.

> Today, the road all runners come,
> Shoulder-high we bring you home,
> And set you at your threshold down,
> Townsman of a stiller town.

That was the funeral.

> Smart lad, to slip betimes away
> From fields where glory does not stay
> And early though the laurel grows
> It withers quicker than the rose.

> . . . Now you will not swell the rout
> Of lads that wore their honours out,
> Runners whom renown outran
> And the name died before the man.

That's the peculiar process of memory.

Like in 1890s England, the fame of early GAA heroes expired not long after they did.

There was once a young man from Eglish parish who was a teenage sensation for Tyrone, a county and Ulster full-back, but who died before his time. His fame lasted but a while.

Malachy Mallon kicked football for Dungannon, for his native parish had no team then. A strapping figure, he debuted for Tyrone at eighteen in 1925. He and his teammate Ned McGee – our granny's cousin, no less – became arguably the county's first star players. Two years on, the prodigious Mallon was full-back on Ulster's maiden

Railway Cup side. He also kicked the first Gaelic football penalty on film; it's on a Gaumont Graphic Newsreel of a 1929 Tyrone match online. (He missed.) In 1931, he won an NFL Division 2 medal with Tyrone – the first squad from the county ever to win anything – before leaving for England. He returned, but died of TB in 1938, aged just thirty-one. His folks were nearly all wiped out by the same disease.

His name echoed for a generation. Fathers about Eglish in the 1950s asked their sons, 'Who'll be the next Malachy Mallon?' But while the new heroes sprang up, memory of Mallon faded. Nobody talked of him in our young day. When I researched his story in 2011, only a handful of old folk had heard tell of him, and his burial place was unknown in Eglish.

Even today, memory can be so evanescent. Another Eglish man was once a Tyrone full-back, though few recollect it now. It was Paul Hughes, though everyone in football called him Buzzer. He played at No. 3 in the 1990 All-Ireland under-21 semi-final against Meath. He too died well before his time in 2012. Five years on, his tragedy seems as terrible and unjust as Cormac's.

They don't make many like Buzzer nowadays. He was a football prodigy: a senior debutant at fifteen, captain for our first minor championship, and a Tyrone under-21 player – all after losing an eye. He played midfield on our Intermediate Championship side of 1997. He was our biggest character: a sing-songer, a winder-upper, and a referee-befriender. We didn't always agree, but you knew he cared deeply for the club. He made a beeline for Cormac after Eglish's '97 minor final, to shake his head and serenade him. Likewise, when Tyrone won in '03, Buzzer chaired Peter Canavan above the crowd.

Buzzer found out he was ill in January 2012. Three months later, he was dead. At forty-two. Leaving behind Noleen and three children. Having neither drunk nor smoked. It made no sense then, nor does it now.

As Housman put it, '. . . silence sounds no worse than cheers / After earth has stopped the ears'. Do medals or memories really matter to a soul in the next life? Probably not. Memorials are about providing reassurance to the bereaved.

How we memorialize is also governed very much by the spirit of the age. People pick and choose the parts of an image that dovetail with their own objectives. Modern society worships sporting winners. Hence Cormac became something of a secular saint of our time. Had he been born decades earlier, or elsewhere, or not been team captain or an All-Ireland champion at that time, his sudden death would not have had the same effect, and the memory of his name would probably not be so strong or enduring.

Other SADS victims have faded from public consciousness. Read through their stories and you find glowing accounts of the character and accolades of young people like Aaron Lundy (nineteen) of Portstewart; Darragh Kelly (twenty-one) of Greystones; Ciara Agnew (fourteen) of Lisburn; Noel Quill (twenty-three) of Wexford; Conor Martin (sixteen), Darius Vasseghi (eighteen) and Robbie Simpson (nineteen), who all died in Dublin in May 2005; Marcella Doherty (twenty-four) of Bellaghy; Patrick Dinsmore (sixteen) of Warrenpoint; Ellen Minihan (twenty-six) of Tallaght; Oisín McGuinness (sixteen) of Newry; Cathal Forde (twenty-eight) of Gort and London; and Daryl Comac (fifteen) of Dungannon. Their lights went out with little or no warning either. Their families carry their pain yet, and with it they carry the torch of remembrance as the world moves on.

For years I vowed to myself that if I ever wrote a book about Cormac, it would profile other SADS stories as well, as they deserve. Now I realize it's too big a task for here. At least 500 young people, likely nearer a thousand, have died of SADS-type illnesses on this island since 2004. To do justice to their cases would require an entire book, a *Lost Lives* of the heart.

Another day, perhaps.

*

The Eglish club's desire to create its own memorial to Cormac co-incided with a pressing need for a second pitch to cater for increasing demand from its various teams. The 'Páirc Chormaic' fund-raising banquet in November 2006 launched the project. It wasn't until 2009 that the clearing and excavation work commenced on the site, in the townland of Brossloy.

But the real digging began two years later, when the ground development draw got under way. The club dispatched ticket-sellers all over the north, from Derry to Dundalk. Mention of Cormac's name sold a lot of tickets, we're told. For that precise reason, I stayed well away. I couldn't stomach cold-calling on the doorsteps; if people recognized me, would they feel emotionally blackmailed? Perhaps I worried too much about such things. The £240,000-plus raised in this way covered much of the bill for the ground.

Páirc Chormaic was officially opened on 27 May 2012. It was a glorious day for the village. The Artane Boys played martial tunes and the people paraded. The priest blessed, presidents spoke, and the plaque was unveiled. Four generations of our family were there.

A huge boulder outside the entrance bore the inscription 'Páirc Chormaic'. It would stand as a new milestone for Eglish.

The park lies around a bend at the foot of a narrow road on the outskirts of the village. Even with signposts up, it's not easy for strangers to find. During the planning, I wasn't keen on the location: it's half a mile away from Fr Connolly Park, so separate parking, fencing and amenities would be required – a pavilion with dressing rooms and a ball alley has just been built.

Its charms won me over in the end. It's a scenic pocket of tree-lined greenery, a tranquil hideaway. Big matches remain largely the preserve of Connolly Park, but this Páirc caters especially for the youngsters, and even some adult players prefer it here.

There hasn't been a regular McAnallen presence about the club for years. My playing days ended in spring 2009, when my hip flexors packed in. Even after an op, I stayed a crock, and for a time it was a struggle even to walk. Comeback hopes dissolved gradually, regretfully. My part in club affairs has been otherwise fitful: research tasks; accompanying red-card appellants to hearings; and Scór-quizzing.

Cormac's portrait hangs in the dressing rooms, looking at the men in black, urging them to do better. The younger generation don't mind his presence; they've seen him there all their playing days, and only as a positive influence.

When time allows, I hope to repay my dues to Eglish, to give something more back. For I'm proud to call it our club. Yes, I've written about cross words and bad feelings over football failings of bygone days, but such are the things that older and wiser colleagues of yore recall with regrets and wry smiles when they reconnect at weddings, wakes and funerals. I've recounted some of them here only as a true part of the big picture of Cormac's life. And in standing back to admire that big picture, I'm reminded how much he was hewn from the rock and clay of his native parish, and sculpted by its people.

That's what I emphasized back on that May day of 2012, speaking on behalf of the family at the opening of Páirc Chormaic. The ground should stand as another monument to the Barretts and Dalys and Donaghys and Jordans and Muldoons and Murtaghs and many others who had built up a club with bare hands and raw materials – not just to the man whose name it would bear.

I recalled also Eglish men who had moulded Cormac but had since departed.

Patsy Jones, a gent who carted us all over to juvenile quizzes, and passed away nine months after Cormac.

Paddy McIntosh, our first coach, and general of a football army, who mourned Cormac deeply. He died before his time at fifty-nine, in the week after Tyrone's 2008 All-Ireland triumph.

And Buzzer. Fresh in our minds, only a month gone from our midst.

Eglish hasn't forgotten Cormac, nor likely ever will. His name might as well be carved in the bark of the trees. Local youths have heard his name and seen his image as often as the times tables. Parents, teachers and coaches have told them. They have gone to his camps and worn the jersey. And now they play on his pitch.

★

March 2014 was an important threshold for us. We went back to Armagh City Hotel for 'Comóradh Chormaic', a banquet to mark the tenth anniversary of his death. Once more, Cormac packed the place out.

Micheál Ó Muircheartaigh started proceedings with a recitation of 'The Beautiful Game'. He had driven from a TG4 recording in

Connemara, through a thunderstorm, to be there on time. Typical Micheál. He has been an official patron of the Trust for over a decade and has spoken at several Cormac-themed events.

In those few moments, he brought us all back to March 2004.

Then a ten-minute photo-reel showed Cormac's life in chronology, to the accompaniment of 'The Long Road'.

It had been a long road. We were there to reflect on it, recognize a decade of good work, and look to the future. We had been bowled over by the generosity of the public. Right through the recessionary years, strangers continued to organize fund-raisers for the Trust: bag-packing, barbecueing, cookbook-publishing, distance-running, house-decorating and skydiving, to name a few. Many of these people had suffered in some way, too. Tonight we had to show our appreciation of major contributors. We also raised funds on the night, and wrapped up with the happy announcement that PwC NI was naming the Trust as its official charity for a second year.

When we took that step back on the night, it was clear to see that an incredible amount had been achieved in combating SADS in the ten years since Cormac's death. Another three years on, it's clearer still. The medical profession and the public are so much better informed and prepared than they were a decade ago. Provision of cardiac screening has increased hugely.

Attitudes have changed, too. The change was driven from ground level. So many county and club teams and individuals were getting screened of their own accord, not wanting to be hostages to fortune. In 2011, Croke Park announced that all county senior teams would be screened as a matter of course. After six years, it had arrived at the destination we had been pointing it towards, only it had taken the scenic route.

Wherever you work, learn, play or shop, chances are you're within shouting distance of a defibrillator. Local councils have installed them in civic spaces. Schools and universities have acquired them and trained teachers to use them. Sports and community facilities have them to hand. Offices have brought them into their H&S policies. The Henderson Spar group has, upon Daddy's suggestion, been working to have a device fitted in each of its 300 NI shops. It's a rare sports or community facility that hasn't one to hand. By 2013, the GAA had subsidized over 1,500 defib purchases. And whereas clubs once locked them away, often out of view, and kept the keys hidden, most now store them in easy-to-open cases. When a defibrillator is needed, every minute counts.

Public awareness isn't yet what it should be. Ireland has one of the highest densities of community-based defibs in the world – roughly one for every 500 people – but many people don't know where their nearest defib is, and a HiQA report criticized a lack of standardization and linkage to emergency medical services.

Nevertheless, we draw solace from stories of Trust defibrillators saving lives.

The Brookeborough club in Fermanagh received a device from the Trust in 2006. Six years later, in August 2012, Peter Boyle was umpiring at one of the club's league games when he collapsed. Someone ran for the defib outside the clubhouse at the far end of the field. A visiting Aghadrumsee player, who was a paramedic, affixed the pads to Peter's chest and side. 'Stand clear!' warned the automated machine voice, and the shock was administered. Peter's heart revived, though he remained in an unconscious state. Three days on a life-support machine later, he awoke. 'I was told in the Royal and by a number of others that, only for the defibrillator, I wouldn't be around today.'

In August 2014, Kevin McCloy (thirty-five), a former Derry dual player, collapsed while playing for his club, Lavey, in a football championship game at Owenbeg, Dungiven. For seven minutes, he had no pulse. The ambulance service defibrillator didn't work. The seven-year-old Trust defib on-site did. Three days later, he awoke.

The device that saved Seaghan Kearney (thirty) was donated by a local pharmacist to Oliver Plunkett's/Eoghan Ruadh, Dublin, in response to Cormac's death. Seaghan was playing five-a-side at the club in 2010, when he collapsed. He was clinically dead for five minutes when an off-duty fireman pressed the red button. He's a maths teacher, born around the same time as Cormac, and is now an expert stats-man for the Dublin football teams. 'It was Cormac's life that saved my own,' he tells anyone who asks.

The provision of defibrillators at all major GAA grounds, another

Cormac legacy policy, has saved more lives. In May 2015, Owen Roe O'Neill (sixty-eight) – a playing colleague of Daddy's with Benburb in the late 1960s – was watching the All-Ireland under-21 football final at Parnell Park when his heart failed. Dr Michael Logan, the Tyrone team doctor, gave him one last electric defib shock when all seemed lost. He revived. Sadly, a Tipperary supporter died at the same match, despite efforts to defibrillate him.

The saving of Bolton Wanderers footballer Fabrice Muamba with a defib in 2012 was the biggest SADS story in England to date. His revival after seventy-eight minutes of being 'in effect dead' was a miracle, a joy and cause for hope. At the same time, it took me back down that long road. Could Cormac have been brought back, if he'd been shocked for that length? Or could I have saved him by using the right CPR the minute I found him? Muamba was the exception, though. They couldn't save Miklos Feher of Benfica; or Antonio Puerta of Sevilla; or Phil O'Donnell of Motherwell; or Daniel Jarque of Espanyol; or Cheick Tiote, formerly of Newcastle.

The screening regimes brought in on foot of Cormac's death have almost certainly saved some athletes' lives too.

Simon Best, the Irish rugby international, retired after a cardiac abnormality was detected.

Seán Prunty, a top-scoring striker and twice FAI Cup winner with Longford Town, had a heart arrhythmia detected by screening in 2008. A loop recorder was inserted, and he retired from soccer.

Cormac Ryan, a Dublin under-21 hurler, was screened and found to have heart-block in 2012, following which he had a pacemaker fitted and resumed playing.

We know of other players closer to home whose post-Cormac screening led to curtailment of activity, or surgery, or retirement.

Survivors have become an extended family to us.

Seaghan Kearney has retold his tale for defibrillator awareness video messages. His parents, Pat and Bernie, sit on the management committee of the Trust.

Cormac Ryan has cycled the thirty-two counties twice with a team of friends, donating thousands of fund-raised euros to the Trust.

Kevin McCloy is now a patron of the Trust, and an active one. He has been a roving ambassador on highways and byways, and attended its nitty-gritty meetings, all while having four young children at home. It's odd how the wheel of life turns. Back in 2001–3, Cormac and Kevin played on Tyrone and Derry sides that often got entangled in squabbles. Now their lives are intermeshed in the most positive, profound way. Kevin has become like another son to Daddy – just look at the number of jobs he gets asked to do.

As a member of the Irish Heart Foundation's 'Prevention of Sudden Cardiac Death Council' for several years now, Mummy keeps abreast of developments and stays in contact with key stakeholders. Since 2009, the Trust has contributed approximately €80,000 to the Mater Hospital, Dublin, starting with €30,000 for its screening clinic, and latterly €35,000 towards research into genetic screening.

Genetic screening is the big-ticket future objective for the Trust. Research into family clusters of inherited cardiac diseases has been advanced considerably in Ireland over recent years. Some day soon it might be possible to identify every person in the land who has a genetic condition within the SADS category.

In the meantime, there are vital, unglamorous and unceasing functions to fulfil from the Trust office in Benburb. To keep communities vigilant, active and ready. To train volunteers to conduct CPR and use a defibrillator; and to provide their refresher training each year. To remind people to check weekly that their defibrillators' batteries and pads are in working order. To co-ordinate fund-raising. To speak at local events. To update the database of defibs distributed. To answer inquiries and provide advice to anyone seeking it. To maintain a presence for the next time SADS strikes.

*

Campa Chormaic has grown beyond our wildest imaginations. It now has seven venues in four different counties. Nearly 1,000 pupils overall attend each year. By now, most of them were born after Cormac died, and none of the others are old enough to remember him as a living person. And two-thirds of the attendees aren't even from Tyrone.

We take part in the admin and try to visit most of the camps, to speak and present awards as requested, year after year. Sometimes the journey can be like a distant wake. We might be going out of duty or obligation rather than pure desire, but when it's over we're glad to have met the people we've met and have said what we've said.

The question arises, though. For how long should we keep it up?

As a family, we're more philosophical about that than onlookers might think.

If interest in memorial projects drops off, so be it. If the time comes to fold up the Campa tent, we'll fold it. If and when the Trust runs out of steam, we'll pack it away. If the International Rules series be discontinued, retire the cup to a good home.

We don't rely on these things for survival, or to keep Cormac alive in our minds and hearts. For the present, we see them continue because others still want them.

Seen in the wider context of post-conflict northern society, projects such as Campa Chormaic and the Michaela Camps (founded in 2012) and the Spirit of Paul McGirr (founded in 2007) project more positive and hopeful ideals than the memorials that went before them around these parts. Living for Ireland, not dying.

In the Eglish club, some say that the camps have re-energized interest at youth level. Lads who picked up a *camán* at Campa Chormaic have become the first Tyrone hurlers from Eglish – Ryan Jones, Seán Muldoon and Kevin Muldoon.

The McAnallen's club in Sydney prospers, supports the Trust, and has spawned several marriages. It'll last. *Just keep it between the lines, lads and ladies*.

Some day we'll give it up. We're just not there yet.

★

The GAA was good to Cormac, and it has been to us. That's important to remember, however frustrating it can be to deal with its byzantine workings from time to time.

I can't imagine that if Cormac had been a member of any other sporting organisation, he would be so praised, blessed, adored and glorified. Certainly not to the point where you could still see his name on so many jerseys over a dozen years after his death.

We've been treated to extraordinary acts of generosity. In the early years after Cormac, Danny Murphy and Miceál Greenan of the Ulster Council presented the McKenna Cup Mark II to us permanently, supplied free tickets on tap, and treated us like minor royalty; ask, and we'd receive. County board men and club officials and elder statesmen went out of their way to help us where they could. Ordinary members couldn't have been kinder. The late Jack Boothman, the former president, became a good friend.

In those early years, I plunged ever more deeply into Croke Park committee-work and other voluntary GAA admin – partly in order to augment our campaign to combat SADS. For a time, it served as a helpful release from darker subjects. I believed in the GAA, religiously; I would have preached its doctrine on anything back then.

That faith was tested, and weakened subsequently, though it holds on. Perhaps it's just that I believed too much in the first place, and I'm now a plain layman with commoner doubts.

I'm referring to a changing ethos in the association, but also the personal touch. It's fine when you're nodding and smiling and shaking hands like you're expected to. I once spoke on a motion at congress for five minutes, bang on time to the last second – I nailed it. And then I got a round of applause for being Cormac's Brother, at the president's prompting. Motion passed.

But when you're on the 'wrong' side of a debate, or expressing an individual viewpoint, some officials can turn on you very quickly. And the magnet of goodwill that comes with being brother of a tragic hero can reverse in polarity. A few times, I've encountered adverse responses that seemed to say, *Lookit now, I had sympathy for ye and all when you suffered your loss. But don't go abusin' your position now, thinkin' you're a big-shot.* It's as if I chose that mantle.

In life in general, and particularly the GAA, I hark back to three pieces of advice that Cormac gave me at different times.

Write your own script; it's not written yet.

Don't be pessimistic, or you'll have self-fulfilling prophecies.

Be careful who you trust.

I wish I had paid more heed to them all, especially the last one.

Our family's trust in people, inside and outside the GAA, has been largely repaid. On occasion, however, it has been short-changed, even mis-spent. There've been a few people who'd attach themselves to Cormac's image, and then do something completely contrary to his values. Sometimes it might've been simply human error. That fundraising money wasn't intended to rest in the account indefinitely. Those words or actions concerning a memorial project probably weren't meant to be insensitive. That liberty taken with Cormac's name may have owed to naivete or immaturity, and no more. These things pass.

I'll try to keep up my trust in people, and in the GAA. And the GAA has given back trust in return – Croke Park announced the Cormac Trust as one of its official charities for 2016, donating €20,000 to the cause.

*

Don't know what I'm doing next year – need to know soon! or going to crack up!

14 June 2016. Fifteen years on from when Cormac wrote those words, I copied them into my diary.

Writing this book and reflecting on Cormac had caused me to focus again on my own life. It ended up taking me down a route that I never anticipated; down a route that would in some ways bring me back closer to him than I had been since the day he died.

For a few years after Cormac's death, I lost sight of my own career path. I became sidetracked by voluntary endeavours and trying to pursue other unattainable goals, like compiling a perfect doctoral thesis about the history of the GAA.

Meeting Pauline in 2008 re-balanced my spirit level. She's The One. As in, 'The One who turned that man around'. She never met Cormac. As a Tyrone girl she knew his story, though she wasn't a hardcore *take-down-that-effin-umbrella* type of fan. She didn't realize the extent to which the carousel of commemoration still carried us around, but she has helped to alleviate its burden.

As we progressed through rites of passage together, she and I have had new reasons to miss Cormac.

He was the absent best man when we got married in 2011.

It was his site that we built our house on and where we live today.

He was the missing uncle and godfather when our three girls were born.

And I might have performed these same roles for him.

For years I hoped to secure an academic history post in a university. I kept plugging away, despite noticing that history-lecturing jobs were being slashed. Then came a moment of clarity.

I was at Queen's University in early June 2016. Generations of students have come and gone, but the university's GAA clubs commemorate Cormac yet. Four months before, they had worn the Trust logo on their jersey in lieu of sponsorship. Today was the occasion of the fifth presentation of the Cormac McAnallen Medal, awarded since 2012 to the student adjudged to be the most committed Gaelic games clubperson at the university. Peter Canavan was there as special guest, to present the 2015/16 medal to Ryan Murray of Antrim. I was also asked to speak, but was warned by club officials not to mention the war.

What war? A week earlier, the vice-chancellor of Queen's said in an interview that 'society doesn't need a twenty-one-year-old who is a sixth-century historian', but rather one 'who really understands how to analyse things, understands the tenets of leadership and contributing to society, who is a thinker and someone who has the potential to help drive society forward'. The secret was out: the filleting of History departments wasn't due simply to enforced cutbacks, but also to an ideological scorn for the humanities.

Now that I'd be speaking about Cormac's time at Queen's, how could I not reflect on him as a twenty-year-old history graduate who had studied the sixth century? I didn't go for the jugular, but I did make a connection between his analytical skills and his contribution to society. Deal done, point made.

On my way home, I found myself thinking hard. Where was I going career-wise? If one so eminent could write off thousands of history graduates, then my stock as a historian must be pretty low in the minds of a lot of influencers. I'd have to do something different for the sake of my family. My mind turned back towards Cormac. Writing this book, I was thinking and writing about Cormac's career crossroads just as I was reaching the same juncture myself. And the signpost was telling me to take the same road he had travelled. This might be how to find my solid perch in the world. So I enrolled at the thirteenth hour for the PGCE at Coleraine, on a reserved place to do the course with Irish. A decade and a half after I had got Cormac into teaching through a back-door route, he was – through inspiration – repaying the favour to me.

The PGCE is a tough, tough year. A tree's worth of paperwork, limited sleep, and daily servings of humble pie. Any pretensions you might have about yourself are stripped away. I was once the youngest boy in my year. Here now I was the oldest. And most of my whippersnapper classmates had no idea about Cormac. Which I found strangely refreshing.

Once we hit teaching practice, though, it started again. On my first morning at St Joseph's, Donaghmore, a girl in 9I, Orlaith Ní Agáin, asked me the question as we crossed the courtyard:

'*Nach tusa deartháir Chormaic McAnallen?*'

The question wasn't entirely a surprise. The school holds the biggest camp of Campa Chormaic, and four years earlier I had presented an award to Orlaith. In a solidly Tyrone school like this, lots of pupils have heard about Cormac as they've grown up. *Beatha le Bua*, a series of booklets about famous lives, are dispersed around Irish classrooms; you'll find copies of one on Cormac, along with Martin Luther King, Patrick Pearse, Mother Teresa, Aung San Suu Kyi, Bono and so on.

The experts in diversionary tactics brought it up in the classroom:

'Sir, are you Cormac McAnallen's brother?'

I wrestled with both awkwardness and pride, but I gave a noncommittal answer, and moved on.

His influence – albeit indirect – will linger on school walls. The defibs are on show, so too is the list of those trained to use them. Pupils who have heart conditions are identified on a display in the staffroom.

The reminders kept coming, in the most unexpected ways. For my university inspection, I had to deliver essentially the same lesson that he had taught on his last day: 'Who should be king in 1066?'

I approached my second placement with a certain trepidation. It was at St Catherine's, the school where Cormac had taught. All roads were leading me back to Cormac.

I started in late February 2017. It was the anniversary week, so I was intensely aware of time as well as place. I had visited the school only a few times since '04. Now, I was walking in his footsteps here as never before. I was treading the same passageways, mapping his former routes, and perhaps getting a closer glimpse of the mental and physical landscape of his last days here. During my first Thursday lesson, the girls of 10M had to tell me I had written the wrong date on the board: '2/3/07'. My head was halfway between '04 and '17.

Some teachers were surprised to see me. For those who remained from back then, it was like a sudden leap back in time. They either knew me from before, or could work me out in a flash. And in the early days, I was called 'Cormac' a couple of times.

He's still remembered at St Catherine's — more than I could have imagined. His image and name are omnipresent in the tapestry of the main corridors. Standing with the school football team in '02. A sponsorship picture with Daddy, players and coaches. Promoting Youth Sport in a suit. A sports day with pupils. The dinner ladies keep him up on the wall of the canteen. The chaplain Matthew hangs a picture of him that his late mother first framed. And in the IMU building, the large portrait of him holding the McKenna Cup in February '04 still greeted everyone in the main entrance. You couldn't not notice him here.

I was up there also, among the collages of snaps of leadership lectures held in his name up to 2010. It's odd to start an apprenticeship, see yourself pictured a dozen years earlier, and say to yourself, *Look at the state of me there*.

Two of the newer teachers were mere Year 8s here when he died, and one played on his under-14 team. Now they take charge of school teams. Some of the lively 8I boys tell me with glee that they played on my brother's pitch yesterday.

With Cormac looking over – or at – me each day, I got through it. I qualified.

★

Cormac's room today is like a large time-capsule.

It's not a shrine – things have been moved, taken in and out – but most of the stuff that was there on the night that he died is still there.

His winning jerseys are here, the medals as well. His spoils of swapped jerseys too. His suits and shirts still hang on the rack. Shoes and boots and balls and kitbags lie around.

There is the VHS stash: '90s Gaelic matches, World Cups, Euros, and the Leonard v. Duran trilogy. *The Canavan Way*. Tapes of NBA matches, each with his own star rating: Spurs v. Rockets, Feb 1996 ★★★★; Bulls–Miami, 97 ★★; Utah–Chicago, 1998 finals ★★★★. Then the comedy stuff: *Police Squad,* Harry Hill and Alan Partridge taped on VHS. *The A-Team* in multiple. *The Day Today*, Reeves and Mortimer, and Ali G, as purchased. Even an *Après Match 1994–2004* DVD.

There are two Travel Scrabble sets, and the *Official Scrabble Words* book.

The bookshelves are full. Tomes of facts: *Guinness World Records*, *Top 10 of Everything*, millennium record books, sports and pop quiz books. A dictionary, thesauruses, and driving-test manuals. Five Bill Bryson travel books. Paperbacks on the Vietnam war and English football hooliganism. *Resurrection Man* and an Irish literature anthology.

There are the sports books he was reading around 2002–3. Autobiographies of John Eales and Martin Johnson. Biographies of Paul Gascoigne, John McEnroe and Diego Maradona. Paul Howard's *The Gaffers. The Tao of Muhammad Ali* and *McIlvanney on Boxing*.

There's a clutch of books that we bought for him after the '03 victory. Mickey Harte's diaries. *The GAA in Tyrone: The Long Road to Glory*, by Joseph Martin. And more.

There's my last present to him in February '04, a history book. *A Terrible Beauty is Born*.

There's so much evidence of his teaching. Exercise books from his own schooldays, used for reference. Textbooks on history and politics. A run of *Newsweek* issues from December '03 to February '04. Large 'Quote of the Day' sheets from classroom displays: Churchill, Gandhi and Gary Player ('The harder I practise, the luckier I get').

There's a shoebox of match-programmes. Another shoebox of good luck and congrats cards. And a box of yellowing newspapers, for the 2001–4 scrapbooks he had never time to make.

Any time I root around in here, I am reminded of something I forgot, or didn't know before.

What strikes me today is his care for his body. His drawers contain every type of gel and balm and ointment and cream that you can imagine, plus Epsom salts. And sellotaped to the wall still, 'Tyrone Players' Safe Medication List'.

Yes, that's the true Cormac. Better safe than sorry.

*

The big dates swing around every year. What hits me hardest is to hear his name read in church – even now, it still sounds intimately raw, and wrong.

Often people remark, at commemorative occasions and in public forums, on all that he would have done, had he lived on. He would have led Tyrone to more All-Irelands. He would have become a principal, a president and more.

All of those things might have come true, had he lived. But such prospects are not what I think about when I imagine Cormac alive. I imagine us as neighbours at Gortmerron, in and out of each other's back doors, raising our families side by side. Pucking and kicking, coaching and collaborating, scribing and scrabbling, jibing and joking, car-pooling to wakes and carping over young ones nowadays. Taking turns at mowing the lawn, and rowing about the strimming.

Epilogue: The Future

What on earth will the future be like?
A question plaguing writers and thinkers alike
It cannot be found, but everyone tries.
When it happens it no longer applies.
The invisible, inaudible fourth dimension,
The will of God, time's extension.
If only we could get a sample,
Put it up as a prime example,
If only we could catch a glimpse of the future.

[A poem written by Cormac, published in the school magazine, 1994]

22 April 2017. It's the day of the fifth 'Cormac Run', a 10k organized jointly by the Trust and the Eglish GAA club.

It's also my first run of any sort in over eight years. For months I have set this as the target for a comeback. Stretching and osteopathing, but not daring to jog, lest I hurt myself.

But today is the day.

Pauline and our daughter Ailbhe, who has just turned five, are doing the 5k course, with the other two in the double-buggy.

Away we go. Somehow I hold together, without putting my back out. I cross the line in 1:01:31. The last man home. But I'm probably the most elated one there.

Still he inspires me.

Watching our children come to terms with the subject of death can be unexpectedly amusing. Ailbhe was three years and nine months of age in January 2016, when the following conversation took place.

Ailbhe [pointing to a knee-strap]: What's this, Daddy?
Me: It's Uncle Cormac's.
Ailbhe: But why did Uncle Cormac leave it behind?

Me [pausing]: . . . Because he died. Because he wanted to see
God.

Ailbhe [pointing]: But why is Uncle Cormac up there in the
sky?

Me: Because he wanted to see God.

Ailbhe: [holding a phone] Is this Uncle Cormac's, Daddy?

Me: Yes.

Ailbhe: But why did he leave his stuff behind in my house?

[Pauline arrives home]

Ailbhe: Mummy!!

Me: Go tell Mummy what you said.

Ailbhe: Mummy, these are Uncle Cormac's and he lives in
the sky.

Pauline: Oh really?

Ailbhe: Yes. He went to see God. But why did he leave these at
my house?

Pauline [mesmerized]: I'm not sure.

Ailbhe: But how will we get his phone and his stuff back to
him?

Pauline: We would need an aeroplane.

Ailbhe: Or a rocket. But I don't know how to build a rocket.

Some parents who wrote to us after Cormac's death mentioned their
difficulty in explaining to their children, amid all the commotion,
where he had gone. A couple told their young Tyrone fans, five or
six years old, that God needed a full-back for his all-star team in
heaven.

Since she started at Derrylatinee P.S., Cormac has become a recur-
ring motif in Ailbhe's days. 'Leabharlann Chormaic' is the permanent
library section at the back of the school corridor. For the November
'month of the dead' project, she learned about and drew Uncle
Cormac.

And so on.

It was around then, aged four and a half, that she started to ask
questions at bedtime:

'Why did Uncle Cormac die?'

'But why was his heart not working properly?'

'Where is he now?'

And she also knew the schedule after Mass. If, for any reason, I suggested we weren't bound straight for the cemetery, she'd start to chant, 'Unk-ill Cor-mac! Unk-ill Cor-mac!'

Lára, our second girl, knows the score already at two and a half. '*Cá bhfuil muid ag dul anois?*' I ask, as we belt her in.

'Unka Caw-mack,' she mouths through her dummy, and amazes me. Iona, at one, will need more time.

I choose to wend our way around the other family graves first, and finish off with Cormac. Daddy – who has mapped every grave in the cemetery for a display board – prefers to go straight to him.

Daisies grow around Cormac's grave, a few buttercups too, where once bouquets were bundled. No longer do the superstitious sort leave coins on the base of his gravestone, thanking him for his service and making a down-payment for the next life.

By the time we get there, however, Ailbhe and Lára are nearly always running riot around the cemetery. Visiting Uncle Cormac, for them, means an obstacle course, a maze, a wide-open space to play chase and pick dandelions. This is the one place where I pray *to* him, as well as for him. Their prayers will come another day.

The legacy of Uncle Cormac will pass to them and their baby sister Iona to uphold. They're the only McAnallens under the age of thirty in Tyrone today. As they grow up, strangers will ask them about him frequently – 'Are you anything to . . . ?' Especially so if they succeed in sport.

Eglish usually does, when it comes to camogie. In March 2017, we took our girls to Croke Park to watch Eglish's finest, the Ulster champions, play in the All-Ireland Intermediate Club final. Two months later, Ailbhe overcame her shyness and turned up for her first under-6 session. When the time came to run, she was a live wire.

So the cycle begins again. She'll be the first McAnallen to play on Páirc Chormaic. Every time she and her sisters swing a *camán*, I'll be pleased, excited and willing them to win. I may also be wary. Look what happened to Uncle Cormac. Maybe I shouldn't. Their fitness regimes ought not to be as punishing as inter-county football, and heads should be well protected. We'll encourage them, but if they decide it's not for them, so be it.

I suspect they'll stick at it, though. As they come to know the backstory of their family, they'll hear of drive and determination and discipline. For inspiration, they'll only have to look towards the wall.

★

Thirteen years is more than half of a Cormac lifetime ago.

We're now more than halfway to the silver jubilee of Tyrone's historic All-Ireland victory of 2003. Then, if not sooner, will start another carousel of commemorations.

Those history boys will be brought together again every so often for the rest of their days, until the survivors number the minority. For the present, thankfully, there's only one of them missing.

When the day comes for them to be honoured at half-time of a final at Croke Park, there'll be a vacancy at No. 3 to be filled. A member of the McAnallen family will be called to deputize. One of us will stand in line, hear the name called out, step forward, and raise a hand to salute the crowd, for five seconds, then turn around and stand back in line.

If it falls to me, I shall be the most emotional man in that parade. As we cross the sward, I imagine I'll be ruminating on many things. Wishing he were here. Reflecting on his noble service to a cause. Casting my mind back to where it all began, the two of us on our lawn.

Acknowledgements

For over a decade these thoughts and words swirled around in my head, without the time or space to write them. The passage of so many years before the publication of a book on Cormac's life may be for the better. Time allows trauma to heal, new perspectives to develop.

When I started, I knew that to unravel truth from legend and give an authentic account of Cormac would involve drawing on his own words, contemporary sources, and those close to him. It entailed two years and more of scouring schoolbooks and scrapbooks, sun-faded old newspapers, programmes and magazines, personal diaries, teaching reflections and match evaluations, brittle video and audio tapes, and the hard-drive of my own memory. After some deliberation, I decided to quote diary extracts, because they express aspects of Cormac's character and views more clearly than I could; insofar as I present them, I hope they do him justice.

The research also comprised many conversations with colleagues, friends and family. They ranged from lengthy late-nighters to snap chats on a corridor. All seemed to hold a precious memory; alas, only some of these details could be used here, and time was too brief to speak to every potential contributor.

First, I thank our parents, Brendan and Bridget, who gave us the love for it all. Just as they steered Cormac towards success, they have helped me in seeing this through to completion. They faced the biggest challenge in recounting better days and reading manuscripts, but as ever they have been brave. *Yes, I have got this book writ.*

To Ferg, thanks for all anecdotes and technical support, unlocking more than a few hidden treasures.

To Ashlene, my sincere appreciation for your cooperation and support; and to Padhraic, Grace and the boys, thanks for your forbearance while we revisited the past.

Sincere gratitude to the extended family who assisted in many different ways: Seán McAnallen, Kevin McAnallen, Hannah McAnallen, Margaret Mannion, Bertha Hughes, Paul McAnallen. Likewise, I wish to thank maternal relatives who played their part: Margaret Allchin, Imelda O'Neill, Marie Burns, Marian Kelly, Anne Mac Airt, the McCartans and other O'Neills – not least Uncle Peter.

I must pay tribute to those who helped to make Cormac the man he was and who passed away before this book got under way. Above all I think of Granny Mary O'Neill, Mary McAnallen (who kept her own archive on Cormac), Mary Daly, Patsy Jones, Paddy McIntosh, Eileen Donaghy, Dave Billings and good old Gandy.

To Eglish (including the Brantry) folk, past and present: *GRMMA*. Particular thanks to Fr Patrick Breslan, Anthony Daly, Conor Daly, Joe Daly, Dermot Donaghy, Paul Feeney, Teresa Ghosh, Gerard Jones, J. P. McGeough and Declan McKeever – and their better halves. I salute also the input of Peter Barker, Gary Daly, Felix Daly, Liz Daly, Brendan Donnelly, Jim Fay, Neil Gildernew, Kieran Hagan, Noleen Hughes, Mary McNeice, Ciaran McVeigh, John McVeigh, James Muldoon, Cathal Murtagh, Conall Ó Máirtín, Greg O'Neill, Pat Treanor, Cillian and Declan Walsh.

A big shout-out goes to SPGA alumni who lent their time, including: Pierce Donnelly, Stephen 'Jacko' Hughes, Conor Judge, Ryan Kelly, Darran McCann, Jonny McGivern, Karol McQuade, Francis McQuade, Willie McSorley, Ronan McWilliams, Paul Mellon, Rory O'Donnell and Paul Toner. Ditto to former teachers, including Paul McGonigle, Paddy Mohan and Damian Woods.

To those who retold tales of university football, míle buíochas: Jack Devaney, Brendan Dardis, Dr John Kremer, John McCloskey, Alan Molloy, Breandán Ó hAnnaidh, Aidan O'Rourke and Dessie Ryan.

To Cormac's former work-colleagues who shared stories, top marks: first, Seán Mulvihill and Éamonn Cosgrove of St Benildus'; Margaret White and Carol Reynolds of the shop; current and former staff of St Catherine's, Armagh, including Mary Corr, Jacqueline Creighan, Therese Donnelly, Kieran Gallagher, Mary Kilpatrick, Fionnuala McGrath, Marie McManus, Peter McNeill, Margaret Martin, Mary Thomas and Ryan White; and past pupils such as Edel

Barrett, Tanya McCoy, Ciara McKeever, Cathy McKenna, Caoimhe McNeill, Niamh Marley, Lori Muldoon and Fiona Swift. I am indebted to Mrs Noeleen Tiffney, Mr Séamus Mac Dhaibhéid, Aisling Bhean Uí Choinn and Mrs Mairéad Fitzpatrick for facilitating me at St Catherine's during 2016/17; likewise to Mrs Geraldine Donnelly, Mrs Annette McGleenan and Mrs Catherine Taggart at St Joseph's, Donaghmore.

My narrative of Cormac's role in Tyrone football has been enriched by the memories of Peter Canavan, Ciarán Gourley, Mickey Harte, Colin and Shona Holmes, Philip Jordan, Marie McElhinney, Siobhán McGuinness, Eugene McKenna, Art McRory, Ryan Mellon, Louis O'Connor, Stephen O'Neill, Brian Robinson and Paddy Tally. Tyrone partisans like Mark Conway, Mickey Donnelly, Connor McCarron, Gerry Mellon have each given a handy tuppenceworth too. Thank you all.

Several medics have kindly given the benefit of their insight into the complex issues surrounding Cormac's death and sudden death in general. Thank you to Dr Joseph Galvin, Dr Valerie Grant, Dr Fearghal McNicholl, Dr Con Murphy and Dr Pat O'Neill, the Northern Ireland Ambulance Service, and the Coroners Service (NI).

To everyone who ever sent us a letter or other message, without reply, and especially those whose words I drew from in my writing, thank you also. Alas, there was not space in this book to list all that was done in the Cormac commemorative projects over the years, nor to list all the people involved – thanks to all anyhow.

Members of the fourth estate helped me along the way, like they did for Cormac in his day. I would like to credit Aeneas Bonner, Eileen Dunne, Michael Foley, John Greene, Oliver McVeigh, Christy O'Connor, Micheál Ó Muircheartaigh, Jerome Quinn, Alan Rodgers and Hugh Russell. Most of all, Eoghan Corry sent me on the right path (again) – *go maire sé*.

I am immensely grateful to Michael McLoughlin and Brendan Barrington of Penguin Ireland for offering this opportunity. To write under Brendan's direction has been truly a pleasure: his meticulousness, kind words and firm pointers were of precious value in the moulding of this work.

Special mention is merited for the following for lifting some of my yoke over the last couple of years: Roddy Hegarty, Joe Canning and Bernard Hagan and the Management Committee of the Cardinal Ó Fiaich Library and Archive; Brian Howley; Dr Alan McCully and Dr Seán Mac Corraidh; all the Whippersnappers at Coleraine; Niamh Burns; Dr David and Joanne Hassan; Dr Paul Rouse; Humphrey Kelleher; Kathleen Ward, Charlie Markey and Neil Rooney; Mary and Francie Conway; Noreen, Justin, Erin and Conor McElduff; Una and Matthew McFadden; Damian Conway; Mary Hughes, Christina McGready and Christianne Hughes.

To our three girls – Ailbhe, Lára and Iona – *go raibh míle maith agaibh as an inspioráid; cuireann sibh gliondar i mo chroí.* To Polly, you started it, you persuaded me to go for it, and you showed saintly patience; you're the onion on my borger.

Finally, to the man himself: thanks for the memories; you make us proud still.

He just wanted a decent book to read ...

Not too much to ask, is it? It was in 1935 when Allen Lane, Managing Director of Bodley Head Publishers, stood on a platform at Exeter railway station looking for something good to read on his journey back to London. His choice was limited to popular magazines and poor-quality paperbacks – the same choice faced every day by the vast majority of readers, few of whom could afford hardbacks. Lane's disappointment and subsequent anger at the range of books generally available led him to found a company – and change the world.

'We believed in the existence in this country of a vast reading public for intelligent books at a low price, and staked everything on it'
Sir Allen Lane, 1902–1970, founder of Penguin Books

The quality paperback had arrived – and not just in bookshops. Lane was adamant that his Penguins should appear in chain stores and tobacconists, and should cost no more than a packet of cigarettes.

Reading habits (and cigarette prices) have changed since 1935, but Penguin still believes in publishing the best books for everybody to enjoy. We still believe that good design costs no more than bad design, and we still believe that quality books published passionately and responsibly make the world a better place.

So wherever you see the little bird – whether it's on a piece of prize-winning literary fiction or a celebrity autobiography, political tour de force or historical masterpiece, a serial-killer thriller, reference book, world classic or a piece of pure escapism – you can bet that it represents the very best that the genre has to offer.

Whatever you like to read – trust Penguin.